ARISTOTLE'S P

SUNY series in Ancient Greek Philosophy
Anthony Preus, Editor

ARISTOTLE'S POLITICS TODAY

EDITED BY
LENN E. GOODMAN AND ROBERT B. TALISSE

STATE UNIVERSITY OF NEW YORK PRESS

Published by
State University of New York Press, Albany

For information, contact State University of New York Press, Albany, NY
www.sunypress.edu

Production by Dana Foote
Marketing by Michael Campochiaro

Library of Congress Cataloging-in-Publication Data

Aristotle's Politics today / edited by Lenn E. Goodman, Robert B. Talisse.
        p. cm. — (SUNY series in ancient Greek philosophy)
    Includes bibliographical references and index.
    ISBN 978-0-7914-7227-9 (hardcover : alk. paper)
    ISBN 978-0-7914-7228-6 (pbk. : alk. paper)
    1. State, The. 2. Aristotle. Politics. I. Goodman, Lenn Evan, 1944–
II. Talisse, Robert B.

JC11.A75 2007
320.092—dc22   2006101109

10 9 8 7 6 5 4 3 2 1

CONTENTS

INTRODUCTION
Lenn E. Goodman and Robert B. Talisse

A well-known philosopher who lived through almost all of the twentieth century used to remark on the penchant some philosophers have for announcing the death of their own discipline. That bad habit isn't confined to philosophers, of course. We've often seen premature obituaries about art in general or figural art in particular, or lyric poetry, or music, or melody, the novel, or religion. It was even thought, around the end of the nineteenth century, that physics was about finished and nothing was left but to fill in the last few decimal places in the key Newtonian constants. That was just on the eve of the Michaelson-Morely experiment, which paved the way for Einstein's work and opened the door to the expanding universe of quantum mechanics, the nuclear age, and string theory. Our philosopher, however, had lived long enough to see metaphysics, political philosophy, aesthetics, normative ethics and normative epistemology, among other branches of philosophical inquiry, revive more than once from the overhasty and sometimes overeager death announcements. His observation was that before it had even become trite to say that this or that variety of philosophy was washed up some young kid would start reading Aristotle, and everything began anew and fresh.

It was Aristotle who said that philosophy begins in wonder. He was too much a believer in cycles of history, too much Plato's student, and too ready to probe the views of the many and the wise to think that *he* had started anything from scratch. But he did lay out in plain terms, without the cloak of dialogue or a thick veil of poetic tropes, many of the lasting questions and inviting answers that have put philosophers to work from his time down to our own. Nowhere was that more true than in political philosophy. But is it true that Aristotle's thoughts on politics have any life left in them for today? What, we might ask, have *we* to learn about politics from an ancient thinker who wrote in Greek and lived at Athens but was not even an Athenian, let alone a committed democrat? What have we to learn in political philosophy from a man who could accept slavery as an institution, who did not see women as men's equals, who had a lively interest in historical and political traditions but nothing much to say about the politics of group identity?

A common answer, we suspect, is that Aristotle has little to teach us modern liberal democrats. Aren't Aristotle's views on the nature and purpose of the state, the meaning of citizenship, and the ordering of political institutions not only archaic, because they rest on an exploded metaphysics, but unacceptable, because they slight the modern staples of political legitimacy: formal equality, individual rights, negative liberty, moral neutrality, and democratic rule. For those who find these fundamentals of normative discourse about politics insufficient today, and who call for more robust commitments to differential equality, group rights, and identity claims, Aristotle's vision of a polity whose purpose is to promote virtue seems even more remote.

The chapters collected in this volume aim to challenge the commonplace perception of Aristotle as a thinker as planted firmly in the "liberty of the ancients"—and therefore irrelevant to those who seek to theorize the "liberty of the moderns," as Benjamin Constant framed the contrast. The chapters represent different methodological and conceptual foci. But they all endeavor to bring Aristotle into conversation with contemporary theorists. In most instances, they find that Aristotle indeed has much to say to us.

Consider the question of equality. Aristotle is a valuable companion in our discussions here, precisely for his openness. He does not share our familiar sayisms about equality. He does not assume that all humans are equal in talent, skill, intellect, or ability. He does not even assume that we are all moral equals. His views here jangle our sensibilities, schooled in the sacredness of human dignity and the rhetoric of democracy. And yet, Aristotle's freedom from the commitments we hold dear makes him a pluralist about the varieties of equality, as he is about so many other topics, from the marks of substantiality to the dimensions of human virtue. He can review the Pythagorean reduction of justice to reciprocity, dismiss the mechanical equation of justice with simply making "a man suffer what he did," and still extract from that crude tit-for-tat a subtler, highly diversified notion of requital. The more nuanced notion will be applicable in commerce; but it is also generalizable to themes of proportion where equality of various kinds preserves the sense of equity that Aristotle finds adumbrated in temples to the Graces. The multifaceted concept he extracts finds its articulacy in context, from the law courts to the tennis courts, and from works of fiction and criticism to relations of intimacy and understanding. Passed through Aristotle's conceptual prism, equity is refracted into all its diverse colors and recombined into a single idea critical to the foundation of any sound polity or society. For the kernel of truth that Aristotle finds in the Pythagorean dictum, through his habitual practice of "saving the appearances," not only visually but in the outlooks of others, is that justice demands a kind of equity without which human beings "would think their position mere slavery" (*Nicomachean Ethics* 1133a7).

The idea of slavery is a firm pivot point for much of Aristotle's political thinking, not because he assumes that slavery is always wrong but because he knows that no one given the freedom to choose would opt to be a slave. Slavery, as Aristotle defines it, is the use of a human being as another's tool. It is, in that sense, the ultimate violation of the Kantian imperative never to subjugate another to the status of a mere means to an end. We human beings, for Aristotle, fulfill and exercise our human nature when we are choosers of our own ends. Slaves, as a condition of their servitude, cannot do that. They have uses, not ends of their own, and those uses are imposed.

That Aristotle failed to find a way of liberating humanity from the trammels of slavery without losing the opportunity for fulfillment that he held so precious for the free matters less today philosophically than does his ability to pinpoint just what it is that makes slavery repugnant and unacceptable. The standard he invokes but fails to apply reaches far beyond the bare demand for emancipation. For it articulates the basis for condemning and combating all forms of invidious exploitation and abuse, from human trafficking and sweatshop labor to meretricious sexuality and environmental poisoning.

It's fashionable today to disparage the idea of human nature. The notion that one can derive moral standards or political norms from a study of the human species and human personhood is viewed with suspicion, if not alarm. Not only do such efforts breach Hume's barrier between *is* and *ought* but they seem to threaten the very fabric of diversity—ethnic, cultural, and moral—that is widely seen as the chief and ripest fruit of democracy, bursting with the seeds of a postliberal dispensation. Diversity, of course, is precious, and not least for what it brings to and draws from the idea of liberty. But human diversity does have limits, and if prescriptive judgments and practical imperatives do follow from the recognition that there are only certain things a human being can stand and only certain things that any human being should be asked to put up with (being ordered to the back of the bus or relegated to a racially segregated school never among them), then we must recognize a common core of humanness that deserves respect and demands dignity; and we must acknowledge that the legitimate distinction between facticity and rightness does not preclude the recognition that there are facts about values and that the human person, qua human, is a locus of inviolable deserts—and obligations.

Some of what Aristotle has to tell us about politics comes in the form of simple home truths that might sound like cliches when spelled out and might seem too obvious to need stating and yet, elementary as they are, have often been forgotten, quite often wilfully and with dangerous or tragic consequences. Sometimes an idea like Arisotle's claim that man is a *zoon politikon*—that is, a social animal, a civic being—sounds so familiar and looks so transparent on the page that we readily lose track of how richly filled with implications these seemingly simple words can be. Reading in Aristotle that habit is *second nature* or that a friend is a second self, one risks losing sight altogether of the full meaning of the words and slips unselfconsciously into the mode of the fellow who said "What's so great about Shakespeare? It's just a bunch of famous sayings strung together!" Seeming familiarity breeds contempt. And one value of the chapters gathered here is that they cast fresh and bright light on thoughts that we might think we have fully explored when in fact we've given only cursory attention to the words in which trenchant and telling arguments have been clothed.

But many of Aristotle's thoughts about politics are subtle and complex, not enshrined in reliquaries or camouflaged by familiar phrases and perhaps elusive of the well-worn pathways of our common language—yet worth snagging nonetheless. Among the home truths and commonplaces to be found in Aristotle is his recognition that even our most basic needs are not met without collaboration. We humans are not a solitary species. We need each other, and not just for mating. None of us would be able in isolation to find or produce adequate (let alone decent) food, shelter, or cover for our bodies.

The subtler truth to which Aristotle is committed is that to live fully human lives, to exercise any of our most distinctive human capacities and to realize any of our most distinctive human potentials, we need each other in quite a variety of ways that are themselves distinctively human: We need language and the opportunity to learn, to share and pass on what we have learned from others. For culture, the transmission of a nongenetic heritage, is both a distinctively human trait and a means by which our own humanity is brought to fruition. We need friendship too, and opportunities to discover and express ourselves in ways not even conceivable beyond a social context. And we need the opportunity to plan our own lives, build our own character, tell our own story, on the basis of our experience—to deliberate within ourselves about the next steps we might contemplate, and with one another about our common needs, projects, hopes, fears, opportunities, and challenges.

Aristotle sees the essences of all living things in dynamic, conative terms: All have aims and goals, ends, as he calls them. And the most distinctively human of our human goals—both those that we share with other members of our species and those that express our individuality—can be reached only through our complex web of interactions with one another in all sorts of formal and informal relationships and institutions whose adequacy and appropriateness, by Aristotle's standards, are to be judged wholly in terms of their capacity to foster the winning of those aims and attainment of those goals—which he sums up under the name of *eudaimonia*, by which he means not just happiness but human fulfillment and active flourishing.

Like the tragic figures that are the focus of his thoughts about Greek drama, Aristotle finds his own greatest strength in the same characteristics that spawn his greatest weakness. His realism, his openness and pluralism, make him far more accepting of the social conditions he sees around him than, say, Plato was. Politically, Plato is a radical—not a democrat, of course, but a radical. When he asks the great question of political philosophy—*What legitimates authority?*—Plato looks around him and sees that de facto authority rests on wealth and military prowess (or the reputation or expectation of such prowess), and on accidents of birth like gender, and lineage, and name. He knows that this is radically wrong, and he will argue that only sound judgment about the good legitimates authority. Indeed, Plato is ready not just to argue but (as his ill-fated Syracuse adventure clearly shows) to risk his life and the lives of many others in the effort to establish his ideal. Chastened by the failure of his efforts at Syracuse and by the blood that was shed in the name of his misguided effort (always a deep thinker but often a slow learner and much more dependent on years and experience than his innatist epistemology might have led us to expect), Plato comes to qualify his expectations. He turns more toward law in his late years and sets less hope in the search for some ideal ruler whose judgment might be trusted without question.

Aristotle too has learned from Plato's experiences. For Plato's tragedy at Syracuse was playing out when the young Aristotle first came to the Academy, and Aristotle's realism, his willingness to rationalize the status quo, an acceptance that might seem at times to border on complacency, arises perhaps as much from the chastening of experience as from the tenor of his own personality. But the weakness has a strength to it as well. Aristotle does not construct utopias or plan revolutions. Without doctrinaire preferences, he sees a better and a worse way to run a monarchy, a democracy, or an oligarchy. In each case, law is what legitimates—constitutional principles, to put it more precisely. If these help stabilize a regime, that stability is won not by arbitrary or violent exercises of authority or displays of force or undermining and corrupting the opposition, but by some form of fairness. And, again, it's characteristic of Aristotle's pluralism that he sees many forms of fairness.

Fairness is both the root and the fruit of the political stability Aristotle teaches. In that sense his realism about the varieties of polis functions much as his ethical teaching does, starting with what everyone knows or thinks he knows (about self-interest in the case of ethics, or about how precious peace and stability are, in the political case) and building outward, dialectically, to less familiar or less commonly acknowledged ground—the discovery of the virtues that foster our fulfillment, in the case of ethics, the recognition that those virtues always need a social theater for their realization; the discovery, in the case of politics, that the bare needs of peace, prosperity, and political stability rest on far broader foundations than may at first meet the eye: law and constitutionalism, measured deliberative openness and participation, social and cultural institutions that foster and affirm a sense of fellowship and belonging among the individuals who constitute a polity and that both foster and affirm the kind of character that will warrant the trust on which such a sense of fellowship depends. Aristotle is never in doubt that the legitimate aim of any polity (and the aim that legitimates its structures of authority) is *eudaimonia*, the flourishing of the individual. Nor is he ever in doubt that the only means ultimately effective in pursuit of that end is education, broadly construed (as Plato himself had taught)—that is, the formation of character, as influenced by all the formal and informal institutions that the society can

constitute in support of that goal. But Aristotle is not averse to arguing dialectically, building from a narrower aim like stability or prosperity to the broader
and subtler goal of *eudaimonia*. The dialectic, again, is modeled on Plato, and
on the Socratic plan of argument that Plato celebrates and canonizes in the
Republic. But the detailed vision of the organic connection that links the
higher goal with the narrower but more familiar one, by way of constitutionalism, fairness, participation, and the like, is distinctively Aristotle's. Its eluci-
dation is the distinctive goal of political science, as he understands that crititical
and in a way magisterial branch of study, so closely parallel, in its own way,
to the biological studies that Aristotle so loved, in which he sought to uncover
the unseen linkages between the forms taken by the organs of living beings and
the peculiar and distinctive goods that those organs serve in promoting the
survival of living creatures and the continuance of their species.

Much of our political discourse and rhetoric today, still centered on the
idea of rights as trumps and on the conception of liberty as noninterference,
hangs in the air because so many of our philosophers and other thinkers have
foresworn the idea of human nature. They predicate their talk of rights and
liberties, entitlements and deserts, on the notion of a social contract—no
longer mythic or historical, but virtual, the thought, that is, of an agreement
that no one actually has made but that hypothetically rational choosers
would or should have signed onto, had they been asked. The effect is to
suspend rights, and duties along with them, from a skyhook. Political norms
become conventional rather than universal. Human rights and obligations
become contingent on social forms not just for their efficacy (as they must
be) but for their prescriptivity. Once that move has been made, we fear,
diversity has been pressed too far. We find ourselves (in the name of the
respect we owe the *other*) willingly and even with relief accepting the exploitation and expropriation, oppression and, yes, enslavement of the other, as
if we were let off the hook morally, simply because that other, conceived *as*
other, does not seem to be subject to our particular conventions, is not a
party to *our* contract, a player in our game, a member of our group.

If rights are products not of compacts or conventions but of our very
being (even though convention and our tacit and emergent compacts with
one another are necessary to their social and institutional implementation),
if rights are demands of what we are, anchored in our common nature, not
because we share it but because that nature makes us subjects, choosers,
persons, beings capable of thought and reflection—beings, in short, whose
very nature is denied when the avenues of choice are closed—then natural
rights are firmly grounded in natural law. And persons, of course, *is* what we
are. We are susceptible to pain, yes, but also to laughter and regret, sensibil-
ity and distaste. We are capable of intellectual honesty and self-deception.
We are beings able to chart our own course individually, consultatively, and
conjointly. We are able, in some measure, to define our own ends. Granted
we do so fallibly and corrigibly. But we also do so responsibly, self-consciously,

even at times self-critically. It is here that the simplest demand of morals comes into play, the demand that we treat beings as what they are. This is the same broad demand that finds its special case in the imperative to acknowledge the truth when we see it. Rights, in that case, are no longer suspended from a skyhook, or hung out to dry in the winds of contingency.

A volume seeking to bring Aristotle into constructive conversation with political theory today could not hope to succeed without a focus on modern ideas of rights. So one of the themes that links the chapters in this symposium is attention to the place of the idea of rights in Aristotle's political philosophy. This focus may seem surprising, since Aristotle does not bathe in the rhetoric of rights, as do so many of our modern political practitioners and the theorists sensitive to their concerns. The dialectic of rights and responsibilities is not Aristotle's cynosure. He's far more interested in the moral basis of society, in ethos and history, statecraft, and the nexus we have mentioned between stability and legitimacy. Constitutionalism is perhaps his great theme—a theme not foreign to our own political discourse, especially if we bear in mind that often, in our rhetoric and casual talk, when we say 'democracy' we mean 'constitutional republic.' But it is precisely because Aristotle's *Politics* does dig for the moral roots of constitutionalism that the theme of rights emerges so insistently from its pages. It's here, as three of the chapters in this volume argue, that Aristotle's political philosophy can be most helpful to us.

As Edward Halper argues, *Aristotle* does not lack an explanation, a political motivation, or a metaphysical foundation for the idea of rights. What Aristotle calls to our attention is the fact that rights *are* nonsense without a philosophy of the human being. It's the lack of an adequate philosophical anthropology that would make absolute rights what Bentham branded them, "nonsense upon stilts." Halper argues that an Aristotelian politics affords a firmer ground for modern liberty than contemporary neutralist liberalism can offer. Pursuing a similar course, Fred D. Miller, Jr., extracts from Aristotle's conception of statecraft a workable set of prescriptions for contemporary politicians and policy makers. Adopting an Aristotelian critical perspective, Peter L. P. Simpson masterfully echoes Aristotle's analyses of constitutions, to bring into relief the ways in which Aristotle might find flaws and blindspots in the American Constitution.

Like so much of the rest of his philosophy, Aristotle's politics begins with observation—characteristically and appropriately biological in this case, the observation we have already reflected on, that man is a social animal. We live human lives by virtue of our ability to cooperate in groups, to differentiate our roles and coordinate our activities in pursuit of a common goal, not just of surviving but of living well, thus realizing our humanity. It is for this reason that all virtues of character are defined by Aristotle in their social context. Courage, liberality, proper pride—all the habits and dispositions that make us effective, successful, and fulfilled as human beings are honed and exercised in interaction with our fellow humans. Friendship is listed among the virtues and anatomized in extenso along with them because friendship is the social bond (extending beyond mere mechanical reciprocity) that makes society possible and the polis effectual—whether its locus is in sheer exchange relations, or whether its practice broadens our relationships to bonds of fellowship and camaraderie, or security in its exercise allows us to rise to the plane of mutual trust, regard, respect, or love that would lead us to take risks and make sacrifices for one another, that is, to treat one another, indeed as "second selves."

As Lenn E. Goodman argues, what Aristotle shows us by his analysis of sodality is that human society is founded not on our fear of nature or of one another but (as Plato had taught), on our capabilities of complementing one another's strengths and building a life together that none of us could even approach on our own. The human virtues, Goodman contends, are not just nominal categories that capture in their verbal net the dispositions that we welcome in our neighbors. They are, like any virtues, strengths that make us more adequate in ourselves and more effective in our roles. And human roles, perforce, are social roles, since social beings is what we are, civic beings, if we are to consider the conditions needed for the fullness of our human life.

Only a god or a beast, Aristotle writes, could live alone—and a human being who lived alone would not long retain the character of humanity but would slip inexorably into the cyclopean mode that Homer had so brilliantly painted in the *Odyssey*. It is our interdependence that makes a human being a *zoon politikon*, but that interdependence is not just a matter of subsistence. It's a matter of enhancing our lives with all the cultural and institutional amenities that a full description of human society would omit from mention only at the cost of the grossest misrepresentation.

The social setting, of course, is not the only basis for Aristotle's grounding of political norms in human nature. If it were, those norms would not extend beyond the formal reciprocities of our conventions—be they vested in institutions like commercial exchange and promise keeping or in the more spiteful ethos of blood feuds and *talio*. There are concrete and, yes, universal material constituents to human nature, capabilities that can be realized only in a social setting but that no ant or bee or termite could exercise or develop, no matter how elaborately organized the social structure in which such creatures lived. The existential basis of human interdependence might start with our needs for food and water, shelter and mates, but it can hardly be confined to that level. It extends rapidly from the procreative urge and the desire to protect our offspring to the more intangible but hardly impalpable human needs for status, recognition, and control—the desire, in Aristotle's terms, for active engagement in the concerns of the community, to deliberate not only as regards individual needs and familial wants but also in the larger, public arena where human societies articulate themselves as states and not just clans or neighborhoods, to have our interests consulted and our voices heard. It is with this thought in mind that Robert B. Talisse's contribution brings Aristotelian themes of intellectual virtue into conversation with contemporary theories of deliberative democracy.

All human drives and wants are distinctively human in form, even those that have counterparts among the animals, even those that have counterparts among the plants. But part of what Aristotle finds most distinctively human is the use of reason in our deliberations, whether in a calculative way that seeks to discover and deploy means to our ends, or in a more reflective way, in the recursive examination of those ends themselves, comparing them with one another and with their alternatives. That reflective phase of the deliberative, which makes it not merely calculative and instrumental but open ended and philosophical, leads naturally from the practical to the speculative, as the work of Plato and the life of Socrates had clearly shown. It is when we think and engage in inquiry for its own sake, as Aristotle sees it, that we are most self-sufficient and godlike.

Reason in this sense fulfills and enacts our humanity. But, as Eugene Garver notes, it is when our deliberations about means and ends become public, when we seek to persuade or be persuaded by one another, that our natures as social beings and as reasoning beings intertwine. And here too our humanity is realized, as the fruits of our reflections about nature and the cosmos, divine wisdom and human happiness, are put to work, in shaping and preserving the institutions that will facilitate the humanization of human life and foster, in our offspring and in new generations, the kind of character that will find its way to lives worth living and not leave that question unexamined. Garver develops these themes strikingly against the contrastive backdrop of Aristotle's reflections on revolt, faction, stability, and change.

Education lies at the core of Aristotle's politics, as it does for Plato, and no doubt even for the historical Socrates as well. It is here, perhaps that Aristotle can be most informative to our political thinking. For we devote a great share of state revenues to educational enterprises and our political and social institutions remain, much as those of ancient Greece were, dependent on the intellectual outlook and moral dispositions of our citizenry. Yet our political theories insistently neglect the subject of education, frown on the very idea of moral education, and vehemently confuse education with indoctrination (or even operant conditioning) in ways that would have made Aristotle cringe. Our political philosophers are perhaps as much in denial about the centrality of education in the mission of the modern state as were those contemporaries of Socrates who wanted to hold *him* responsible for the character of Alcibiades and failed or refused to see that it was they and their institutions that had struck that counterfeit coin.

What Aristotle offers here is no political panacea, unless what we are after is the kind of self-validating argument that promises to end all political and moral difficulties if only we could learn to train our youngsters soundly. That kind of formula rests on a promissory note. It assumes, without offering much support, that we can somehow discover and agree on, and indeed implement, just the right kind of education. It ignores the fact that education for the young and for adults as well begins with *us*. For our actions are the models that the young and others too most follow. Children learn swiftly to be as adept as we are in saying one thing, doing another, and believing a third. Where Aristotle is perhaps most helpful here is not in showing us just what behaviors we should model. Like Plato he is skeptical that any mere behavioral rule will capture the full texture of the life of virtue. He is not likely to think it possible that some behavioral formula or nostrum will spell out the true nature of the good life.

Experience, judgment, practical wisdom are never out of place in the thick reality of our daily lives, once we get beyond the bare minima of human decency that laws and moral systems seek to articulate. Given Socrates' teachings about the moral primacy of practice over precept and the need for habits of mind *and* action to be internally appropriated, to be made part of our character and identity and not merely heard or mouthed before we can call them our own, mere formulae are not something that we could hope would do us any good, even if Aristotle (or anyone else) were equipped to provide us or our children with the relevant instruction. Only sophists would profess to do that, whether they wear the garb of advocates or marketers, demagogues or preachers. But what Aristotle can give us is the recognition that education is not a matter of conditioning and still less of indoctrination, that the moral habits we acquire, by doing not by speaking, are in the first instance habits of the mind, habits of acting thoughtfully, with due consideration of who and where we are, what our aims and the consequences of our acts might be, how our choices affect others and ourselves, how they become expressions of who are and of who we wish to be.

The good life, as Aristotle argues at some length, is not a collection of goods and services or even a body of passive experiences. Rather it is a hierarchy of actions, organized around our human capabilities for thought, deliberation, reflection, and self-governance. In thinking that thought and communicating it to us, Aristotle, like Plato, refuses to segregate the moral from the political or the political from the moral: Our individual choices are political, not only in the sense that they take place in a social context and have social antecedents and consequences, but also in the sense that they demand adjudication among potentially conflicting claims and in that sense presage and prepare us for our public and communal deliberative roles. Our public choices are moral too, not only in the sense that they portend value judgments and wreak their effects upon our fellow human beings—our neighbors to be sure, but also distant contemporaries, as we now know—and our successors, and even (as the people of traditional societies are not prone to forget) the good name and vanished hopes of our ancestors. They are moral in another sense as well. For they call upon and express, expose and define our character and the character of the society that is the product of our interactions. In light of Aristotle's coupling of good politics with the human good, questions of global politics naturally arise. In his treatment of these issues, Lloyd P. Gerson develops an Aristotelian account of moral agency that he proposes belongs in contemporary theories of international relations.

Aristotle is sometimes blamed for the scholastic uses that were made of his philosophy. Nothing, we think, could be more unfair. Scholasticism, as we understand it is the marshaling of doctrines into schools rigidly attached to their own fixed methods, agendas, and assumptions. Typically, the reference is to the Christian schoolmen of the Middle Ages. But scholasticism is not confined to theology or to medieval authors and teachers. It is found wherever knowledge is limited, opinions are many, and access to the avenues of thought is controlled by a demand for prior commitment to premises safeguarded from inquiry. The balkanization of discourse is self-aggravating, as rival groups are insulated by refusal to criticize shared assumptions or to engage the insights of outsiders charitably. Gatekeepers and coded language often guard the boundaries and borderlands of discourse, making scholasticism inimical to philosophy and to all free inquiry. The chief symptom of scholasticism, in this regard, is a kind of fractal structure that is more than evident in much of contemporary philosophy and in other disciplines as well, especially where value judgments are in play and the players loathe or dread canons of judgment divergent from their own. By a fractal structure we mean an ever-narrowing dialectic, where the open universe is negated and denied by the arbitrary or dogmatic constriction of inquiry within the confines of accepted premises whose truth is not examined and whose alternatives are not even entertained. Each new turn of thought is not an opening but a narrowing, responding only to what preceded it and in a bizarre way mimicking and miniaturizing its insights as the demands of specialization and overspecialization constrain the scope of discourse to ever smaller domains, ignoring or finessing ever-larger bodies of concern and caricaturing the original broad interest that sparked an inquiry, by generating only commentaries upon commentaries and metadiscourse at ever-higher (but never loftier) degrees of abstraction.

The confinement of much current political discourse to a contractual paradigm is a case in point. John Rawls won plaudits for reinvigorating normative political philosophy in the last half of the last century, and much of the praise is well deserved. But, as Rawls freely admits, he did not *open* a new discourse or create a new framework of political analysis ex nihilo. He presented the familiar Lockean and Kantian contractual arguments in new imagery; and to the extent that political philosophy since that time has committed itself to commentaries, expositions, or even rebuttals to Rawls's ideas—hundreds have been written, including a handful by Rawls himself—the effect of his work was not to liberate or renew political philosophy but to hem it in, to aggravate and exaggerate the trend toward scholasticism that is already at work in modern intellectual disciplines for a variety of reasons, mostly connected with the social structure of our academic institutions.

Here Aristotle's political philosophy, far from being scholastic in its potential, can have just the opposite effect. Because it does not presuppose a contractualist framework, it can work to open up the trammels of contemporary scholasticism in political philosophy. Like Asian philosophy or any unfamiliar outlook, ancient or modern, Aristotle's philosophy can stun by its foreignness. But, perhaps more importantly, it can enable triangulation, precisely because it stands outside the familiar nostrums and givens that hem in dogmatic thinking. In that sense, Aristotle's philosophy in general and his political philosophy in particular can be liberating. Picking up on this theme, May Sim explores the resources in Aristotle and Confucius for a new conceptualization of human rights and international justice.

Of course, this volume does not pretend to be the final word on the contemporary relevance of Aristotle's political theory. The chapters presented here represent at best suggestions for further work, sketches of future research programs. We hope that readers will find some of what they read here inviting of response and provocative of their own creative efforts in unlimbering their more independent thoughts. If our chapters prove stimulating in this way, this book will have achieved some of our best hopes for its impact.

1

ARISTOTELIAN STATECRAFT AND MODERN POLITICS

Fred D. Miller, Jr.

INTRODUCTION

Aristotle still has much to offer to modern politics. Although many today would reject his aristocratic ideal (not to mention his endorsement of slavery and the disenfranchisement of women, artisans, and laborers), his conception of statecraft transcends his historical and political perspective. This chapter will offer a reconstruction of Aristotelian statecraft (*politikē*) and a brief overview of Aristotle's suggestions as to how statecraft should be applied. The main thesis is that Aristotelian statecraft is still of value to modern political theorists, even those who repudiate his view that the highest aim of the state is to make men virtuous. To underscore this point, I shall consider a modern proponent of the minimal state—a political ideal far removed from Aristotle's.

FUNDAMENTALS OF ARISTOTELIAN STATECRAFT

Aristotle's political theory rests on two fundamental analogies. The first is between the city-state (polis) and a living organism. A city-state exists "by nature" in two respects: it develops out of natural human impulses for association, and it promotes the natural ends of the citizen (*politēs*). For example, even where no political communities exist, men and women join together out of a natural urge to procreate, and families combine in villages to meet long-term needs. In time the city-state emerges with the aim of supplying resources sufficient for the happy and flourishing lives of its citizens. "It comes to be for the sake of living [i.e., survival], but it remains in existence for the sake of living well" (I.2.1252b29–30).[1] Aristotle does not mean that city-states spring up like plants or that human beings are biologically programmed to

13

live like citizens. His point is that humans are naturally disposed to live together and cooperate, and they have natural aptitudes for political life, including linguistic ability and a moral sense. As Ernest Barker succinctly put it, "Art cooperates with nature: the volition and action of human agents 'construct' the state in cooperation with a natural immanent impulse" (Barker 1946, 7 note 1).[2] Aristotle concludes: "Hence, though an impulse toward this sort of community exists by nature in everyone, whoever first established one was responsible for the greatest of goods" (1253a29–31).

This leads to Aristotle's second analogy. The person who is qualified to establish the political community is a statesman (*politikos*), or, more precisely, a legislator (*nomothetēs*). Such a political expert is compared to a craftsman (II.12.1273b32–33; VII.4.1325b40–1356a5). The analogy can be understood in terms of Aristotle's four causes: the material, formal, efficient, and final causes. For example, when a craftsman (e.g., a potter) produces an artifact (say, a vase), the clay (material cause) is molded into a vase shape (formal cause) by the potter (efficient or moving cause) so that it can contain liquid (final cause). Similarly when a legislator establishes a political community, this can also be understood in terms of the four causes.

Materially, the city-state is composed of parts such as households, economic classes (e.g., the rich, the poor, and the middle class), or demes (local political units). But, ultimately, the city-state is composed of individual citizens, who, along with natural resources, are the material cause or "equipment" out of which the city-state is fashioned (see III.1.1274a38–41; VII.14.1325b38–41).

The formal cause of the city-state is its constitution (*politeia*), which Aristotle defines as "a certain organization of the inhabitants of a city-state" (III.1.1274b32–41). He calls the constitution "the form of the compound" and argues that the identity of a city-state over time depends on the constancy of its constitution (III.3.1276b1–11). The constitution is not a written document but an immanent organizing principle analogous to the soul of an organism. In that sense, the constitution is the way of life of the citizens (IV.11.1295a40–b1; VII.8.1328b1–2).

As for the efficient cause, on Aristotle's view, a community of any sort can possess order only if it has a ruling element or authority. If the city-state is a going concern, this element is its ruling class or governmental body. This ruling element is defined by the constitution, which sets criteria for political offices, particularly the sovereign office (III.6.1278b8–10; cf. IV.1.1289a15–18). On a deeper level, however, there must be an efficient cause to explain how the city-state came into being. This is the legislator or statesman who "first established" the political community, someone like Lycurgus who founded the constitution of Sparta, or Solon who reformed that of Athens.

Finally, the city-state has a final cause: "we see that every city-state is a community of some sort, and that every community is established for the sake of some good." Because the city-state encompasses all other communities (households, villages, etc.) and has the highest authority, its good has the most authority (I.1.1252a1–7). Its proper aim is the good life or happiness (2.1252b29–30; cf. III.6.1278b17–24; 9.1280b39; VII.2.1325a7–10)—or, more broadly, the aim specified by its constitution (IV.1.1289a17–18).

To sum up, the city-state, like any artifact, is the product of four causes: an efficient cause (the statesman or legislator) who imposes a formal cause (the constitution) on a material cause (the inhabitants) for the sake of a final cause (the aim).

Building on his two analogies—between city-state and living organism, and between statesman and ordinary craftsman—Aristotle discusses the different but interrelated tasks of statecraft (*Politics* IV.1) with an illuminating comparison between statecraft and gymnastics. Each must study a wide range of issues concerning its subject matter. A knowledgeable gymnastics coach should provide the sort of physical training that is beneficial for each sort of body. A skillful coach can train an athlete who is "naturally the best" to become a champion. But a good coach should also know what training is appropriate to prepare a less capable athlete for the contests. Further, some might come to the coach with more modest aims; they might want just to get in shape and not aspire to compete in athletic contests. A competent coach should be able to help them as well. Other craftsmen, including physicians, ship builders, and clothing manufacturers, carry out a similar array of tasks. Analogously, "the good legislator and true statesman" will make it his business to know each of the following:

1. "What the best constitution must be like if it is to be most ideal, and if there were no external obstacles." (1288b21–24)

2. "Which constitution is best for which city-states. For achieving the best constitution is perhaps impossible for many." (1288b24–27)

3. "Which constitution is best given certain assumptions. For a statesman must be able to study how any given constitution might initially come into existence, and how, once in existence, it might be preserved for the longest time. I mean, for example, when some city-state happens to be governed neither by the best constitution (not even having the necessary resources), nor by the best one possible in the existing circumstances, but by a worse one." (1288b28–33)[3]

Task (1) involves *ideal theory*, prescribing the best constitution a community could have under the most favorable circumstances: a population of the highest physical, intellectual, and moral capacities, which has at its disposal all the natural resources needed to develop these capacities. Aristotle describes this constitution as "ideal"—provided such a constitution is in principle attainable and does not rely on Panglossian assumptions about human nature or the available resources.

Task (2) involves *second-best theory*, prescribing a constitution that is best for an actual community, making allowance for the insurmountable limitations of its citizens and resources. Aristotle calls this a "second sailing" (*deuteros plous*), a nautical euphemism for hauling out the oars when the wind is too weak to fill the sails.[4] In fairness to Plato it should be noted that he too assigns this job to the legislator in the *Laws*: "Reflection and experience will soon show that the organization of a state is almost bound to fall short of the ideal." Assuming the legislator lacks the power to impose such a constitution, "the right procedure is to describe not only the ideal society but the second and third best too, and then leave it to anyone in charge of founding a community to make a choice among them" (*Laws* V.739a–b).[5] Although communism is the ideal for Plato, this "is a practice too demanding for those [citizens] born and bred and educated as ours are." The second-best solution is that individual families hold portions of land in perpetuity, although they continue to regard it as the common possession of the entire state (740a). Ironically Aristotle's own ideal constitution in the *Politics* borrows (without attribution) fixtures, such as the scheme for parceling out private property, from the second-best constitution of Plato's *Laws*.

Task (3) involves *commonplace or ordinary political theory*, prescribing how to reform an actually existing constitution. After surveying the political systems of 158 city-states of his day, Aristotle concluded that most fell short of being the best they could be, even allowing for the limitations in aptitude of the populace and the available resources. These shortcomings might be due, for example, to the prevailing culture or to class warfare. He observed that the rich tended to prize wealth above anything else, whereas the poor valued equality and the freedom to satisfy their own wishes. Many city-states were divided between rich and poor, with violent revolutions as one class overthrew the other. Aristotle contends that statecraft has something to contribute even in such adverse circumstances.

By studying actual systems, political experts can recommend reforms that will make an existing system more stable and long lasting: "If we know the causes which destroy constitutions, we also know the causes which preserve them; for opposites produce opposites, and destruction is the opposite of preservation" (V.8.1307b27–30). For example, political instability may result from failure of the citizens to obey the laws. Disobedience often develops little by little, starting with minor infractions that no one takes seriously when they occur separately but that eventually result in widespread indifference or contempt for the law. If the laws are frequently changed or arbitrarily enforced, the citizens may not develop habits of obedience to them, eventually resulting in a general disregard for the legal system. Obvious remedies would be to enforce even minor laws consistently and to make it more difficult to change the laws.

Aristotle issues a sweeping rebuke to his predecessors for neglecting this third task:

One should not study only what is best, but also what is possible, and similarly what is easier and more attainable by all. As it is, however, some seek only the constitution that is highest and requires a lot of resources, while others, though they discuss a more attainable sort, do away with the constitutions actually in place, and praise the Spartan or some other. But what should be done is to introduce the sort of organization that people will be easily persuaded to accept and be able to participate in, given what they already have, as it is no less a task to reform a constitution than to establish one initially, just as it is no less a task to correct what we have learned than to learn it in the first place. That is why . . . a statesman should be able to help existing constitutions. (*Politics* IV.1.1288b37–1289a7)

Aristotle chides Plato and other theorists for pontificating from their ivory tower and refusing to dirty their hands with everyday politics. His injunction to "introduce the sort of organization that people will be easily persuaded to accept and be able to participate in, given what they already have" recalls a remark of the Athenian legislator Solon, who when asked whether he had enacted the best laws for the Athenians, responded, "The best they would accept."[6] Real statesmen should be capable of improving the situations they face. The ideal should not be the enemy of the (attainable) good.

Political idealists might retort that Aristotle's approach leads to a crass pragmatism. If the statesman merely recommends minor changes that supporters of the constitution are willing to accept, these may simply perpetuate an unjust regime. In that case they will not be genuine reforms, changes that make the city-state better in an absolute sense, but merely quasi reforms—that is, changes that merely make the system more viable. For example, supposing the statesman advises that the regime will be more stable if all laws are enforced—what if the laws are thoroughly unjust? The Aristotelian statesman sounds like a Machiavellian consultant for hire, promising to preserve any regime no matter how evil.

This criticism, however, ignores an important Aristotelian principle, which may be explained as follows: Assuming G is our ultimate good or end, we stand in three possible relations to G. We may already possess and enjoy G, or we can get to G through one or more actions, or we can never make it all the way to G. Aristotle uses health as an example. Some of us are already in good health, others can become healthy by reducing their weight or exercising, and others can never become healthy because of an incurable disease. The person who is capable of becoming healthy by exercising and reducing should clearly do so, but even the person who can never become entirely fit (perhaps having suffered a stroke) should try to become as healthy as possible—say, by exercising as far as possible under the circumstances. In the light of this example Aristotle offers *the principle of approximation*: "While it is clearly best for any being to attain the real end, yet, if that cannot be, the nearer it is to the best the better will be its state." (*De Caelo* II.12.292b17–19; cf. *De Generatione et Corruptione* II.10.336b25–34).

Second-best theory, mentioned above, turns out to be a special case of the principle of approximation. This principle has wide application in Aristotle's philosophy. He employs it in biology to explain sexual reproduction (cf. *Generation of Animals* II.1.731b24–732a11) and in his ethics, where he counsels that although it is hard to be perfectly virtuous, we should try to act as virtuously as we can: "since to hit the mean is hard in the extreme, we must as a second best (*deuteros plous*), as people say, take the least of the evils" (*Nicomachean Ethics* II.9.1109a34–35).

Aristotelian statecraft is realistic, but it is not a forerunner of *realpolitik*. Aristotle's statesman is better described as an *approximist* than a perfectionist. He recognizes moral principles and wishes that actual society could be organized according to them. But he does not take the all-or-nothing stance of the utopian perfectionist, who either dreams of a "heavenly city" or stands aloof from politics (Kraut 2002). For the Aristotelian statesman the best constitution serves as a *regulative ideal*. Practical politics should aim at reforming the existing system so that it approximates this ideal as closely as is feasible.

It is important then to get clear on how Aristotle understands the political ideal. Our word "ideal" freely translates the Greek expression "according to prayer (*kat' euchēn*)," what we would "pray (*euchesthai*)" for. The "most ideal" constitution is the one that would obtain "if there were no external obstacles" (IV.1.1288b23–24). It would have the most favorable resources, location, and a population of appropriate size, natural aptitude, and class structure (IV.11.1295a29; VII.4.1325b36; 5.1327a4; 10.1329b25–26; 11.1330a37). Consequently the ideal constitution is beyond the reach of most citizens and city-states (IV.11.1295a29–31). Compared to actual legislation, ideal theorizing is easy, because it simply postulates conditions that depend on good fortune (VII.12.1331b21). Actually creating the best city-state would require a combination of luck and careful planning: "We pray that our city-state will be ideally equipped with the goods that luck controls (for we assume that luck does control them). When we come to making the city-state excellent, however, that is no longer a task for luck but one for scientific knowledge and deliberate choice" (VII.13.1332a29). In spite of the role of luck, Aristotle insists that the ideal must be possible: "We should assume ideal conditions, but nothing that is impossible" (II.6.1265a18; cf. VII.4.1325b39). Hence, Aristotle's regulative ideal is not utopian in the literal sense (*ou-topia* means "no place").

APPLIED STATECRAFT: ARISTOTLE'S PRESCRIPTIONS

What then *is* the regulative ideal for the Aristotelian statesman? According to Aristotle the aim of the city-state is happiness, and the happiness of the city-state as a whole includes the happiness of every citizen. "A city-state is

excellent because the citizens who participate in the constitution are excellent; and in our city-state all the citizens participate in the constitution"
(VII.13.1332a32–35). Individuals become virtuous only by realizing their
highest potentials: "For what is most choiceworthy for each individual is
always this: to attain what is highest" (14.1333a29030). The aim of the ideal
state is thus the *common good*, a state of affairs in which every citizen is able
to achieve full self-realization without impeding another's happiness.

This sets the stage for the fundamental claim of Aristotle's constitutional theory: "constitutions which aim at the common advantage are correct and just without qualification, whereas those which aim only at the
advantage of the rulers are deviant and unjust, because they involve despotic
rule, which is inappropriate for a community of free persons" (1279a17–21).
The distinction between correct and deviant constitutions is combined with
the observation that the government may consist of one person, a few, or a
multitude. Hence, there are six possible constitutional forms (*Politics* I.7):

	CORRECT	DEVIANT
One ruler	Kingship	Tyranny
Few rulers	Aristocracy	Oligarchy
Many rulers	Polity	Democracy

This six-fold classification (adapted from Plato's *Statesman* 302c–e) is the
starting point for Aristotle's inquiry into the best constitution, although it is
modified in various ways throughout the *Politics*. In a kingship or aristocracy
the rulers are fully virtuous and aim at the common advantage of all the
citizens. In a polity (or republic) the ruling group is more extensive (prefer-
ably encompassing a moderately wealthy class), but they possess only a lesser
grade of "military" virtue. The deviant systems are so called because the
rulers are vicious and privilege their own interests. The tyrant seeks power,
and in an oligarchy those in power—literally the few (*oligoi*) but ordinarily
the rich—are concerned with their own wealth. Finally, democracy is rule of
the people (*dēmos*), that is of all free-born citizens. When the majority are
poor and uneducated, they often empower unprincipled demagogues who
cater to their whims at the expense of the rich. Nevertheless, democracies
are generally more moderate than oligarchies, which in turn are more so
than tyrannies. The point is clearly that political virtue or vice is exercised
more effectively when the government is concentrated, because more rulers
make for disagreements and problems of coordination. These considerations

suggest a provisional rank ordering of constitutions with kingship as the "most divine" and tyranny the "worst." This yields the following ranking from worst to best in terms of how far they deviate from the ideal:

TYRANNY → OLIGARCHY → DEMOCRACY → POLITY → ARISTOCRACY → KINGSHIP

Statesmen should be familiar with all six forms and apply the principle of approximation. First, they should try to establish the best constitution permitted by the circumstances. For example, if no "godlike," supremely virtuous person is available to be king, an aristocracy should be established, provided there are candidates with full but human virtue. Second, statesmen should try to reform constitutions in a similar manner, by altering an existing constitution, reforming it so that it more closely resembles the systems above it in the hierarchy. For example, an oligarchy might be reformed by expanding the franchise to include more citizens, and a polity, by adding merit requirements for the highest offices. But the statesman must recognize a practical constraint: the target constitution must be one that "people will be easily persuaded to accept and be able to participate in, given what they already have."

As Aristotle examines actual constitutions in detail, it soon becomes evident that his initial ranking is too crude. For there are different types of democracy and oligarchy, ranging from moderate to extreme. The most extreme form of democracy, in which a mob takes the law into its own hands, is worse than a moderate form of oligarchy in which the ruling minority respects the legal rights of most subjects. In general, deviant constitutions with the rule of law are better than ones subject to the arbitrary rule of men. Aristotle ends up redefining polity as a *mixed constitution*, that is, one that combines features of different constitutions. This revised account may be summarized as follows: In the ideal commonwealth every citizen possesses freedom, ample wealth, and most importantly virtue. This is not so in actual city-states, which are divided between the rich and the poor and are fortunate to have any virtuous citizens at all. Still a constitution that assigns citizenship and offices to different groups on the basis of free birth, wealth, and virtue at least resembles an aristocracy and may be called an aristocratic polity. If the virtuous class is empty or too small to have an influence, the constitution is still a polity if it respects the political rights of both rich and poor (see *Politics* IV.8.1294a9–29). This allows a more complex way of applying the principle of approximation, since one can approach the same political ideal from the direction of democracy or oligarchy:

Aristotle also suggests criteria by which constitutions can be evaluated. One criterion is *unanimity*: A well-mixed constitution "should survive because of itself and not because of external factors, and because of itself, not because a majority wishes it (since that could happen in a bad constitution too), but because none of the parts of the city-state as a whole would even want another constitution" (*Politics* IV.9.1294b34–40; cf. II.9.1270b21–22).[7] Unanimity is a reasonable test of justice, because the citizens will tend to support the government when and only when they view it as protecting their interests. But such a requirement is beyond the reach of most deviant constitutions such as democracy and oligarchy, because different groups disagree about what the aims of the state should be or because resources are not sufficient to satisfy everyone's demands. In such cases Aristotle offers a fall-back criterion of *superiority*: "the part of a city-state that wishes the constitution must be stronger than any part that does not" (*Politics* IV.12.1296b14–16; cf. IV.13.1297b4–6; V.9.1309b16–18; VI.6.1320b26–28). This requirement could clearly be met by unjust constitutions, because it permits cases where the stronger group that supports the regime benefits at the expense of the weaker group that does not. But it may be as close to unanimity and justice as that city-state can come. And it is better than having an individual or small group that clings to power by means of intimidation, misinformation, and divisive tactics. For example Aristotle recommends that an oligarchy admit as citizens "a sufficiently large number of the people that those who participate in the constitution will be stronger than those who do not, and those who do share should always be drawn from the better part of the people" (VI.6.1320b26–28). By satisfying the criterion of superiority in this way the oligarchy becomes "better mixed" and thus more stable as well as more just. In the process the oligarchy also becomes more moderate and a better approximation of the regulative ideal.

Political theorists and practicing politicians who are guided by ideals may commit serious mistakes. The first sort of mistake may concern the political ideal itself. This is Aristotle's complaint about Plato's ideal in the *Republic*. Plato assumes "that it is best for a city-state to be as far as possible all one unit" (*Politics* II.2.1261a15–16; cf. *Republic* IV.462a), which leads him to advocate an ideal constitution in which "the citizens share children, women, and property with one another" (II.1.1261a4–5). Aristotle rejects Plato's principle that unity should be maximized: "the more of a unity a city-state becomes, the less of a city-state it will be. For a city-state naturally consists of a certain multitude; and as it becomes more of a unity, it will turn from a city-state into a household and from a household into a human being. . . . Hence, even if someone could achieve this, it should not be done, since it will destroy the city-state" (2.1261a17–22). Aristotle argues that Plato's ideal is unattainable even in principle. In particular, he rejects the communistic scheme of the *Republic*, because he believes that collective ownership of property and communal families will not work even under ideal circumstances.[8] Because human beings have a natural tendency to care more about what belongs to them personally, collectivized assets will tend to be neglected, resulting in what is now called a "tragedy of the commons" (Hardin 1972, 250–64). For example, unenclosed range lands tend to be overgrazed, because each rancher derives a benefit from increasing the size of his herd but the costs of doing so are spread to all users of the commons. But if the land is privately owned and fenced off, each rancher must directly bear the cost of adding to his stock. The privatization of property permits the internalization of costs and more efficient use of resources. Aristotle offers other arguments in support of private property as well, based on the premises that human beings are naturally self-interested and that moral agents need to control private spheres in order to practice virtues like generosity and friendship. But the argument as to internalizing costs does not depend on these added premises. Aristotle's conclusion is that communism should not be an ideal. For a political ideal to be relevant, it must be realizable; and a realizable constitution must include private property and separate households.

In addition, statesmen can easily go off the rails in trying to apply their ideals to actual circumstances. A case in point is Phaleas of Chalcedon, a contemporary of Plato who advocated equalization of property. Besides viewing the aim of leveling wealth as misguided, Aristotle points out practical problems with Phaleas's proposals—for example, a rule that the rich can give but not receive dowries and the poor can receive but not give dowries. Even if this could be done, it would be necessary to regulate the numbers of children. If offspring outstrip estates there will be a class of dispossessed persons descended from wealthier persons, some of whom are likely to become revolutionaries (II.7.1266b8–14). Further, Aristotle objects, merely equalizing property cannot ensure a just society unless the people have been adequately educated under the legal system (1266b28–31). Political reformers like Phaleas neglect the importance of culture and education. If these are not taken into account, political reforms may be ineffective or even yield unintended deleterious consequences.

Such mistakes can arise if political reformers are confused about their task. Recall the analogy with the gymnastics coach. An inflexible coach who subjects a pupil who is in poor physical shape or bad health to the same regimen as an Olympic athlete would probably not benefit the pupil and might cause serious harm. Similarly a would-be reformer who tried to impose on a troubled state laws suitable for an ideal state would probably fail and could precipitate social and economic dislocations or even civil war. Political radicalism typically involves this sort of confusion about the level of political change that is feasible. "Radical" derives from the word *radix* meaning "root," and the political radical wants to reform society from the roots, regardless of the costs and risks. The Aristotelian statesman must take the status quo seriously and consider carefully the possible outcomes of any change in laws or customs. Moreover, as noted earlier, any change, even for the better, has a cost: "If the improvement is small and it is a bad thing to accustom people to casual abrogation of the laws, then some of the rulers' or legislators' errors should evidently be left unchanged, since the benefit resulting from the change will not be as great as the harm resulting from being accustomed to disobey the officials" (II.9.1269a14–18). So Aristotelian statesmen are cautious about undertaking reforms; but they are not traditionalists, opposed to any departure from the past. They are *approximists*, committed to implementing their political ideals so far as circumstances permit.

ARISTOTLE FOR THE MINIMAL STATESMAN

A THOUGHT EXPERIMENT: *Imagine you are a legislator in a modern political state, who is in a position to bring about significant political change. After considering different possible regimes, you conclude that the best is that which affords the greatest liberty for its citizens. You accept Max Weber's definition of the state as "an association that claims the monopoly on the legitimate use of violence" (Weber 1947, 156). The proper role of the state, so defined, is to use force in order to protect individual rights to life, liberty, and the pursuit of happiness. The best regime would thus be a* minimal *state, in which individuals achieve justice by respecting each other's rights and cooperating for mutual advantage.*

Obviously, modern states are far from minimal. Every nook and cranny of modern life is subject to legislation and regulation. Yet contemporary societies continue to suffer serious problems including crime, unemployment, inadequate health care, and so forth. You doubt whether existing public programs are effective, and yet there is increasing pressure for a greater role by the state. Although there are different political factions, they seem to disagree over what things government should control or how it should control them, rather than whether government should have so much control over people's lives. In sum, in the modern world the minimal state looks like an anachronism.

Casting about for solutions, you are intrigued by Aristotle's theory of statecraft and his principle of approximation: that is, try to reform an existing system so that it approximates the ideal as closely as is feasible. You wonder whether this theory could be of use to you, even though it is hard to imagine a more un-Aristotelian ideal than the minimal state. You have heard that Aristotle offered advice to non-Aristotelian politicians of his own day: to democrats, oligarchs, and even tyrants. If you could ask Aristotle, what sort of advice might he offer to a "minimal statesman"?

Recall that Aristotelian statecraft involves three distinctive levels of application:

1. On the level of the *ideal*, to prescribe the best constitution a community could aspire to under the most favorable possible circumstances:

a population of the highest physical, intellectual, and moral capacities, which has at its disposal all the resources needed to develop these capacities.

2. On the level of the *second-best*, to prescribe the constitution that
    is best for an actual community making necessary allowances for
    the limitations of its citizens and resources.

3. On the level of the *commonplace or ordinary*, to prescribe how to
    reform an actually existing constitution.

These tasks may apply in turn to the minimal state.

On the level of the *ideal*, the task is to describe the best state, understood as the state which provides the fullest protection of individual liberty.
In such a state all citizens would have the right to do whatever they chose
with what they own—their own persons, their labor, and the private property they have legitimately acquired—unless their actions infringe on the
rights of other individuals. Others' rights are violated most importantly by
initiating the use of physical force or coercion against them, but also by
taking what belongs to others by threat, fraud, or theft. Rights violators are
liable to forfeit rights of their own, for example, by being punished or forced
to provide compensation to their victims. Individuals may choose to waive
or transfer a particular right (e.g., to a piece of property) to other individuals,
so that sales, gifts, contracts, and transfers of agency are legitimate. Individuals have a duty to respect each other's rights, and if they are rational they
will cooperate in a voluntary manner for mutual advantage. Within the
society property is privately owned, including consumer goods and capital, so
that the economic system would be a form of laissez-faire capitalism. The
purpose of government is to enforce individual rights by protecting life,
liberty, and private property, enforcing voluntary contracts, and punishing
rights violators. The ideal minimal state would perform this function without
violating the rights of the citizens. The aim of government would be justice,
consisting in respect by individuals of each other's rights and in voluntary
cooperation for mutual advantage.

The foregoing description is deliberately schematic. Nothing is said
about the origin or precise character of these rights. There are many different
theories of the minimal state, and these theories imply important differences
of detail concerning the constitution of the minimal state.[9] For example,
theorists may disagree over the status of individuals who are (completely or
partially) unable to exercise their own rights effectively: children, for example, who must remain under the authority and protection of adults until
they reach maturity, and adults suffering from severe mental or physical
disabilities. Different theories of rights will imply different ways in which
rights must be understood in special cases. Recent theorists of the minimal
state have not allowed human beings to be treated as the property of others

under any circumstances. Slavery or any other form of involuntary servitude (except as punishment for rights violations) is prohibited. But again different theories may disagree on what exactly constitutes impermissible servitude.

There is considerable room for disagreement and error when it comes to fleshing out the proper role of the minimal state. What exactly rights like the right to self-ownership, property rights, and rights of association amount to will vary, depending on the underlying theory of rights. For example, libertarian proponents of the minimal state have divided into two camps, sometimes called right and left libertarians. Although both wings endorse the right of self-ownership without qualification, they disagree on private property. The former endorse strong property rights, whereas the latter hold that "natural resources . . . may be privately appropriated only with the permission of, or with significant payment to, the members of society" (Vallentyne and Steiner 2000a).[10] The controversy echoes in a way the ancient dispute between Aristotle and Plato over ownership in the ideal state. How the problem is resolved will clearly have far-reaching implications for the minimal state as a regulative ideal.

On nearly every theory of rights, the legal system must play a role not only in enforcing individual rights but also in giving them greater precision. For example, Locke's theory that individuals legitimately acquire private property by "mixing their labor" with previously unowned natural objects, leaves the scope of property rights indefinite. As Robert Nozick points out, one can't acquire an entire ocean by mixing a can of tomato soup in it (1974, 174–75). This example does not show that the Lockean theory is mistaken, only that it is inherently vague. It does indicate that legal conventions are necessary to resolve such vagueness if there are to be clear and predictable expectations about the exercise of rights. The fact that a certain arrangement is conventional does not mean that it is arbitrary; one solution to a problem is frequently more reasonable than another. Thus property owners do not fully enjoy the benefits or incur the costs of using their own property; these are called positive and negative "externalities." For example, a boater may produce pleasure or annoyance in a homeowner on a lake. Or a homeowner's beautiful landscaping may increase the value of his neighbor's home. Or he may keep his neighbor awake at night by operating loud machinery. Laws to internalize externalities are difficult, since there are significant costs of enforcement. Hence, it is reasonable to internalize only the more proximate, weighty, and measurable externalities, for example, by adopting nuisance laws to protect property owners from neighbors who produce noise above a certain decibel level after dark.

This raises another question. If protection of rights is costly, how is the cost to be borne? One view is that public officials should conform to the same moral side constraints as everyone else. Hence, they may not use force against private citizens to collect revenues to finance state activities, on the grounds that taxation is on a par with forced labor (Nozick 1974, 169). An "ultraminimal" state, solely dependent on voluntary contributions would probably be too weak to press its claim to exclusive legitimacy and would likely sink into a functional equivalent to anarchy, leaving individuals to defend their own rights or rely on private protective associations. It has been suggested that the financing of the minimal state should be voluntary, involving fees for service, for example by imposing a fee *ex ante* on all enforceable contracts commensurate with the contracted amount (Rand 1964, 157). Such an arrangement, if workable, would obviously place very stringent financial constraints on government.

The above considerations concern ideal politics. In contrast, *second-best* must take into account actual limitations on the population and resources, even supposing the ideal has strong political support. The ideal minimal state does not interfere in individual transactions except to enforce contracts and protect the rights of outside parties. An obvious problem involves threats from foreign enemies. A well-regulated militia might suffice for "the city of our prayers," one with few enemies. But in the twenty-first century national defense can be provided only by government, and it is extremely expensive in a world plagued by belligerent states with large standing armies and weapons of mass destruction. Moreover, the recent rise in terrorism highlights the problem of controlling movements of personnel across national borders. The problem arises because defense is a *public good*: that is, everyone would benefit from it, but it cannot be withheld from just anyone selectively. So individuals who do not coordinate their actions have little incentive to contribute to it. They could free ride, leaving others to pay. Such underproduction of public goods is a classic example of market failure: The private producers of laissez-faire capitalism have no way of requiring users to pay for a public good (e.g., national defense) since they have no way of excluding noncontributors from using or benefiting from such goods. Granted the case for public defense, what about similar collective goods like pollution control, environmental protection, public safety, public health, and disease control? In our actual world, such goods, it might be argued, can only be provided by government, and it is hard to see how their provision could be funded without some mode of taxation.[11]

Another problem involves *eminent domain*, the power of the state to take private property for public use. If the government decides it is necessary to construct a military base, the ideal solution might be to purchase any property needed from the private owners. But if they are unwilling to sell or if they insist on holding out for an exorbitant sum, it may be necessary to take it from them coercively. This possibility was recognized when the U. S. Constitution stated that the property owners in such a case must receive "due process of law" and be provided "just compensation."[12] The principle has been applied to the taking of land for public roads, railroad throughways, and so forth. This is a second-best solution: It assumes an infringement of property rights strictly construed, but it protects the property owner through reasonable compensation (Epstein 2005).

To sum up, second-best theory recognizes that untoward circumstances may seriously impede the cooperation for mutual advantage of free individuals, and makes appropriate provisions in the constitution to meet these contingencies, while keeping it as close as possible to the minimal state.

Finally, *commonplace or ordinary* theory is concerned with reforming actual laws and institutions. This is a difficult task requiring practical wisdom as well as knowledge of the social sciences. Indeed, the modern proponent of the minimal state is in much the same position as an Aristotelian legislator in a deviant constitution such as the Athenian democracy.

The last century witnessed a rapid expansion of government into every sphere of social life. Especially remarkable was the emergence of totalitarian regimes inspired by ideologies such as communism, fascism, and national socialism. Although once endorsed by many intellectuals, these maximalist states have now been widely repudiated, having issued in tyranny, world war, genocide, millions of deaths, and untold misery, the outcomes of political repression and failed social experiments. Democratic societies also experienced a rapid and continuing expansion of government, motivated partially by responses to the totalitarian menace, but even more by the desire to regulate the economy and to establish a comprehensive welfare state. This has involved not only public support for the needy (e.g., the young, elderly, sick, disabled, and unemployed who cannot provide for themselves) but also programs for the universal provision of education, health care, and pensions. In addition, there is a natural tendency for government expansion, as illustrated by the example of protective tariffs or price supports. A domestic group (e.g., wine growers) is directly benefitted by a tariff and thus has an incentive to expend its resources in order to establish or retain the protection from competition. But because the costs are spread throughout the population, it is difficult to organize political opposition to the protective measure. Likewise it is difficult to eliminate existing programs even when they are no longer justified, because entrenched interests have an economic incentive to preserve them. This phenomenon is called *rent seeking*: economic actors use political means to obtain special benefits beyond what they could earn through voluntary exchanges (Tullock 2005). Although rent seeking benefits special interest groups it can be very costly to society as a whole, since it impedes competition and a free flow of goods and labor. For example, protectionist legislation may increase the revenue of a particular domestic industry but such interventions in the market are inherently inefficient; protectionist regulations tend to produce shortages and other economic dislocations and to provoke retaliatory protectionist measures by foreign countries, which harm other economic enterprises. Further, with greater governmental power there are more opportunities for corruption. Although more laws and regulations may be adopted when egregious acts reach the light of day, clever individuals and groups will predictably seek and find ways to evade the rules.

Despite all this, the fact is that big government has widespread and firm support throughout the contemporary world.[13] It would be quixotic to try to run for high office on the platform of transforming the modern welfare state into a minimal state. Aristotle would offer the modern "minimal statesman" the same sort of advice that he offered the democrat, oligarch, or tyrant of classical Greece—to practice *incremental approximism*: identify key programs that are obviously not working, because they are failing to meet their putative goal or generating unpopular costs, and devise politically palatable changes that will lead to less governmental control and more individual choice. The policy prescriptions will often involve some device for privatizing public programs. For example, government may contract with a private company to manage a public operation (e.g., an airport, wastewater plant, or prison); give vouchers to clients instead of providing services directly (e.g., for housing, education, health care); offer funding to private nonprofit organizations to provide services (e.g., charities or churches); enlist volunteers instead of employing bureaucrats to perform its desired functions; transform governmental agencies into private corporations or autonomous quasi corporations; or sell public assets to individuals or private companies.[14]

Two recent reforms in the United States illustrate the privatization strategy. The first was welfare reform. Although welfare was originally justified as a social "safety net," the reality was that many people lived their entire lives on public support as did their children, resulting in dynasties subsisting on welfare. Also, programs such as Aid to Families with Dependent Children (AFDC) seemed to give women an incentive to have children out of wedlock and to remain unemployed. The welfare system was fundamentally reformed by the Personal Responsibility and Work Opportunity Reconciliation Act of 1996. The principle was abandoned that people on welfare were entitled to their benefits. The aim of the new law was to help families exit from welfare by providing block grants to the states to fund benefits for needy families to help support their children while requiring them to make verifiable efforts to find employment and avoid illegitimate births. AFDC was replaced by a new program, significantly called Temporary Assistance to Needy Families (TANF). Following the reform, a number of people in fact left the welfare rolls and found employment. The number of disadvantaged single mothers employed increased significantly, and the welfare rolls dropped by more than 50 percent. In the years following the reforms there were over two million fewer people living on welfare.[15]

The other reform involved public housing. In the mid-twentieth century there was an extensive program of urban renewal and public housing. Much low-income housing in the cities was bulldozed away and replaced by large tenements like Cabrini Green in Chicago, on the premise that those relocated would lead a more stable and structured life there. But public housing was very expensive (costing 30 to 100 percent more to build than comparable privately built units), and the public structures rapidly deteriorated and were infested with crime and drugs. Public buildings costing billions of dollars had to be demolished, including the bellwether Pruitt-Igoe complex in St. Louis in 1972. In 1974 a significant reform provided for Section 8 tenant-based certificates to increase low-income tenants' choice of housing. During the 1980s the U.S. Department of Housing and Urban Development introduced new policies to permit occupants a much greater degree of control over their homes and living spaces. Institutions were established to assist low-income individuals to buy homes through entities like the Government National Mortgage Association (Ginnie Mae), the Federal National Mortgage Association (Fannie Mae), and Federal Home Loan Assocation (Freddie Mac). By the year 2000 over seventy million American families owned their own homes. New programs were also instituted to enable low-income persons to purchase their own homes. The premise was that housing would be of higher quality if individuals could exercise ownership over their own homes, or if they enjoyed some approximation to ownership, and that this would give them a greater opportunity to develop self-esteem and an enhanced sense of responsibility and control over other aspects of their lives.[16]

Both reforms are noteworthy because they had bipartisan support. They were widely viewed as successful, and they arguably helped to bring about a closer approximation of a free society. Ironically, these two reforms resemble proposals Aristotle himself made to the democrats of his day:

> When there are revenues, one should not do what popular leaders do nowadays. For they distribute any surplus, but people no sooner get it than they want the same again. Helping the poor in this way, indeed, is like pouring water into the proverbial leaking jug. But the truly democratic man should see to it that the multitude are not too poor (since this is a cause of the democracy's being a corrupt one). Measures must, therefore, be devised to ensure long-term prosperity. And, since this is also beneficial to the rich, whatever is left over from the revenues should be collected together and distributed in lump sums to the poor, particularly if enough can be accumulated for the acquisition of a plot of land, or failing that, for a start in trade or farming. [*Politics* VI.5.1320a29–b1]

From Aristotle's vantage point the aim of the reform is to enable the poor to assume greater responsibility and self-sufficiency. That, in turn, will make the democratic system more stable. The minimal statesman favors the reforms for similar reasons. The aims of virtue and freedom here converge in a common practical strategy.

CONCLUSION

Aristotle's theory of statecraft has enduring value for the modern political theorist. The modern statesman would do well to follow Aristotle in distinguishing three levels of political prescription: the ideal, the second best, and the ordinary. This approach is incremental approximism. It involves devising important reforms that are politically feasible and that will move the existing system closer to the regulative ideal.

Modern statesmen are also well advised to keep in view Aristotle's suggestions for practical politics. For example, his concept of the mixed constitution remains relevant. An actual constitution may be more just and more stable and efficacious if it combines features representing different political values. In today's political context *democratic capitalism* may represent a viable synthesis of two principles: where political order is subject to representative democratic rule, and economic order is largely the result of decisions by individuals possessing rights of property, contract, and enterprise (Novak 1982). Furthermore, modern statesmen should not forget Aristotle's warning about the hazards of political change. Political change by its nature is destabilizing. It weakens established institutions and threatens habits of obedience. Moreover, alterations often have unintended consequences, bad as well as good, affecting other parts of the political system. The would-be reformer should consider such potential consequences as carefully as possible and include the risks in his calculations.

Modern statesmen should keep in mind that they can err by going to either of two extremes. One is the unprincipled pragmatism espoused by the sophists and practiced by the tyrants and demagogues of Aristotle's day. On this view ideals are irrelevant to politics, and one should aim only at power over others. Any "reform" is merely a quid pro quo among competing factions without regard to moral principles. The opposite extreme is utopian perfectionism as espoused by Plato. On this view, the statesman should never depart from the ideal, since any effort at accommodation is evil. If the ideal is unreachable, one should stand aloof from politics. This sort of attitude is found in many modern splinter parties that refuse to make common ground with the major party closest to their own position and may even forge alliances instead with other radical factions whose principles are diametrically opposed to their own. This misguided utopianism results from confusing the task of ideal theory with that of ordinary politics. It is comparable to the mistake of a gymnastics coach who tries to impose on run-of-the-mill pupils a regimen appropriate for Olympic champions.

Radical utopians are vulnerable to two sorts of fallacies. First, the "slippery slope" argument is that any departure from the ideal will inevitably lead to the worst possible outcome. For the radical minimal state theorist, "having a little government is like being a little pregnant." This fails to recognize that a proposal should be selected on the grounds that it approximates the ideal. There are principled reasons for resisting a further deviation from this position. Second, the "lesser of two evils is evil" argument rests on a misleading tautology. It is of course wrong to take a less evil course when a better is available. But if one selects the least bad outcome because it is the closest attainable approximation to the ideal, one is not betraying the ideal.

The basic principle of Aristotelian approximism may be summed up as follows: It is possible to compromise without compromising one's principles.

NOTES

1. All translations of the *Politics* are from C. D. C. Reeve (Indianapolis: Hackett, 1998).

2. A similar interpretation is defended in (Miller 1995). The interpretation of Aristotle's account of statecraft in this essay also draws on the latter work.

3. Aristotle mentions a fourth task: to prescribe "which constitution is most appropriate for all city-states." (1288b33–5). This seems to be a special application of the other tasks.

4. Aristotle offers a *deuteros plous* rationale in connection with ostracism, the practice in the Athenian democracy of banishing citizens who were regarded as a threat to the regime although they had not been convicted of a crime warranting exile. "It would be better, certainly, if the legislator established the constitution in the beginning so that it had no need for such a remedy. But the next best thing (*deuteros plous*) is to try to fix the constitution, should the need arise, with a corrective of this sort" (*Politics* III.13.1284b7–20). Although ostracism is unjust, strictly speaking, it may be justified in order to eliminate a threat to a constitution, for example if an individual appears who is so powerful or rich that he presents an imminent threat to the constitution. Aristotle adds however that ostracism was open to abuse, for example to eliminate political opponents. Aristotle's qualified endorsement of ostracism may be compared to a provision in the U.S. Constitution: "The privilege of the writ of habeas corpus shall not be suspended, unless when in cases of rebellion or invasion the public safety may require it" (Article I, Section 9).

5. Translated by Trevor J. Saunders in *Plato: Complete Works*, ed. John M. Cooper (Indianapolis: Hackett, 1997).

6. Plutarch, *Life of Solon*, 15.2. This anecdote was reported by Pierce Butler during the debates on the United States Constitution in 1787, and was echoed in the Federalist Paper No. 38 by James Madison.

7. A weaker version occurs at VI.5.1320a14–17: "all the citizens should be well disposed toward the constitution, or, failing that, they should at least not regard those in authority as their enemies." It should be noted that unanimity is only a *criterion* of correctness. Aristotle is not anticipating modern theories of popular sovereignty by deriving the legitimacy of government from the will of the governed. Aristotle holds that a government is legitimate to the extent that it promotes the common advantage, and he assumes that a government that promotes everyone's interests will have everyone's approval.

8. Aristotle's critique is not altogether on target because he represents Plato as advocating communism for all the citizens, whereas the *Republic* prescribes it only for the comparatively small guardian class.

9. The thesis of this section—that Aristotelian statecraft would be useful for a proponent of the minimal state—is intended to apply to a wide array of such proponents, regardless of special doctrinal issues over which they happen to disagree. This is in no way to suggest that these issues are unimportant or to deny that it is incumbent on the protagonist of any political ideal to justify it on theoretical grounds. Early proponents of the minimal state were John Locke, *Two Treatises of Government* (1689) and John Stuart Mill *On Liberty* (1860). Two influential recent defenders are Ayn Rand in *The Virtue of Selfishness* (1964) and *Capitalism: The Unknown Ideal* (1966) and Robert Nozick, *Anarchy, State, and Utopia* (1974).

10. See also Vallentyne and Steiner 2000b. So-called right libertarianism is represented by Machan (1982), Narveson (1982), and Boaz (1997). Advocacy of the minimal state must to be distinguished from libertarianism (which encompasses a broad spectrum of views that repudiate the initiation of force) since not all defenders of the minimal state are libertarians and some libertarians are anarchists, arguing that the state necessary involves criminal aggression and violation of individual rights: e.g. Rothbard (1982).

11. For an argument along these lines see Morris (1998, 273–4). The classic work on public goods is Olson (1965).

12. United States Constitution, Amendment V, "nor shall private property be taken for public use without just compensation," and Amendment XIV, Section 1, "nor shall any State deprive any person of life, liberty, or property, without due process of law."

13. Although President William Jefferson Clinton declared that "the era of big government is over" (State of the Union address on January 23, 1996), the state in fact continues to be massive in all modern nations. Paul Charles Light (1999) argues that government is in fact much vaster than it appears. For example, the United States government employs not only 1.9 million full-time civil servants but also indirectly 17 million nonfederal workers in carrying out public programs. The latter belong to what Light calls "the shadow of government," which greatly exceeds the visible government.

14. An early treatise on privatization was Poole (1980). Recent studies of privatization as a political phenomenon are Bos (2001) and Feigenbaum, Hamnett, and Henig (1998). The Reason Foundation publishes an *Annual Privatization Report*.

15. See Mead (1997) on the rationale for welfare reform.

16. See Husock (1997) on the rationale for public housing reform.

2

ARISTOTLE AND THE LIBERAL STATE

Edward C. Halper

On the surface the contrast between Aristotle's political aims and
those of the modern political state—I shall refer to it as the "liberal
state"—could not be more stark. Whereas the very first sentence of
the *Politics* asserts that all political associations aim at some good (1252a1–
2), the liberal state does not aim to realize a public good but to insure that
each individual is able to pursue his private vision of the good, so long as it
does not interfere with others' pursuits of their own goods.[1] Clearly, where
Aristotle sees a positive role for the state in the attainment of individual
good, the liberal state ascribes to the state only the negative, prevention-of-
interference role. Although it is not always fully understood, the positive
political good that Aristotle advances consists rather simply in the citizen's
participation in mutually beneficial activities, not least of which is the governance and administration of the state itself.[2] There are, in fact, a huge
number of these administrative and governance activities; as a mark of just
how many, let me suggest that one peruse the number of local telephone
listings in the government section of a telephone book of a small municipal-
ity like Athens, Georgia, where I live. The existence of the state creates the
need for these functions, but it also provides citizens with opportunities to
cultivate and exercise their human capacities by performing the jobs that
sustain the state. Since virtue is the capacity to exercise one's faculties well,
the state opens up possibilities for virtue, at least on Aristotle's view.

Of course, the liberal state must also allow for mutually beneficial
activities, but it conceives of them under the rubric of individual choices: if
people share interests, there is no obstacle to their pursuing them together;
indeed, it is precisely such pursuits that the state makes possible. Government service, however, is conceived, at least in theory, as the forsaking of
one's private interests to serve others' needs and, thus, as motivated by a
noble personal self-sacrifice. Now, we do not, in fact, believe that all our
public officials are entirely noble: lust for power and, perhaps, greed often
seem plausible motives. More interesting than the question as to which of

these alternatives is true of any particular person is the fact that there are just two, that is, that proper service to the state is always posed (at least officially) as a sacrifice of personal interests and contrasted with improper, self-interested service. My aim here is to argue that the state needs a common good. This is a significant modification to the theory of the liberal state, but I will argue that it not only leaves intact its fundamental principles but strengthens them.

THE BEGINNING AND THE END OF THE STATE

One of the foundations of modern philosophy was a critique of Aristotle's notion of final causality. The objection was that a final cause could never actually be operative because it is attained, at best, at the end of some process. But proper explanations, it was claimed, would invoke causes that operate to produce consequences.[3] It was assumed as a result of this critique that the Aristotelian claim that the state aims at the good had to be thrown out. What replaced it were accounts that emphasized the *origin* of the state, that is, accounts in terms of what were traditionally called "efficient causes." Specifically, in the modern period the state is assumed (by Hobbes, Locke, Rousseau, and the entire "natural rights" tradition) to have arisen in response to conditions in a state of nature when people made a covenant that limited and prescribed behaviors necessary for their peaceful coexistence. This initial covenant was to be prescriptive for further decisions made to preserve the state. Now leaving aside the general lack of historical evidence for any such covenant, indeed, its utter historical implausibility, we should ask whether there is any real and intrinsic difference between a state conceived from its *origin* and one conceived from its *end*.

What makes it doubtful that there is a difference is that, from whichever direction we begin, it is necessary that self-preservation loom large in political decision making. In a state defined by its *origin*, future decision makers aim to preserve a state that fulfills its initial function, and to do so, they must arrange its institutions so that they are likely to produce citizens capable of making appropriate decisions to preserve the state. Such decisions require citizens or leaders with a rational perception of the purpose of the state and the ability to act upon that rational perception, that is, a capacity for free or autonomous agency. Equally, the state defined by its *end* requires leaders or citizens capable of making decisions that will preserve it, and for them to preserve the state is also to preserve their own role in the state. Hence, in this state, too, citizens are required to act with autonomy: their agency is for its own sake.

To put this point another way, the good that Aristotle sees as the *end* of the state is not something separate from the state, no more than the good of human life, happiness, is separate from human life; the good of the state is the state's functioning well, but that is no different from the individuals in the state performing their tasks for the sake of maintaining the state in its fully functioning condition; and that, in turn, is no different from the citizens in the state choosing to act with the freedom or autonomy requisite to preserve the state. In short, the good functioning that is the *end* of the Aristotelian state seems no different from the autonomous agency that is the *beginning* of the liberal state.

But this identity obscures three significant differences that it is important to appreciate. First, because the liberal state is constituted by individuals entering into a covenant, it presupposes that the individual good preexists the good of the state, and the state's task is taken to be limited to preserving the individual good, in contrast with the Aristotelian state that creates a good that individuals would not have on their own, namely, the exercise of human faculties in running the state. A second but related difference is that the Aristotelian state is itself a fulfillment of human nature, whereas the liberal state is an artifice, not natural in itself, that serves merely to preserve individual nature. Third, with its limited ends, the liberal state seems to require much less of individual citizens: they must only have some ability to act collectively so that all citizens can continue, to the extent possible, to function autonomously without interference from others; whereas the Aristotelian state requires individuals with real insight into the state's end and the ability to advance it, a rarer ability that is put to more demanding use. Hence, given the minimal demands it places on its citizens, the liberal state seems intrinsically democratic and the Aristotelian state, requiring more from its citizens, seems intrinsically aristocratic; but that is somewhat illusory, I shall argue later.

In short, we have something of the same autonomous activity involved in citizenship and government in both the liberal and Aristotelian states, but it is conceived quite differently. The crucial point of difference is the value of that governing activity: is it a mere necessity or a positive value in its own right? This is just the question I started with, but the point to see is that the autonomous or self-preserving activity of governing is much the same in both cases. What differs most is how to interpret it.

VIRTUE AND GOVERNANCE

One of the most basic but least understood ideas of Aristotle's political philosophy is that the self-preserving political activity fundamental to the state is identical to the activity in accordance with virtue that he identifies with happiness (*Nicomachean Ethics* I.7.1098a16–18; *Politics* VII.1328a35–b2).[4] In other words, the activity necessary to sustain a state is the very activity that fulfills human potential; so a person lives the best life he can by engaging in those political activities that, in fact, constitute the state. To be sure, philosophy represents a different and higher type of human fulfillment, and its special status may be what fosters the persistent notion that Aristotle sees the state as protecting a privately realized happiness. However, Aristotle's philosopher is not removed from the state; he, too, fulfills his responsibilities as a citizen, and these activities contribute to the development of the practical wisdom he needs to pursue philosophy (Halper 1999, 133–35). Aristotle thinks that the best life is lived in a good state, not because such a state removes obstructions to private fulfillment, but because the state itself provides opportunities for personal fulfillment in performing those very activities that the state needs to sustain itself.

In the best state, each citizen is assigned a job that fulfills his abilities to the greatest extent possible. Of course, there is no way to guarantee perfect assignments, and we are all uncomfortable with Aristotle's notions that (a) someone else would know each of us so well that he could decide for another person, better than that person could decide for himself, what job would best suit his abilities and that (b) there will be some people of such puny abilities that slavery would provide them the best opportunity to fulfill their potential. But these are merely problems of application. Setting them aside, we can appreciate the principle that the ideal arrangement is that citizens and state be so well matched that the one could not be what it is without the other's being what it is.

The corollary of this type of unity between perfect citizen and perfect state is an analogy between the character of a citizen and the character of the state in which he lives. The best-known treatment of this analogy is in books IV, VIII, and IX of the *Republic* where Plato describes the parallel between the soul and state in the ideal state and in the states that fall away from this ideal. Aristotle endorses the same analogy. In the first two chapters of the *Nicomachean Ethics*, for example, he describes the relation between the various activities, some of whose ends are subordinate to or included in the ends of others. An example is bridle-making whose end, the bridle, is used by the horseman, whose activity is, in turn, used by the general to attain his end, victory in war. But all activities in the state are used by the ruling art to achieve its end, the preservation of the state and the continued happiness of its citizens—an end identical with the proper functioning of the state.

This hierarchy of arts in the state is meant to parallel the manifold activities of which human life is composed, all of which are subordinate to the activity of living. The science of living well is parallel to politics: each is a knowledge of how to subordinate lesser activities to greater activities and to use their products for those greater activities. Thus, a person who knows how best to use his own abilities and how to engage in different activities in a way that furthers his own happiness—that is, that furthers his own best use of his faculties—has a knowledge that resembles that of the person who knows how best to use the various arts and activities of citizens so as to preserve the state and promote human happiness. Later in the *Nicomachean Ethics*, Aristotle maintains that the two types of knowledge are, indeed, the same, although they are not the same in being since the one concerns the state and the other the individual (VI.8.1141b23–29). Still later, near the end of the *Nicomachean Ethics*, we learn that one of the two good lives is the political life (X.7.1177b16–24; 8.1178a25–27; cf. I.5.1095b17–19; *Politics* III.13.1284a1–3).

In *Politics* III.4, Aristotle argues that the identity between good person and good citizen holds only for the ruler. However, it is also clear that other citizens exercise derivative forms of the virtues by fulfilling the jobs they have in the state (1277b13–29). The point is that there is a parallel between the character of the state and the character of citizens of that state because the personal faculties individual citizens exercise to maintain a state are a function of its character as a state, and cultivated faculties are virtues.

PARADOXES OF THE LIBERAL STATE

Let us now try to apply this analogy to the liberal state, modern democracy. There are well-known remarks that Plato makes in the *Republic* about citizens of a democracy: just as everyone is equal in this state, so too everything that his soul seeks is equal; so the democratic man might just as well pursue philosophy as engage in any other activity (561a–d). There is a certain resonance here with our nonjudgmental, "every person is valuable" society. However, we do not really live in the sort of democracy that Plato had in mind; for, normatively, an ancient democracy would have sought the good for its citizens, whereas the political institutions of modern democracy seek only to insure that its citizens are able to pursue their own good individually. Plato's democratic man pursues pleasures randomly "as if chosen by lot," just as Plato's democratic state chooses its officials, and this state selects, as if at random, what it happens to desire at any particular time. Yet, both democratic man and democratic state, as Plato sees them, act to pursue positive ends, even if the choices of those ends are random and fickle. Today's liberal state is different. Its end is *negative*; it aims to prevent others from interfering with an individual's pursuit of his own happiness, as he conceives it. Since this is a case where the state's negative end is supposed to allow, indeed, presupposes the individual's having his own private positive end, it might seem that the analogy of state and individual simply does not apply. That is to say, since the end of an individual in the liberal state is whatever he has chosen to pursue, and since that state has no end of its own except to allow the individual to pursue whatever end he has chosen for himself (provided it not interfere with others) and to prevent others from interfering with him, the ends of the state and the individual are so different that there seems to be no analogy between them.

This conclusion is, I submit, overhasty. First, let us notice that the purpose of the liberal state, to allow individuals to pursue their own notions of happiness, presupposes that happiness is an *individual* pursuit. From Aristotle's point of view, this assumption is wrong. He argues that happiness is an end that is not for the sake of something else and that it is self-sufficient (*Nicomachean Ethics* I.7.1097b6–16). By the latter, he means that a person with happiness does not need anything else, and he explains that this would not be true of a person who lives his life alone, but only of someone who lives with "parents, children, wife, and friends and fellow citizens, since man is by nature a social and political being." Aristotle goes on to define "self-sufficient [as] that which taken by itself makes life something desirable and deficient in nothing" (1097b14–15). The point is that happiness is not attained by an individual living in isolation but by his working together with family, friends, and fellow citizens. "Working together" is exactly the right phrase here because Aristotle argues that happiness is not a state but an activity, not how we feel but what we do. There are solitary activities, but there are also activities in which we can engage only with others or so significantly better with others that they are rightly called group activities. One can hit a tennis ball against a wall, but playing tennis requires another player. Aristotle's contention is that the best activities we engage in as human beings involve doing things with others. His exemplary virtuous activities are courage displayed on the battlefield, justice manifested as legislator or judge, and moderation in the pleasures of taste and touch, all activities that occur only or, at least, best with others. Even philosophy, the most solitary of virtuous activities, is still best done in conversation with others.

If Aristotle is right about happiness, there is something incongruous about the liberal state. It is dedicated to allowing individuals to pursue their individual visions of happiness, but happiness is fundamentally social or communal. It is tempting to say that in promoting individual freedom the liberal state is actively working against happiness. But this is too strong; for the liberal state allows individuals to associate and work together with whomever they please. The problem is subtler. First, at the theoretical level, the liberal state conceives itself as enabling each individual to pursue his own ends. So from its perspective a group activity must be understood as the sum of the individual activities in the group; a tennis game would not be a single activity but two acts of two individuals, each of whom is playing tennis. Suppose that tennis were among the activities that constitute happiness. In fostering individual happiness, the state might encourage each individual to play tennis, but it would also encourage each individual to see happiness as something individual. As a result, even individuals who are playing or working together see themselves as isolated and separated from others, each pursuing his own happiness apart from the others. Even while promoting individual activity and free association, the liberal state is promoting the sort of *individual* activity that does not constitute human fulfillment.

This conclusion may well be hard to accept. Let us approach it from a different perspective. Consider an individual living in a liberal state who reflects on which ends to pursue. He is aware of his own ambitions and desires, but he judges it nobler to pursue larger ends. What end could be larger than the preservation of his society? But the aim of society is merely that individuals be allowed to pursue their individual ends. Hence, for him to dedicate himself to society is for him to allow others to be in the position of choice that he is in—but that can be no more of an end than his own choices in the circumstances. So it makes no sense for him to choose the public good. Once again, all lives are private lives in the liberal state.

This is just the beginning of the difficulty. As a citizen of a state, I am obliged not just to pursue my individual ends but also the ends of the state; for it is only because the state allows me to pursue my ends that I can do so. The state is ultimately what allows or proscribes individual pursuits. But what does it mean to pursue the end of the liberal state? The liberal state does not really have its own end. It aims to allow individuals to pursue their ends. So in addition to whatever personal goals I have, I must foster the non-end of the state. Now all states must preserve themselves. If they allow certain behaviors, it is because they recognize them as either beneficial or nonthreatening. Behind the liberal state is the idea that individuals ought to make their own decisions autonomously, provided those decisions do not prevent others from making and acting on their own decisions. (There is constant debate about how precisely to apply this principle because it is not always clear when personal decisions do impact others; in particular, drug use has seemed to many to be a personal decision, but it is usually proscribed as a social threat.) To generalize, the liberal state proscribes all behaviors that could harm others or the social order and allows everything that is insignificant to the social order. The problem here is precisely this assumption of the insignificance of individual actions. As an individual in a liberal state, I am free to do what I want, provided it is of no significance. But, it will be objected, the act can have significance for *me*. Yet, what kind of significance does an individual have? Just because his choices are limited to himself or to facilitating others' making choices for themselves, his significance must be minimal. This is what strikes me as the supreme irony of the liberal state: individuals are free to do nearly everything, but only because nothing that any of them could do is deemed really to matter. It is just because everyone's choices are personal choices that no choice has real significance.

If this conclusion seems hard to swallow, we should think of characters that have become familiar fixtures of our imagined world and, sometimes, of the real world of the liberal state. I have in mind characters like the corporate manager, the public official, and the political activist. The corporate manager has been trained to maximize profits; he conceives himself as producing the most at the least cost. His skill has little or nothing to do with the particular product or service of the company. The public official searches for the common good, but is able to see only a plurality of conflicting special interests. There is no policy or legislation that will not be championed by some interests and condemned by others. It is possible to distinguish the more widespread interests from the less so, but the "common good" evaporates into competing interests. Finally, the political activist is motivated by his desire to pursue a good beyond his narrow self-interest. But he faces the dilemma that if he imposes his notion of a good on someone else, he deprives the other of the autonomy that makes a person really worth caring about; whereas if he does not so impose but opts to assist another in pursuing the other person's goals, he may well find himself promoting ends he does not share and the other, for his part, may well see the activist's end (aiding others) as alien and decline or resent his assistance. The perfect solution to the problem is animal rights: by aiming to help animals, one has a good beyond himself, but he can dictate a good to beings that cannot exercise autonomy or decline his assistance. This is an end that is larger than an individual end but does not impose itself on others. But, of course, it is confined to nonpersons.

These characters, each cockeyed in his own way, exemplify the liberal state and what is wrong with it. They pursue their ends without being able to connect with others or work together on common ends. Each seems to be working toward good and reasonable ends, but considered closely, each end is seen to be insignificant because it does not promote the common human good. To be sure, we can all think of hardworking individuals sincerely dedicated to noble goals; the beauty of the liberal state is precisely that it allows for such individuals. My claim is not that the liberal state excludes these individuals, but the more subtle and tendentious claim that it tends to work against them. The liberal state allows them to exist, indeed prides itself on their existence; but it tends to imbue individual ends with the same purposelessness that it has. In order to pursue the ends that I choose, I must live in a state that allows me to do so. Hence, I must work to preserve the state that allows me to pursue my ends. But it allows me to pursue my ends because it is essentially indifferent to them. Hence, while striving for my ends, I must also strive to preserve a system where those ends do not matter. Nietzsche (1974, 166) spoke of the boredom that afflicts modern societies: how could there not be ennui if in order to pursue my own ends, I must acknowledge that they are only mine, do not impede others' actions, and are not of larger significance? The analogy between the state and the individual manifests itself in the individual's indifference to his own ends—a characteristic familiar enough from literature.

AN ARISTOTELIAN SOLUTION

In the final section of this chapter, I will briefly sketch a solution that derives from Aristotle. I begin with an observation. It is often said that the American state is rooted in the political philosophies of Hobbes, Locke, and

Rousseau, and this is surely true. But there is another source that I think has been neglected, Aristotle's *Politics* IV. In the first three books of the *Politics*, Aristotle is concerned with the best state; in the fourth with the best *possible* state. The difference is that this latter is a state whose realization does not depend on the presence of people with special virtues. Because Madison and the authors of the Federalist Papers were deeply concerned to prevent faction, also a central concern of Aristotle's here, the polity Aristotle describes in book IV is an important model for the American state.[5] Aristotle's image of a state governed by gentlemen farmers who follow laws enacted by assemblies that can afford only temporary absences from their small farms to assemble to enact laws resembles Jefferson's vision of democracy and is reflected in the brief annual legislative session mandated in Georgia and other states.[6] The "natural rights" philosophy that imbues the Declaration of Independence and the thinking of the founding fathers is not, in my view, antithetical to Aristotle's political philosophy: it, too, accepts some positive end for the state. However, this philosophy was effectively replaced in the nineteenth century by the theory of the liberal state propounded by John Stuart Mill and others. That Aristotle's polity was a model for an American state founded by thinkers who saw a positive role for the state suggests that institutions created by the framers of the Constitution were conceived as attaining positive ends. Again, the difference between Aristotle's polity and the liberal state is that the polity aims at a good, and that good is or includes living in the state, whereas the liberal state aims only to remove obstructions to individuals pursuing individual aims.

Here then is my proposal: because the institutions of the liberal state are not necessarily different from the institutions of the polity, we can, without large institutional changes, abandon the ideology that makes us regard ourselves as having a liberal state and begin to see ourselves as a society that aims at the public good. Consider what that would mean: instead of extolling the businessman because of his efficiency, we should see his occupation as a realization of his talents; instead of seeing the politician as someone who has sacrificed his interests for the sake of others, let us understand, what is obvious anyway, that in being a political leader he exercises his own abilities in a manner that is no less demanding than the athlete but, because he has a hand in sustaining the state and thereby enabling others to exercise their faculties, far more valuable. Let us see the scientist not, as James Watson (1980) proposes, someone out for fun and fame, but as someone whose activity advances knowledge and improves the human condition.

What is discomforting about seeing the state as aiming at some good is the thought that it might exclude certain pursuits and thereby limit autonomy. There are plenty of critics of the liberal state who would indeed do so. But it is precisely here that Aristotle stands to make the greatest contribution to contemporary political theory, that is, in teaching us how to have ends without their dictating choices. Aristotle's ends are functional human communal ends that do not force us to accept a particular doctrine but to put our faculties to the greatest use. Whatever particular choices the citizens of a state make, they need to keep in mind the state's positive goal of allowing its citizens to realize their human potential through political activity. In the very act of promoting this goal through political activity, the citizens are realizing it. Hence, the realization of our human faculties in politics is a positive human good that, so far from limiting freedom and autonomy, opens a way to exercise autonomy. Concern that the state's pursuing a positive good would stifle dissent and democracy must be set aside if the state's aim includes the exercise of citizenship and participation in national policy debates. Discussion and disagreement are essential to the state, properly conceived. We do not need to sacrifice personal interest to pursue the public good. We can achieve our personal good in the act of fostering the public good. This personal good that is also a public good is within the reach of nearly all. It requires only the simplest and most difficult of changes: to think of ourselves differently.

NOTES

1. As John Stuart Mill puts it in *On Liberty*: "The sole end for which mankind are warranted, individually or collectively, in interfering with the liberty of action of any of their number, is self-protection. The only purpose for which power can be rightfully exercised over any member of the civilized community, against his will, is to prevent harm to others" (1947, 9).

2. Until recently, the predominant view in the literature assimilated the Aristotelian state to the liberal one and, accordingly, saw the state's role as making possible private pursuits of individuals. One expression of this view occurs in Mulgan (1987, 7). Mulgan denies that a life of moral virtue is "primarily concerned with specifically public or political activity" (32–33). Another occurs in the introduction to Stephen Everson, *The Politics* (1988, xxvii). On the other hand, Julia Annas thinks that political activity is a necessary *part* of human activity; our lives would be "stunted" without participation in it (1993, 150–52). A. H. W. Atkins uses the function argument of *Nicomachean Ethics*. I.7 to argue that the virtues Aristotle describes in his ethics are meant to be exercised in the governance of a state (1991, 75–93). C. D. C. Reeve claims that "ethics and statesmanship coincide" (1998, xxvi).

To speak of the state as having a good of its own requires that it be something capable of having its own end, that is, that it be a substance of some sort. That Aristotle considers it to be such, I argue in Halper, 1995 (14–23). Aristotle claims "when they come together, the multitude is just like a single human being, with many feet, hands, and senses, and so too for their character traits and wisdom" (III.11.1281b3–7, *Politics* Reeve trans.).

3. One version of the critique appears in Baruch Spinoza, *The Ethics* [1677], part 1, appendix (1982, 57–62), and part 4, preface (1982, 154–55).

4. *Politics* III.4 qualifies this identity. Aristotle asks whether the good man is also the good citizen. He argues that one can be a good citizen without being a good

man, but there is one case where the two are, indeed, identical, the ruler (1277a27–29; cf. 1277b25–26). This qualification of the *scope* of the identity does not undermine the *fact* of the identity between the individual good and the political good. Even though most good citizens do not attain the type or degree of the virtue possessed by a good man, they do attain some semblance of that good through their offices in the state.

5. Madison's *Federalist* No. 10 (Hamilton et al. 1961, 77–84) is one of the best discussions of this central theme. His claim that "the most common and durable source of factions has been the verious [sic] and unequal distribution of property" seems to stand behind Aristotle's endorsement of the middle constitution: "the middle constitution is best since it alone is free from faction. For conflicts and dissensions seldom occur among people where there are many in the middle" (IV.11.1296a7–9; *Politics* Reeve trans.). The "middle constitution" is between oligarchy and democracy because its people are neither rich nor poor.

6. See *Politics* IV.6.1292b25–34. Aristotle calls this the first form of democracy, but it closely resembles his first form of oligarchy (1293a10–20) in that both are governed by laws made by citizens who meet property requirements. Aristotle claims that polity, his best of the *possible* forms of government, is "a mixture of oligarchy and democracy" (8.1293b33–34). He seems to mean that there ought to be many gentlemen farmers and that the property requirements should be low.

3

WHY DEMOCRATS NEED THE VIRTUES
Robert B. Talisse

I n this chapter, I pursue two related themes. First, I contend that the deliberative turn in contemporary democratic theory is as yet incomplete. Second, I propose some reasons for thinking that deliberative democrats must turn to Aristotle if they hope to complete their project. Thus the following pages are not focused upon some detail or other of Aristotle's text, nor do I claim to be presenting a view that Aristotle himself would endorse. The point is rather to suggest that contemporary deliberativism needs Aristotle. To my mind, there could be no better vindication of Aristotle's political thought than to show that it is essential for developing a viable political theory today. The argument requires lots of stage setting, so please bear with me as I work through some of the issues driving the current debates.

The deliberative turn can be seen as a response to the liberal-communitarian debate.[1] The communitarian critique of liberalism proposed that liberal political philosophy rested upon a viciously atomistic view of the individual and consequently could not countenance an adequately robust vision of democratic citizenship. That is, the critics of liberalism maintained that liberal politics could not eschew what Jane Mansbridge (1983) fittingly characterized as "adversary democracy." On the adversarial model:

> Voters pursue their individual interests by making demands on the political system in proportion to the intensity of their feelings. Politicians, also pursuing their own interests, adopt policies that buy them votes, thus ensuring accountability. In order to stay in office, politicians act like entrepreneurs and brokers, looking for formulas that satisfy as many, and alienate as few, interests as possible. From the interchange between self-interested voters and self-interested brokers emerge decisions that come as close as possible to a balanced aggregation of individual interests. (Mansbridge 1983, 17)[2]

The communitarian case was bolstered by the widespread concern over dwindling civic association and political participation that received its most popular expression in Robert Putnam's "Bowling Alone" (1995) article and related work.[3] Michael Sandel succinctly captured the sting of the critique, writing that liberalism "cannot secure the liberty it promises," because it "cannot inspire the sense of community and civic engagement that liberty requires" (1996, 6). What liberals needed was a way to reunite the atomic individuals that resided at the basis of their theory, to socialize the essentially asocial. The prospects for liberalism seemed bleak.

The liberal defense consisted mostly in counterattack. The liberal critique of communitarianism took a Millian tack and raised concerns of community tyranny, conformity, and intolerance.[4] To the communitarian call for a politics of settled identities and social allegiances, a community of shared values, and a morally nonneutral state, Amy Gutmann replied, "The enforcement of liberal rights, not the absence of settled community, stands between the Moral Majority and the contemporary equivalent of witch-hunting" (1985, 132). In a more diagnostic tone, Stephen Holmes observed:

> [Communitarians] rhapsodize about neighborhoods, churches, school boards, and so forth; they never provide sufficient detail about the national political institutions they favor to allow us to compare the advantages and disadvantages of illiberal community with the vices and virtues of liberal society as we know it. . . . What does a commitment to "solidarity" or "consensus" imply about the authority of majorities over dissident minorities? (1993, 178)

Communitarians needed to devise a way in which essentially social and "encumbered" selves could adopt a self-critical stance that could weed out the oppressive, intolerant, and homogenizing tendencies of community without re-invoking liberal notions of civil liberty and individual rights. In other words, they needed a conception of community that was at once binding *and* plastic, a politics that was both formative and fluid. Again, the prospects seemed bleak.

Enter the deliberative turn. Although the literature on democratic deliberation is less polarized and thus may seem a decisive improvement over the impasse it dislodged, it is my contention that each camp of the earlier adversaries has seized upon the idea of deliberative democracy as a reparative measure. Accordingly, the fundamental liberal-communitarian problematic persists.

To see this, consider first the host of deliberative proposals associated with John Rawls. Central to liberal deliberativism is the "ideal of democratic citizenship" (Rawls 1996, 217) in which citizens come together in a "public political forum" (Rawls 1999, 133), a realm in which "free public reason among equals" (Cohen 1996, 412) operates. Within this realm, participants regard one another as equals; they aim to defend and criticize institutions and programs in terms of considerations that others have reason to accept, given the fact of reasonable pluralism and the assumption that those others are reasonable; and they are prepared to cooperate in accordance with the results of such discussion, treating those results as authoritative. (Cohen 1996, 413)

On the liberal view, then, "reasonable pluralism" demands that citizens must conduct public debate in strictly Rawlsian, "political not metaphysical" terms. Consequently, the liberal places restrictions not only upon the *kinds of reasons* citizens can employ, but also upon the *kinds of questions* suitable for deliberation. Issues that cannot be debated in "political" terms are removed from the agenda (Rawls 1996, 157). Liberal democratic deliberation is thus subject to what Bruce Ackerman calls "conversational restraints":

> When you and I learn that we disagree about one or another dimension of the moral truth, we should not search for some common value that will trump this disagreement.... We should simply say nothing at all about this disagreement and try to solve our problem by invoking premises that we do agree upon. In restraining ourselves in this way, we need not lose the chance to talk to one another about our deepest moral disagreements in countless other, more private contexts. (1989, 16–17)

So liberals advocate public discussion and debate, but place the basic commitments and principles of liberalism beyond the reach of political deliberation.[5] Gutmann and Thompson are explicit on this point: "Even in deliberative democracy, deliberation does not have priority over liberty and opportunity" (1996, 17). On their view, basic liberty and fair opportunity are "constraints on what counts as a morally legitimate resolution of disagreement" (1996, 17). Indeed, they are "partly independent" values (1996, 366, n.18).

This feature of liberal theories invites the objection that liberal deliberative democracy is "fixed" to favor liberal outcomes.[6] Theorists as ideologically diverse as Robert George (1999), Iris Young (2000), Stanley Fish (1999), and Chantal Mouffe (2000) argue that liberal deliberativism is in fact exclusionary because it silences those whose concerns cannot be articulated within the confines of public reason as "liberally" construed. So liberal theorists of deliberative democracy retain precisely the element that rendered liberalism problematic: the view that citizens come into the political arena as distinct, discrete independent entities with irreconcilable and incommensurable fixed interests and fundamental commitments that are always separable from who they are.

Next consider communitarian conceptions of deliberation. Where liberals attempt to avoid moral controversy, communitarians are obsessed with moral consensus. On their account, shared moral discourse among citizens is the means by which a fragmented community may "recover its civic voice" (Sandel 1996, 324) and change "*me* language" into "*we* language" (Barber 1998b, 13). That is, shared "moral dialogue" *restores* community by appealing to "overarching values" implicitly shared. Through dialogue, citizens come "to affirm new, renewed, or some other set of values" (Etzioni 1998, 186–90). Barber explains:

> A public voice expressing the civility of a cooperative civil society speaks in terms that reveal and elicit common ground, cooperative strategies, overlapping interests, and a sense of the public weal. (1998, 116)

Communitarians are confident that commonality, shared purposes, and overlapping interests underlie all or most political disagreement. Public deliberation is the process by which this deep agreement, suppressed by the deracinating tendencies of liberal politics, can surface and flourish. The value of deliberation lies in its power to realize the immanent sense of community among seemingly divided persons.

Hence the problem: Communitarian accounts of public discourse *presuppose* that fundamental agreement at deep levels *already exists* among persons who *merely seem* to be divided. So deliberation is not a process by which persons confront *real* differences and try to forge common ground. Rather all differences are merely apparent, and common ground will always be *found*. But such confidence in underlying commonalities only reinforces liberal anxieties about community tyranny and suppression of individuality.[7]

Perhaps more importantly, as they believe that the materials necessary for harmonious community lie dormant within citizens, communitarians see deliberation as a *prelude* to politics, a process by which the latent Common Will comes to realize itself in shared purposes, commitments, and ideals. But where there is widespread agreement and a shared moral vision, there is no need for deliberation! Deliberation is thus merely of instrumental, temporary value; once a truly *political* community is realized, through deliberation, deliberative processes may be discarded.

Liberals, then, offer a theory of deliberation that restricts vocabularies and agendas to such a degree that there is ultimately precious little to deliberate *about*. Communitarians, by contrast, promote a view according to which deliberation, understood as the process of excavating a shared political will, is ultimately unnecessary. Neither approach is satisfactory.

Recognizing this unhappy situation, some have proposed a view of deliberative democracy that is both *decentered* (Habermas 1996; Bohman 2004) and *epistemic*. A decentered deliberativism rejects the idea that all political deliberation must be focused upon the State and the essentials of its constitution (Rawls 1999). Rather, the primary sites of deliberation are the multiple voluntary associations of civil society, and the subjects of deliberation run the gamut from the minutely local to the grandly global. An epistemic deliberativism holds that the purpose of public deliberation is ultimately to "rationalize" politics (Habermas 1996; Benhabib 2002), to "inform" citizens (Dryzek 2000), or to arrive at decisions that are "wise" (Young 2000) or even "true" (Nino 1996; Estlund 1993b, 1997).

There is a kind "trickle up" strategy involved in such proposals: deliberation begins in small voluntary associations and, since these associations overlap and intersect in myriad ways, eventually affects higher levels of organization. The proposals often implicitly endorse Mill's ([1859] 1991) point that continuing processes of open critical discussion among citizens are destined to lead to epistemically better decisions and better informed citizens. The combination of decentrism and epistemicism seems to remedy nicely the problems with liberal and communitarian proposals. The decentrism obviates liberal restraints on deliberative agendas, and the epistemicism means that consensus is not in itself the aim of discussion. I myself am very sympathetic to the decentered and epistemic view of deliberative democracy; however, there are complications.

Let us leave aside questions concerning what it could mean for one political policy or decision to be true or epistemically better than another; these are not the complications I intend to discuss. Instead I call attention to the experimental findings as to *group polarization* discussed by Cass Sunstein in several recent works (2001a; 2001b; 2003a; 2003b). Group polarization, found all over the world and in many diverse tasks," means that "members of a deliberating group predictably move towards a more extreme point in the direction indicated by the members' predeliberation tendencies" (Sunstein 2003b, 81–82). In groups that "engage in repeated discussions" over time, the polarization is even more pronounced (Sunstein 2003b, 86). The implication is that ongoing political deliberation among small groups in civil society can be expected to "produce a situation in which individuals hold positions more extreme than those of any individual member before the series of deliberations began" (Sunstein 2003b, 86).[8]

There is a tension, then, in the very idea of a decentered and epistemic deliberativism: When the primary sites of deliberation are small groups in civil society, the epistemic aims of deliberation are frustrated. Group polarization makes small deliberative enclaves *epistemically unstable*, that is, they are prone to irrational shifts in belief toward increasingly extreme views. If the aim of deliberation is truth, voluntary associations in civil society are unlikely to get it and hold on to it.

These results are even more unsettling once it is noted that the phenomenon is found no less among judges, juries, presidential cabinets, members of congress, and boards of directors as among local citizen's groups (Sunstein 2003a). The remedy Sunstein offers goes like this: democratic governments must contrive institutional blocks to group polarization. Toward this end, Sunstein proposes that democratic governments enhance democratic deliberation by expanding the "argument pools" (Sunstein 2003a, 90) to which citizens are exposed. This can be done, he suggests, by fostering a public sphere in which dissent and controversy are welcomed (Sunstein 2003a). How might this be accomplished? To cite one example, Sunstein recommends what he calls "must carry" rules for internet websites that are especially partisan. The idea is that citizens should not be able to use the internet as a "filtering device" that enables them to preselect the political messages and viewpoints they encounter; the government should require political websites to carry links to sites that feature opposing views (Sunstein 2001a, 169).

I tend to agree with Sunstein here. If democracy is deliberative, and if deliberation is epistemic, then certain deliberation-enabling institutions must be in place. Such institutions must ensure that citizens encounter a wide variety of political views, voices, sources, and arguments; they must make it difficult for citizens to band together in isolated epistemic communities listening only to "louder echoes of their own voices" (Sunstein 2003b, 82). However—and here, finally, is where Aristotle begins to come into my story—institutional guarantees that political websites carry links to sites promoting opposed views are certainly not enough. As any student of contemporary political discourse knows, political partisans often make repeated reference to their opponents: they call their opponents "lying liars" (Franken 2003) and propose to offer a "no-spin zone" (O'Reilly 2001) in which "fair and balanced" analysis can commence. The "crippled epistemology" (Sunstein 2003a, 12) of narrowly partisan enclaves does not thrive because partisans are unaware of or unexposed to their opponents' views; they are rather fully aware of and often highly sensitized to the views of their adversaries. How else could ad hominem be possible?

The problem is not just the self-imposed *isolation* of deliberating groups. So the remedy cannot be just encouraging more *exposure* to diverse viewpoints. Rather, the problem lies in the *epistemic insularity* of political groups, their unwillingness to consider that views opposed to their own might not only be *reasonable* but *correct*. That is, the real issue concerns the *way* in which citizens view opposing positions and those who propose them. That is, the issue is the *epistemic character* of the citizens. This is not a problem that can be solved by "must carry" laws or similar legal interventions. Aristotle saw this in his *Politics*:

> For the many, each of whom is not a serious man, nevertheless could, when they have come together, be better than those few best—not, indeed, individually but as a whole. (1281a42)

Contrary to some recent interpretations, Aristotle is not in this passage endorsing the neo-Rousseauian view I above attributed to the communitarians. Aristotle's point is not that public discourse magically transforms "me language" into "we language." The claim is rather that imperfect individuals can collectively form a reliable and responsible deliberative group, *provided they individually embody certain epistemic traits*. We may characterize the traits necessary for proper deliberation as "deliberative virtues." The main thrust of these virtues is well captured by Iris Young's use of the term "reasonableness." She writes:

> Reasonable participants in democratic discussion must have an open mind. They cannot come to the discussion of a collective problem with commitments that bind them to the authority of prior norms or unquestionable beliefs. Nor can they assert their own interests above all others' or insist that their initial opinion about what is right or just cannot be subject to revision. To be reasonable is to be willing to change our opinions or preferences because others persuade us that our initial opinions or preferences . . . are incorrect. . . . Being open thus also refers to a disposition to listen to others, treat them with respect, make an effort to understand them by asking questions, and not judge them too quickly. (Young 2000, 24–25)

When citizens embody deliberative virtue, their deliberations are more likely to avoid group polarization and similar pitfalls. The participants will be able to benefit from expanded "argument pools," because they will be able to *engage* opposition, *evaluate* alternative views, and, when appropriate, *revise* their own commitments. Citizens embodying the deliberative virtues collectively comprise a *community of political inquiry*. And the cultivation of such a community is a key objective of democratic politics.

I have argued that democracy must be deliberative, that deliberation must be decentered and epistemic, and that for decentered and epistemic deliberation to succeed, citizens must embody certain epistemic traits, those that I have called "deliberative virtues." If this is correct, it follows that a successful democracy cannot be liberal democracy. That is, democracy cannot thrive under a neutralist and proceduralist state. Democracy needs the state to take part in what Michael Sandel, following Aristotle, called the "formative project" (1996, 324). But where civic republicans like Sandel see this formation as essentially *moral*, I have suggested that it is ultimately *epistemic*. In the deliberativism I have sketched, the state's formative role is not that of promoting a substantive vision of the moral good but that of cultivating the epistemic habits requisite for deliberating collectively about the good. I contend that the next step deliberativists must take is to work out a general account of the deliberative virtues. Such an account must identify and describe in detail the nature of these virtues and must investigate the means by which they can be cultivated. That is to say, a properly deliberative democratic theory cannot be "political" in the narrow Rawlsian sense common to much recent political philosophy. The focus of such a theory cannot be simply the state or the constitution. Rather, deliberative democratic theory must engage questions of education, art, culture, law, and civic responsibility. Aristotle's *Politics* provides a model here, and even if one does not endorse Aristotle's own conclusions, a reinvestigation of his principal insights is essential to the development of a viable democratic theory today.

NOTES

1. See Mulhall and Swift (1996) for a full discussion; see also the essays collected in Avineri and de-Shalit (1992) and Sandel (1982).

2. Cf. Habermas (1996, 22); Dryzek (2000, chap. 1); Young (2000, chap. 1); Bohman (1998, 1–3); Nino (1996, chap. 4); Cohen (1989, 411–12); and Gould (1988, 97).

3. See Bellah (1985); Dionne (1991); Elshtain (1995); Etzioni (1993); Iyengar (1991); Janowitz (1983); Page (1996); and Phaar and Putnam, eds. (2000).

4. Stephen Holmes provides the most sustained example of this kind of liberal reply to communitarian criticisms. He sees communitarianism as a species of a more general tradition of "antiliberalism." On his view communitarian thinkers like Alasdair MacIntyre and Roberto Unger belong to the same intellectual tradition as Leo Strauss and Carl Schmitt (1993, 176).

5. Cf. Fish (1999, 90–91).

6. See Knight's (1999) discussion of Gutmann and Thompson for an elaboration of this point.

7. On this point, see Cohen (1998, 222–24).

8. It is important not to misunderstand Sunstein's use of the term "extreme." The point is not that deliberation in ideologically homogenous groups will lead individuals to embrace views that are increasingly "extreme" by some extraneous political measure. The point is rather that such deliberation will lead individuals to endorse increasingly extreme versions of the views they held prior to entering the deliberation.

4

VIRTUE-ORIENTED POLITICS: CONFUCIUS AND ARISTOTLE

May Sim

On the face of it, Aristotle's view of politics seems quite different from Confucius's. Aristotle defines the polis and the citizen and analyzes them according to a teleological understanding of nature.[1] Confucius not only lacks explicit definitions but also lacks any explicit theories about nature and teleology. Aristotle sharply distinguishes the political rule of statesmen from the household rule of fathers. Confucius assimilates political rule to household rule: political government is simply the father-son relationship writ large. Aristotle offers an analysis of different regimes, an ideal constitution and the best constitution in actuality. Confucius never offers a theoretical analysis of possible or actual constitutions and concentrates, for the most part, on the benevolent rule of a sage-king. They also differ with respect to the role that laws should play in the governance of a state, and the role that the masses could and should play in deliberating on affairs of the state.[2] Aristotle favors the use of laws and praises a regime in which the masses participate in public deliberations; Confucius is skeptical about both the rule of law and the masses' role in political deliberations. Aristotle claims that virtue is achieved only by the few. Confucius articulates a life of virtue accessible to all or most.

Yet, there are similarities. Confucius and Aristotle agree that people must play different roles and functions in a state. Both men maintain that the aim of government is to make people virtuous. They agree that virtuous men make the best rulers. Accordingly, education is of central concern in governance. The two philosophers also think that justice consists in acting for the common advantage rather than for one's self-interest.

I shall examine the differences and similarities between Aristotle's and Confucius's views of politics and then consider the strengths and weaknesses of each thinker's positions, hoping to shed light on the resources each offers for rectifying the other's shortcomings. I'll then show that their shared vision of the ultimate goal of government—namely, the promotion of moral virtue, if we take it to heart today—can transform our contemporary discourse about human rights.

FAMILIAL RULE AND HOUSEHOLD RULE

Aristotle maintains that the union of man and woman and the family are for the sake of satisfying their most basic needs. Villages stabilize family relations but also constitute a new sort of unity that gives voice to needs that go beyond what recurs on a daily basis (*Politics* I.2). The union of villages in a way that reaches self-sufficiency is the culmination of the previous human associations, and also yields a new form of unity: the polis. The family and village are natural associations that exist "for the sake of mere life," but the polis exists "for the sake of a good life" (1252b28–30).[3] It completes and surpasses the work of family and villages. So it too exists by nature, because it is the culmination of associations that exist by nature:

> Because it is the completion of associations existing by nature, every polis exists by nature, having itself the same quality as the earlier associations from which it grew. It is the end or consummation to which those associations move, and the nature of things consists in their end or consummation; for what each thing is when its growth is completed we call the nature of that thing, whether it be a man or a horse or a family. (1252b31–1253a)

Aristotle also maintains that the polis is prior in nature to the family and to the individual even though these are prior in time. This is because the polis is a whole of which the individual and the family are parts. He claims that the individual and the family are essentially what they are only when they can perform their functions. But without the self-sufficiency that the polis makes possible the individual and the family cannot perform their functions. Just as a hand that no longer belongs to a whole body cannot function as a hand, an individual that doesn't belong to a polis cannot function as an individual. As Fred D. Miller, Jr., puts it, ". . . it is very clear that for Aristotle political life is deeply rooted in human nature. For life in the polis is a necessary means for the attainment of human natural ends, so that one cannot exist as a human being without it" (1989, 196). One who lives alone is either a beast or a god (1253a29). Aristotle assumes that everything has a function natural to it; its end is to perform its function well (cf. *Nicomachean Ethics* I.7).[4] For the human being, this is achievable only in a polis. Hence the polis, like the fulfilled individual, is part of nature.[5]

Confucius, as we have said, offers no theoretical analysis of the state and political rule, nor has he a teleological view of nature that informs his view of the state and the way people are governed. Yet we can perceive an inchoate view of nature and teleology in Confucius, since he is quite clear that there is an excellence that all are to attain, that this is fulfilling for the human being and that a certain sort of culture is required for its cultivation. Specifically, the highest human virtue is humaneness,[6] *ren*, which some translate as benevolence and others render as authoritative conduct or human-heartedness. Ren means progressively extending one's natural love for one's own family members, albeit in a less intense form, to others in the community.[7] But although *ren* is the virtue that Confucius encourages everyone to attain, he does not offer a full-blown view of nature from which he systematically works out an account of the state and the relations of ruler to ruled.[8] Still there is an implicit teleology of roles: for Confucius the state is essentially a bigger family that requires that the reverence that is to be expected between sons and fathers should be recapitulated between ministers and rulers, and between the people and government officials.

Aristotle defines political rule in terms of the citizen, where a citizen is one who is authorized to share in the deliberative or judicial offices of a state. The state is a collection of such persons sufficient in number to achieve a self-sufficient existence (1275b18–22). This definition seems to exclude all those among the ruled who are not actively engaged in governance.[9] Confucius does not draw a sharp line between the rulers and the ruled, nor does he exclude the ruled when he speaks about the state. Thus he responded to a query regarding his not being employed in an official position: "It is all in filial conduct (*xiao*)! Just being filial to your parents and befriending your brothers is carrying out the work of government" (2.21).[10] Similarly, in response to a question about how one is to govern effectively, Confucius says that the ruler, minister, father, and son should fulfill their respective roles (12.11). Aristotle agrees that all should fulfill their roles, but he excludes family relationships from political life.[11]

The state for Confucius is affected by everyone's actions, not only the actions of officers. Confucius speaks eloquently for the view that a virtuous leader inspires virtue in the people. A vicious ruler by contrast would inspire vices (13.6; 12.18; 12.16). Confucius also believes that the effectiveness of a ruler is bound up with the way he interacts with his family. Being filial toward his elders and faithful to his friends will enable the ruler to earn the respect and loyalty of his people (2.20) and lead his people to aspire to the same humaneness (*ren*) that he possesses (8.2; 1.2).

Aristotle would agree that a virtuous man with practical wisdom (*phronēsis*) who treats his family and friends as is fitting would also make a good leader. If he lives in an ideal state he may also be happy (*Politics* III.4). But Aristotle would disagree with Confucius's extension of family rule and love to political rule and friendship or love among fellow citizens. Even though Aristotle compares the rule of the head of the household to monarchical rule, monarchy is not a universal ideal since it is appropriate only for a certain kind of people with a very special sort of monarch (*Politics* I.7; *Politics* III.17). Given Aristotle's remarks on virtuous monarchy, it might seem that he would agree with Confucius's extension of the virtues of household rule to the state, but such a comparison quickly falls apart. I shall consider three points of contrast: Differences in the aim, in the role of self-interest, and in kind of amity (*philia*) that is appropriate in the public and private spheres.

According to Aristotle, household management concerns itself with the goods needed for daily life. Political rule concerns itself with the good life for citizens and the self-sufficiency of the whole polis. Since a household is never self-sufficient, the principles adequate to the rule of a household are never completely adequate for ruling a state.

Household management rules over wife, children, and slaves. But political rule, for Aristotle, is exercised over free men who are equal (*Politics* I.7). In the good polis, the citizen rules and is ruled in turn. But the head of a household ought never to be ruled by his slaves or by his wife and children. Household management aims to benefit the family, including the father's own interest (*Politics* III.6). But Aristotle holds that ruling in the polis is never just when the rulers consider their personal interest. So the master's self-interested rule over his slave falls outside of political rule.

Aristotle differs with Confucius's idea that love of our fellow citizens is simply a more diffuse form of love for our family members. He agrees that there is a difference in intensity between the love of family members and that of fellow citizens. But he would insist that there is also a difference in kind. For the basis of the amity (*philia*) and the relations involved are different.[12]

Amity between family members is natural and based on a common life. Thus the friendship between a man and a woman is natural, because they share a household for the sake of child bearing (1162a17–24). Parents have a natural love for their children, because they brought them into existence and because the children are in a sense a part of themselves (1161a16–17; 1161b27–29). Parents share a life because they are responsible for nurturing and educating their children (1162a6–9). Brothers love each other because they have the same parents and share the same upbringing (1161b30–1162a3). Again there is a life in common. Friendships among citizens, tribesmen, voyagers, and the like, like friendships between hosts and guests (1161b13–16), are based on some kind of agreement rather than on nature or a common life. Sharing parents, upbringing, and education makes brothers closer than hosts and guests, or mere fellow travelers, or strangers who have agreed to share some utility or pleasure for a time. Similarly, shared parental responsibilities and day-to-day living bring spouses closer than citizens who gather to deliberate and act in regard to the general conditions of their lives.

The other reason for the difference in kind between the amity that binds family members and that which binds citizens is the need for equal virtue in the latter case. Citizens must act in harmony regarding the big questions about the good life. They need to be more or less of one mind about what is good and agree about the right kinds of actions to be taken in pursuit of their common goals (1167a33–1167b4). They must also share in a certain laxness about the level of detail at which common efforts should be demanded in the state. These requirements can be met only if the citizens are similar in virtue. Familial relations by contrast are between unequals. Parents must inculcate the virtues in their children. So they must be superior in virtue. Aristotle also thinks that the virtues of a man are different from and superior to those of a woman. Men and women, moreover, complement each other by performing different functions (1162a21–24).

Another way of looking at the distinction between Aristotle's and Confucius's views of familial love and love of fellow citizens is this: While Confucius thinks that our political relations are just extensions of our love for our relatives, Aristotle thinks that friendships differ in terms of relation, virtue, or usefulness (1165a27–33). More specifically, Aristotle thinks that we owe our relatives, say, our parents, the kind of honor that is appropriate to them and not every kind of honor—say, that which is appropriate to a wise person or a general. Family members and relatives are the ones to be invited to weddings and funerals. And more than anyone, we owe our parents support, because we owe them our existence (1165a14–27). Aristotle also thinks that we should honor the old "by standing up, giving up seats, and so on" (1165a28). He claims that we should share everything with brothers and speak freely (1165a29–30). To fellow tribesmen and citizens, he thinks that we should accord the honor appropriate to their virtues or usefulness. Given these different ways in which we are to honor familial relations and fellow citizens, it follows that one is not just an extension of the other, differing from the other only in degree. Rather, there are different kinds of friendship and being good at one does not translate to being good at the other. So Aristotle would not agree with Confucius's view that one who is filial toward parents will also have the virtues of a good ruler (Analects 8.2). In reference to the family, Confucius and Aristotle are quite close; but not in reference to political rule. In short, household management is essentially different from political rule for Aristotle.

Perhaps it is overly simple to regard Confucian political rule as a direct parallel to family rule and political amity as of the same in kind as family love. One might point to Confucius's distinction between the virtue of *ren* (humaneness) and the virtue of *yi* (appropriateness).[13] *Ren* does extend one's love for relatives to others in the society. But *yi* is concerned with the appropriate way of conducting oneself. So plainly *yi* will vary from situation to situation. *Yi*, moreover, pertains especially to matters of benefit and burden or profit and loss (16.10; 14.12; 7.16). So just as Aristotle recognizes a different way of bonding with fellow citizens and honoring them, *yi* would enable one to relate to others appropriately and accord them due honor or profit. For *yi*, like justice, implies recognizing others according to their merit or desert. Even so, *yi* does not imply a difference in kind sharp enough to satisfy Aristotle's conception. Confucius would still claim that it is by *ren* that one can appropriately accord others their due. Knowing how to love one's relatives and others appropriately is what allows one to give all their due—familially or in the public sphere. Aristotle would disagree. If *yi* depends on *ren*, and *ren* is predicated on extending familial love to others, then an appeal to *yi* will not adequately underwrite the difference Aristotle wants to draw to our attention between family and political relations.

Aristotle would argue that too strong an analogy between family feeling and political life obscures important differences and leads to confusions about justice. For what is just according to Aristotle varies with different relationships (1160a1; 1162a30–34):

> It is not the same for parents towards children as for one brother towards another, and not the same for companions as for fellow-citizens, and similarly with the other types of friendship. Similarly, what is unjust towards each of these is also different, and becomes more unjust as it is practised on closer friends. It is more shocking, e.g., to rob a companion of money than a fellow-citizen, to fail to help a brother than a stranger, and to strike one's father than anyone else. What is just also naturally increases with friendship. (1160a1–8)

Aristotle stresses that there are different types of justice in different kinds of relations, particularly between equals or between unequals (1158b12–17; 1160a1–8; 1162a30–35; 1162a34–b4). One is always a debtor to one's father and can never disavow him. But a father, as a superior, can disown his son (1163b20). Confucius would agree. But he would say the same of politics! For Aristotle, political justice is not applicable in familial relations. For him, political justice is always "among associates in a life aiming at self-sufficiency, who are free and either proportionately or numerically equal" (1134a26–27). Only here can there be action by citizens for the sake of a good and self-sufficient life, guided by the common interest (1279a31–32; 1283b40–1284a3).[14]

Aristotle sees different kinds of justice for different groups of people. But the core idea of justice for him is political. It involves citizens who live in some kind of relation of equality and is not a natural extension of other kinds of justice. Rather, the polis is prior in its existence to villages, families, and individuals. So political justice is prior to all other forms of justice (1253a19–1253b). Indeed other forms of justice are rightly called just insofar as they resemble political justice (1134a27–29).

POLITICAL CONSTITUTIONS AND RULE BY LAWS OR RITUALS

Aristotle offers a generous analysis of different regimes, proposes an ideal constitution and describes the best constitution for practical purposes. He recognizes that different types of constitution befit different groups of people and might best lead them to good rule and virtue. Confucius never offers descriptions, theoretical analyses, or evaluations of different constitutions. He concentrates, for the most part, on the benevolent rule of a sage-king. He does compare cultures—Zhou and Shang—as befits his emphasis on culture over law or regime.[15] But in politics, Confucius takes for granted the feudal system prevalent in his time. He assumes a hierarchy of king, minister, lords, and common people. The people work the land and pay taxes. The government looks after the economic well-being and safety of the people. It is responsible not only for the administration of law and punishment of criminals (14.19; 13.3; 12.11; 12.7) but also for the ritual proprieties (*li*). Confucius does not much consider other political systems, except to call them barbaric. Aristotle is also known to call certain regimes barbaric, for example, when discussing the ways that the Persians use to preserve tyrannical rule: either by eliminating outstanding men or by preventing associations that might foster friendship or mutual confidence (1313a34–b17). But in general, Aristotle is keenly aware that the Athenian constitution is not the only form of political association. He derives the available types of constitution from divisions based on wealth and poverty and the economic occupation (farmer, mechanic, tradesman) of the dominant group. There are good and bad types, where good rule has a view to the common interest, while bad rule has a view to the private interest of the ruler(s) (*Politics* III.7). Whether kingship, or aristocracy, or polity is more appropriate depends on the makeup of the society:

> The society appropriate to kingship is one of the sorts which naturally tends to produce some particular stock, or family, pre-eminent in its capacity for political leadership. The society appropriate to aristocracy is one which naturally tends to produce a body of persons capable of being ruled, in a manner suitable to free men, by those who are men of distinction in their capacity for political rule. The society appropriate to government of the constitutional type [i.e., the polity] is one in which there naturally exists a body of persons possessing military capacity, who can rule and be ruled under a system of law which distributes offices among the wealthy in proportion to merit. (1288a7–15)

Even though Aristotle holds that aristocracy and an exceptional sort of monarchy are more ideal, a constitution based on the rule of the middle class (also called a polity) is the practical best (*Politics* IV.11). He claims, nonetheless, that "in relation to particular circumstances . . . there is nothing to prevent another sort from being more suitable in the given case; and indeed this may often happen" (1296b10–13; cf. *Politics* IV.12 for specific discussions of what constitution befits what sort of people). So in addition to recognizing a best form of constitution, Aristotle also recognizes that different groups of people under different circumstances require different types of constitution and rule.

Confucius and Aristotle also differ in their attitudes toward the rule of law: Aristotle advocates it. Confucius is skeptical about it:

> Lead the people with administrative injunctions (*zheng*) and keep them orderly with penal law (*xing*), and they will avoid punishments but will be without a sense of shame. Lead them with excellence (*de*) and keep them orderly through observing ritual propriety (*li*) and they will develop a sense of shame, and moreover, will order themselves. (*Analects* 2.3)

Confucius is also against violence when dealing with people who do not obey the government. Ji Kangzi asked Confucius about governing effectively (*zheng*), saying, "What if I kill those who have abandoned the way (*dao*) to attract those who are on it?" "If you govern effectively," Confucius replied, "what need is there for killing? If you want to be truly adept (*shan*), the people will also be adept. The excellence (*de*) of the exemplary person (*junzi*) is the wind, that of the petty person is the grass. As the wind blows, the grass is sure to bend" (*Analects* 12.19; cf. 13.11). Confucius's view is that the most effective form of government is founded on an exemplary ruler whose actions are so virtuous (excellent, *de*) that the people are naturally inspired to virtue. Penal law might keep people in line when they are being watched, but that will not be internalized—as a sense of shame is in the virtuous, even when they are not being watched. People may appear to be excellent (*de*), abiding by all the laws, and yet be inwardly bankrupt, with no sense of *ren*, or *yi*. They might carry out the letter of the law without living by the spirit of the law. This is why Confucius says, "The village worthy's excellence (*de*) is excellence under false pretense" (*Analects* 17.13, my translation). But Confucius goes further:

> The Governor of She in conversation with Confucius said, "In our village there is someone called 'True person.' When his father took a sheep on the sly, he reported him to the authorities."
> Confucius replied, "Those who are true in my village conduct themselves differently. A father covers for his son, and a son covers for his father. Being true lies in this." (*Analects* 13.18)

Reporting a theft is, of course, what the law demands. But for Confucius, the father-son relationship should take precedence. By blindly following the law, the "true person" of She is not doing what is right. Penal law alone is not sufficient for cultivating virtue, it may even run counter to filial piety; over-reliance on law may lead people to trust too much in external conformity.

Confucius's skepticism about penal law is coupled with his esteem for the unwritten ritual proprieties handed down from the Zhou. Even though the norms of *li* were not written down in Confucius's time, they were captured in the traditional practices of filial piety, reverence for the elders, and the rituals and ceremonies surrounding ancestor worship, mourning, and the like. The glory of the Zhou may be vanished, but fragments of the proper way survive. In response to the question "With whom did Confucius study?" Zigong replied:

> The way (*dao*) of Kings Wen and Wu has not collapsed utterly—it lives in the people. Those of superior character (*xian*) have grasped the greater part, while those of lesser quality have grasped a bit of it. Everyone has something of Wen and Wu's way in him. Who then does the Master not learn from? Again, how could there be a single constant teacher for him?" (*Analects* 19.22)

The *Songs* are also a source of the *li*, thus Confucius encourages his students to study the *Songs* saying,

> Reciting the *Songs* can arouse your sensibilities, strengthen your powers of observation, enhance your ability to *relate to* others, and sharpen your critical skills. Close at hand it enables you to serve your father, and away at court it enables you to serve your lord. It instills in you a broad vocabulary for making distinctions in the world around you. (*Analects* 17.9, italics denote my trans.; cf. 16.13)[16]

Li, then, prescribes proper behavior for every role in society—ruler, minister, duke, father, son, and all the rest. Obviously its prescriptions do not address every detail of behavior. There is room and need for individual adjustments and family amendments. Still, a definite manner of action and attitude seems to be inculcated by the proprieties. I do not find in the *li* quite so much flexibility or so much room for individual creativity as have recent commentators such as Tony Cua and Roger Ames. Confucius stresses the importance of following the Zhou *li*, as well as his own role as a transmitter rather than an innovator of tradition. Whatever creativity we find in Confucius is limited, then, by the existing norms and tradition. For instance, he speaks of substituting a hemp cap for a silk one because hemp is more economical. But the practice of wearing a certain type of cap for ceremonial purposes is not one that is open to individual creativity. One can imagine Confucius balking at an individual's substituting a baseball cap for such ceremonies. Thus I favor a more conservative interpretation of the Confucian *li*.[17] To cultivate both *ren* and *yi* will allow one to act harmoniously in a society where others adhere to a similar mode of behavior and belief. Cultivated from a young age *li* is more effective than mere laws that may be evaded:

> Through self-discipline and observing ritual propriety (*li*) one becomes *humane* in one's conduct. If for the space of a day one were able to

accomplish this, the whole empire would defer to this *humane* model. (12.1, italics denote my trans.)

Confucius tells Yan Hui, a disciple, that one must not look at, listen to, speak about, or do anything that might violate ritual propriety (*Analects* 12.1). Indeed observance of *li* will have a positive effect on the people:

> If their superiors cherished the observance of ritual propriety (*li*), none among the common people would dare be disrespectful (*Analects* 13.4); and,
> If those in high station cherish the observance of ritual propriety (*li*), the common people will be easy to deal with. (*Analects* 14.41).

Li is the crown of the other virtues like *ren* and *zhi* (knowledge):

> When the knowledgeable can apply their knowledge (*zhi*) through humaneness (*ren*), and can govern with dignity but cannot inspire through ritual propriety (*li*), they are not yet adept (*shan*) at it. (15.33, my trans.)

Li is the content of cultivation. It is what structures the social hierarchy and harmonizes the parties to it into a virtuous functioning whole. *Li* can and law cannot accomplish this, according to Confucius.

Aristotle certainly relies on custom and habit in his ethical and political thought. But he argues for a more positive view of law.[18] For example, monarchy is more enduring if constitutional, that is, ruled by law. There are types of democracy and oligarchy where the rule of law is better than rule by citizens who lack leisure for political activity.

> When the farming class and the class possessed of moderate means are the sovereign power in the constitution, they conduct the government under the rule of law. Able to live by their work, but unable to enjoy any leisure, they make the law supreme, and confine the meetings of the assembly to a minimum. (1292b25–29)

On the other hand, in a democracy where a large increase in population and wealth affords the majority means and leisure for political activity, the people rather than the laws are sovereign.[19]

Aristotle allows for the rule of a virtuous leader. But he argues that such individuals are rare. Politics therefore cannot count on them. Recognition of human failings and of the tendency for strong monarchies to become tyrannies leads him to counsel forms of the rule of law for a variety of situations. Confucius contrasts the rule of law to the inspirational rule of an exemplary individual and the power of *li* in the cultivation of virtue. But

Aristotle readily combines the rule of law with custom and habituation. Laws can help inculcate virtuous habits. But, law, for its part, needs virtue for its formulation and implementation. As Bernard Yack says, the laws "have their origins in practical reason. In a passage that comes close to suggesting a general definition of law, Aristotle writes that law is 'a rule of reason from some practical reason [phronēsis] and intellect [nous]' (NE 1180a21)." Yack (1993) also points out that Aristotle doesn't rank written laws higher than unwritten laws.

In constitutions based on the rule of law, Aristotle maintains that just laws should be sovereign (1282b1–6). Still the generality of laws prevents them from making usefully exact pronouncements about particular cases. Here a human mind is needed:

> Rightly constituted laws should be the final sovereign; and personal rule, whether it be exercised by a single person or a body of persons, should be sovereign only in matters on which law is unable, owing to the difficulty of framing general rules for all contingencies, to make an exact pronouncement. (1282b1–6)

Aristotle does make law more sovereign than the rule of man (1287b5–8). But the contrast with Confucius should not be overstated. For Aristotle is speaking not just of formal rules but also of the counterpart of the normative patterns of li, as becomes clear when we consider the role Aristotle assigns to habit and ethos in the cultivation of virtue. As Bernard Yack puts it, "Law's capacity to shape moral dispositions through the inculcation of certain habits is . . . one of its greatest contributions to political life. Unwritten laws perform this function better than written laws do, since the habits they shape are more spontaneous and less alien to the individual. They are thus 'more supreme' in the way that they shape moral character, and they deal with 'more supreme matters' in that they are concerned primarily with the most important political goal: moral education" (181, 204). Again, Yack says, "Moral dispositions rather than political institutions define the Aristotelian rule of law" (201).

Confucius and Aristotle hold similar views as to the diversity of the people who live in the state. Aristotle's discussion comes in the form of his treatment of unity in the polis. He maintains that there should be the right degree of unity to keep the polis a polis. Too much unity will make it too much like a household. A self-sufficient polis needs different and complementary capacities (Politics II.2). Unlike a military alliance, which may be strengthened by a large number of similar people, a polis "must be made up of elements which differ in kind" (1261a23–24). This leads Aristotle to a corollary: Even when some are better than others at ruling, nonetheless, "through the natural equality of all the citizens" (1261b1), it is better that citizens take turns to rule:

This means that some rule, and others are ruled, in turn, as if they had become, for the time being, different sorts of persons. We may add that even those who are rulers for the time being differ from one another, some holding one kind of office and some another. (1261b32–36)

So, even with offices, diversity and complementarity are central. While recognizing that too little unity will cause problems for a political association, since the people may lack a common goal and may even be acting at odds with each other, too much unity will also destroy a polis (*Politics* II.5): "It is as if you were to turn harmony into mere unison, or to reduce a theme to a single beat" (1263b35).

The need for different elements in a state that yet harmonize with each other is also crucial for Confucius. But he pursues a harmonious functioning of persons in their roles—rulers and subjects, ministers and dukes, parents and children. As he puts it: "Exemplary persons seek harmony, not sameness; petty persons are the opposite" (13.23). As to effective government: "The ruler must rule, the minister minister, the father must be a father, and the son a son" (12.11; cf. *Doctrine of the Mean* 1.5; 15.1–3). Because Confucius holds that harmonious home relations extend to the state, he is broadly concerned with everyone's fulfilling his or her particular role. As with Aristotle, he makes the point in terms of music. But also ritual is tied together with music in his view: "One stands to be improved by the enjoyment found in attuning oneself to the rhythms of ritual propriety (*li*) and music (*yue*)" (16.5). Again, "It is said in the *Book of Poetry*, 'Happy union with wife and children is like the music of lutes and harps. When there is concord among brethren, the harmony is delightful and enduring" (*Doctrine of the Mean* 15.2). *Li* articulates roles; *yue* (music) harmonizes them.

Still Aristotle and Confucius differ in their willingness to allow for a variety of arrangements that are politically and morally legitimate. Confucius, as we have seen, does not concern himself with political associations beyond his own ideal, which rings the changes on the Zhou model. But Aristotle allows for human differences that he thinks call for varieties of regimes. For example, he discusses five types of democracies and four types of oligarchies (*Politics* IV.4–5). There could be a democracy where the poor count as much as the rich; or another where only those with property can participate, but the property qualification is so low that the many can qualify; yet another where birth determines one's share in office; and another where birth does not matter. Then there are democracies where the law is the final sovereign and others where the people rather than the law have ultimate authority. Apart from these differences, the economy will contribute to a democracy by making it, say, a democracy that is primarily agricultural or trade oriented. The people's lack of leisure for political activity can make the law sovereign. Aristotle's willingness to admit all of these factors stems in part from his principle of self-sufficiency. This is because he sees that many different functions and skills go into making a self-sufficient polis that does not focus on only one kind of function or rule, as Confucius does. Rather, he recognizes that just as different people within his ideal polis need to do different jobs, so there can be different constitutions with emphases on different occupations and functions, giving each constitution its own distinctive character. He conceives of as many flavors of constitution as there are ways of distributing office among the members of polis. Not all of these possibilities are morally legitimate, but many are. Aristotle's allowance of different legitimate constitutions, appropriate for different people, reflects no moral relativism on his part but a recognition that the pedagogy of virtue demands different starting points for people with different histories, characters, customs, strengths, and interests.

FAMILY, MORAL, AND POLITICAL VIRTUES

Aristotle's admission that several regime types have moral legitimacy— even the second best is good enough for practical purposes—makes for a different attitude toward the populace than we find in Confucius. For one thing, the excellences of different classes differ in kind, Aristotle does not demand that the same kind of virtue be sought in every class. There are special excellences for ruling and obeying, for mechanics and merchants, and so on. Moreover, Aristotle's admission makes for a different attitude toward practical wisdom. Certainly everyone should strive to cultivate moral virtue and practical wisdom. But Aristotle does not suspend the political fortunes of every sort of state upon a virtuous ruler or citizenry. He welcomes regime types based on the rule of law where self-sufficiency and the good life can be achieved in the absence of ideal rulers or even an exemplary populace. Virtue is required in the formation and implementation of law. But neither the exemplary excellence of a single leader, nor the perfect excellence of all or most citizens is required for the life of an acceptable regime.

Confucius's idealized Zhou feudal system does require the discovery of a wise sage-king and will not survive or thrive without the practical wisdom of such a statesman sage. This might seem to imply that the mass of people need no virtue of their own and need only follow this paragon. But that would be too hasty an inference. Confucius's analogy between family relations (especially fathers and sons) and government relations (especially the ruler and ruled) proposes in effect that the mass of people in his ideal state (the men, at least) would have the same kind of virtue as the ruler. His virtues are not just a paradigm for them. They are also an emblem of the practices that permeate this ideal society. Confucius does lean on the special excellences demanded of distinct roles. But moral virtue is very much of a piece for him. Political virtue and family virtue are essentially the same. Good fathers share in and exhibit essentially the same kind of virtue as sage-kings.[20] So the permeation is not just top-down but through and through in an ideal state. But the sage-king is the initial cause of such an ideal just as good fathers are the cause of good children.

In Aristotle's ideal constitution, only the ruler—or the citizen in his temporary role as ruler—can exercise genuine practical wisdom on a public plane. Nor can one exercise the ultimate of virtue in a constitution of the wrong type. In Confucius's view however, it seems that the good private person is also the good citizen and the virtuous man. This is clear when Confucius responds to the question as to why he is not in government, saying "It is all in filial conduct (*xiao*)! Just being filial to your parents and befriending your brothers is carrying out the work of government" (2.21). Where Aristotle more sharply distinguishes the virtues of the citizen from the virtues of the good man, and separates both from any excellences that might pertain to his family relationships, Confucius blends them. Perhaps in a way Confucius allows more people to attain genuine moral virtue, the same kind of virtue as the ruler or *junzi*. They act in their private capacity, as Aristotle would see it, still looking for participation. But their seemingly familial and communal virtues are of social and political significance in Confucius's view. For Confucius the virtues of the *junzi* are accessible even within one's family. This contrast between Aristotle's and Confucius's views on political virtue also reveals two different responses to political exclusion. Whereas Aristotle still hopes for the citizen's rule in an ideal constitution, Confucius accepts the good citizen's exclusion from political rule by stressing the political impact of the private person's virtue.

But Confucius recognizes only one ideal, and accordingly encourages one to seek rule only when the system is not corrupt. Otherwise one must withdraw. As he puts it:

> Be steadfast to the death in service to the efficacious way (*shandao*). Do not enter a state in crisis, and do not tarry in one that is in revolt. Be known when the way prevails in the world, but remain hidden away when it does not. It is a disgrace to remain poor and without rank when the way prevails in the state; it is a disgrace to be wealthy and of noble rank when it does not. (*Analects* 8.13; cf. 15.7)

So even though Confucius allows more people to attain the same kinds of virtues as the *junzi* or moral leaders, he urges them to refrain from exercising their virtues in the public sphere when the state is not in wholesome condition. Aristotle on the other hand, has fewer people achieve the virtues of a true ruler, but his practical proposals for less than ideal situations and less viable constitutions can legitimately be worked on by less than ideal rulers.

RESOURCES FOR POLITICS AND HUMAN RIGHTS

Having discussed some key similarities and differences in the virtue-oriented politics of Confucius and Aristotle, let me next sketch more briefly the shortcomings of each and how the other might offer resources to rectify those shortcomings. More briefly still, I shall say something about the implications of the points gleaned from this comparison for our contemporary discourse of rights.

First, Aristotle's account of the nature of the state and its end enables him to justify his view that the polis exists for the sake of achieving a good life. Confucius would agree with Aristotle that achieving the life of virtue is of the utmost concern to the ruler and the state. Yet he simply declares it and never provides an argument to that effect. Here Aristotle's discussion of the nature of the polis and the nature of the human soul and its ends could help. If human beings are so constituted that certain activities are better than others, one can show that the ultimate aim in life is to live in such a way that our higher parts are cultivated and these higher goals sought. Confucians do not have the resources to persuade someone who does not already believe that the best way of living is to cultivate the Zhou *li*. Indeed without some such grounding in a theory of human nature and the human good, a would-be follower of Confucius does not actually even understand the ground of his own master's normative pronouncements. I have argued elsewhere that there are, tacitly or incipiently, such resources in Confucian tradition, but they are largely undeveloped.[21]

On the other hand, Confucius's account of ritual propriety (*li*) could help supplement Aristotle's all too brief account of unwritten laws. Aristotle needs, but does not supply, an extended account of ethos as the conditioning context for action and habituation. Such an account could have led to a more inclusive view of moral cultivation. Since unwritten laws, like Confucius's *li*, are all-pervasive in culture, Aristotle could have developed an account where moral cultivation is not restricted to the well born but is accessible to common folk as well. This account could act as a bridge between the fortunate citizens and the unfortunate noncitizens, so that Aristotle need not discriminate against noncitizens in respect of virtue. Following Confucius, Aristotelians would be able to see that *li* can pervade our everyday lives and serve as a vehicle for cultivating the virtues.[22] (For example, one would not need to be born into an aristocratic family in order to have the opportunity to cultivate moral excellence.) A move in this sort of direction could make the life of virtue accessible to laborers, tradesmen, farmers, mechanics, and even women. The goal here would be to extend Aristotle's vision of moral virtue into the family and daily life—while maintaining a distinction between household and political contexts more robust than Confucius intended.

Third, Aristotle's analysis of law could help Confucians understand that the rule of law need not be antithetical to the rule of custom or the cultivation of moral virtue. Adherence to the law need not amount to mere external conformity, at least not in the context of certain sorts of regimes. It might be possible to persuade Confucians not only that a sage-king could make good laws that would work hand in hand with normative rituals, but that an assembly of incompletely but moderately virtuous persons could articulate out of custom a set of laws or lawlike rules to guide the masses toward the way of virtue.[23] The rule of law need not deprive people of their sense of shame, nor adjourn the rule of virtue.

Fourth, Aristotle's understanding of the variety of constitutions and their causes might help Confucians to understand that there are other legitimate forms of rule than that of a sage-king. Since Confucius agrees that a state is made up of people who do different jobs and play different roles, Aristotelians might persuade Confucians that states could vary depending on which roles are dominant and the numbers of people who play them. That analysis paves the way to a recognition of the moral acceptability of regimes other than the single highest ideal. As long as the people can live in such a way that they observe *li* attuned to their circumstances and the cultivation of moral virtues, they need not be dismissed as barbarians. Both Aristotle and Confucius take moral education to be the principal means and among the chief ends of political rule. This is manifest in Aristotle's view that the polis exists not merely for the sake of life but for the good life, and in Confucius's insistence on having a virtuous leader to inspire virtue in the people. Confucius thinks that moral education can and should always arise from family virtue. Aristotle recognizes—more realistically, I think—that moral education, like any other, must begin from where people and their culture actually are. The key here is a recognition that political and social circumstances are pedagogical conditions.

One important lesson that both traditions can learn, from the sheer existence of the other philosophical school as an exotic tradition of virtue— and also from the fortunes of varied virtue traditions in the long history of civilization—is the difficulty of achieving virtue. Both men knew that virtue is a precarious achievement in the individual and in society, but I suspect that this point would stand out even more were they alive today to survey historical developments. What does this precariousness of virtue imply for the theory and practice of virtue, Confucian and Aristotelian? Let me tease out just a few implications, beginning by revisiting the four points of comparison just concluded.

I argued that Aristotle's account of nature and teleology better enables him to justify his way to a virtue-oriented politics, in contrast with the Confucian way, whose strategies of validation are all rhetorical. Once a direct appeal to the Zhou *li* is rendered inept by time and distance, the appeal becomes an invocation of Master Kong himself as an authoritative sage, or religious founder, what Aristotle would call a "godlike man" (1253a29). Admittedly, Aristotle has a similar problem when Aristotelian science, logic, and metaphysics are rejected. Even if Aristotelian ideas in these areas are still viable, most people believe they are not. They have lost their persuasive power. In the face of these troubles, an argument to the effect that a virtue-oriented politics is compatible with at least some form of rights theory might help to make it persuasive again, at least to people concerned with excellence and appropriateness in human affairs.

I claimed that Aristotle's understanding of the variety of constitutions and their causes might help Confucians see that beyond the rule of a sage-king there are other legitimate forms of rule. And I argued that one or another of these forms may be more pedagogically appropriate in a given circumstance, although acceptance of this fact may require a more catholic experience than was available to Confucius. Still, a Confucian—especially a contemporary one—might be brought to accept this broader zone of tolerance. Confucians, no less than Aristotelians, ought to recognize the moral legitimacy of certain alternative political arrangements and so tolerate or even welcome them. The language we use to discuss and endorse this tolerance is the language of pluralism of rights. We say that many forms of political rule have the moral right to exist. Now it is widely supposed that virtue traditions are inimical to modern ideas of rights. For most extant rights theories, and certainly the dominant ones, are based on notions of autonomy and possessive individualism that are alien to both Confucian and Aristotelian traditions.[24] I wish to float the programmatic suggestion that Aristotelian and Confucian traditions, precisely to the extent that they have listened to each other, will be more open to an acknowledgment of key moral rights.[25]

The opening occurs just in the moment of mutual recognition, where each identifies an exotic tradition of virtue in the midst of radical cultural differences. It is the recognition that a tradition different enough to argue with (indeed so different that it is sometimes difficult to know where to begin), nevertheless deserves respect and is somehow *entitled* to explore its own vision of political virtue. Exactly at this point of mutual recognition, in the thick of radical cultural difference, there is an experience that translates readily into the language of rights.[26] It may or may not be possible for each tradition to appreciate that it ought to accept alternative personal visions of virtue. That would mean recognizing rights of individuals. But whether the primary locus of rights for these types of virtue traditions is the society, the family, the tradition, or the individual is part of what needs to be argued out between them. For any virtue tradition the limit of openness depends on recognizing these alternatives as visions *of virtue*. No virtue tradition will readily acknowledge the pursuit of ends other than virtue (pleasure, power, wealth, expediency) unless these externals are assigned some sort of subordinate place. But so long as a way of life can be recognized as a pursuit of excellence of character and custom—no matter how radical the cultural differences otherwise—it ought to be able to be and to flourish.[27] It is my conviction that an acknowledgment of rights of this sort can grow directly from the experience of mutual recognition that occurs when Aristotelians and Confucians recognize one another as speaking for alternative traditions of virtue.

I have argued above that Aristotle's analysis of law could help Confucians understand that the rule of law need not be antithetical to recognition of the power and potential benefits of custom and cultivation of moral virtue. Indeed if most people most of the time need good laws in order to make room and even breathing space for virtuous citizens and institutions, and even the exercise of virtues, then in the name of virtue people ought to claim that they have a right to a legal system in which good laws are made and enforced. With a politics that takes its orientation from virtue, laws and rules are not the point. They are means and supplements to virtue. Remember that virtue too is a means to an end (the good life, i.e., the life in accordance with virtue). Not only is virtue a means to the end of the good life, but it is also for the sake of acquiring virtue. Good laws then, are compatible with the cultivation of virtue insofar as they too, are means to the acquisition of virtue. But if a sound system of law is in general a necessary support of virtue, then for the sake of virtue people ought to claim that a system in which good laws can be formulated and enforced is their due. It is something owed to people because it is needed for most people to attain to virtue and because people should claim a right to the necessary conditions of virtue.

I also claimed that Confucius' account of ritual propriety (*li*) could supplement Aristotle's all too brief account of the unwritten laws since Aristotle does not as fully as he might supply the needed account of ethos (and the means of its cultivation). Both traditions could then appreciate that the normative customs that pervade our everyday lives can be the vehicles for the cultivation of virtues in ways that make the life of virtue accessible even to the most ordinary of persons and the most menial of laborers. This possibility rests on a Confucian recognition that the life of virtue does extend into family relationships and in fact has its roots there. Beyond that, both Aristotle and Confucius recommend that a society care for its least advantaged members. Beyond that both seem to base this recommendation on the caring of those who have an abundance of resources, that is, on the generosity and magnificence of people of means. In other words, they see this responsibility as dependent on the exercise of virtue. But surely those in need ought to be helped because they have a right to assistance, when there is a real possibility of affording such aid. This right is not at all antithetical to a virtue-oriented politics, once this politics admits that primary moral rights are rights to the conditions of virtue. Assistance can be justified on the grounds that pursuit of virtue is impossible unless at least the minimal needs of life are met. It is neither noblesse oblige nor a holdover from some fictitious state of nature that underwrites these entitlements. They can be—and should be—claimed in the name of virtue. That is the justification that, if it confirms a somewhat narrower array of rights, confirms them for a moral reason: the cultivation of virtue.

My thesis, then, is that the most basic moral rights are rights necessary to the development and practices of virtue. This is the way to human rights that a virtue-oriented politics recommends. The argument is simple. If one ought to be virtuous, then one ought to have the means of developing and exercising virtue. When there are means available, they should be made available on just these grounds. The exercise of virtue requires subsistence rights, rights to education and indeed certain rights to political access. It will not and it should not imply all the rights standardly listed by the classic liberal rights theorists or by the political manifestoes of the day. But a rich and distinctive approach to rights springs from virtue-oriented politics. It has the power to develop a path of its own. It holds promise also as a *standpoint* of critique that might give pause to many an advocate of the regnant views about rights. I believe that the dialogue between Confucius and Aristotle— fascinating and instructive in itself—is even more notable as an important springboard for such developments.[28]

NOTES

1. A proponent of intercultural incommensurability might ask if I could legitimately compare the political views of Aristotle and Confucius. I argue for the possibility of comparing these two culturally diverse thinkers in (Sim 2004b, 58–77). See also Lee 1999; Hamburger 1959.

2. I use the word "state" when discussing Aristotle's polis and Confucius's state in the same sentence. This term is employed more loosely than either author's use of the concept. Thus used, it simply means the unit constituted by the ruler(s) and the people (whether they are citizens or not), and the qualities that accompany their lives. I provide a detailed explanation of how Aristotle could explain his concept of a polis to Confucius in Sim (2004b).

3. All references to the *Politics* are taken from *The Politics of Aristotle*, E. Barker, trans., New York: Oxford University Press (1958). Bekker page numbers are from the Loeb edition of the *Politics*, H. Rackham, trans., London: Harvard University Press (1932).

4. References to the *Nicomachean Ethics* are taken from T. Irwin's translation (Indianapolis: Hackett, 1985).

5. See Miller (1989, 201, 206, and 211) for discussions of how his thesis that human beings are by nature political is based on Aristotle's teleology of metaphysical naturalism.

Some commentators puzzle over how Aristotle can maintain the polis as a natural association and yet talk about the role of the statesman in its construction. David Keyt (1987) argues that there is a real contradiction. See Miller (1989) and Chan (1992) for arguments against Keyt's position.

The influence of Aristotle's teleological understanding of nature on his *Politics* is evident in a number of his analyses beyond his discussion on the polis. For example, he detects in all compounds a ruling element and a ruled element and maintains that, in general, it is natural and better for the higher or superior element to rule the lower or the inferior element. This principle is exemplified in the rule of the soul over the body, of the master over the slave, and of the man over the woman (*Politics* I.5; cf. *Politics* VII.14 for the hierarchy of the parts of the soul). As Aristotle puts it, "all men who differ from others as much as the body differs from the soul, or an animal from a man . . . all such are by nature slaves, and it is better for them, on the very same principle . . . to be ruled by a master" (1254b17–21). Aristotle's view that there are free men and slaves by nature not only enables him to justify the rule of masters over slaves but also enables him to dismiss the view that permanent sovereignty over everyone is the highest good. He says, "in a society of peers it is right and just that office should go on the principle of rotation, which is demanded by the ideas of equality and parity" (1325b 7–9). Again: "the world would be a curious place if it did not include some elements meant to be free, as well as some that are meant to be subject to control; and if that is its nature any attempt to establish control should be confined to the elements meant for control, and not extended to all" (1324b36–39). Holding that youth is naturally endowed with vigor while age comes with wisdom, Aristotle can argue that the youth should make up the military force of the state while the mature should make up the deliberative part. He says, "the order of nature gives vigor to youth and wisdom to years; and it is policy to follow that order in distributing powers among the two age-groups of the state" (1329a15–16; cf. *Politics* VII.14).

6. I find three senses of *ren* in the *Analects*, which I discuss in detail in Sim (2001, 454, n.5).

7. The five relations between rulers and ruled, parents and children, spouses, brothers, and friends embody the traditional roles for Confucius. For the significance of these five relations to the cultivation of the individual, see Tu Weiming (1986) and King (1985).

8. This is clear from the lack of any systematic account of nature in the *Analects* and the explicit assertion from one of his disciples, Zigong, to the effect that Confucius never talks about our nature or the nature of heaven (5.13). For a detailed contrast between what determines the human good in each of these thinkers, teleological metaphysics for Aristotle and ritual propriety (*li*) for Confucius, see Sim (2001, 460–61).

9. As Peter Simpson says, "Aristotle's definition of city (a multitude of those who share in deliberation and judgment) effectively identifies the city with those who are in control of the city and hence with the regime" (1998, 138). R. G. Mulgan says, "Because he defines citizenship in terms of participation in deliberative and judicial office, the citizen body in any constitution will be coextensive with the supreme body" (1977, 61). In discussing the topic of political distribution in Aristotle, Martha Nussbaum (1988) notes that there is a "whole-part" conception that predominates in Aristotle's discussion in *Politics* VII.9–10. The effect is "to justify the exclusion of manual labourers and farmers from membership in the city." The reason for their exclusion is that "manual labourers and farmers cannot achieve goodness, because their lives lack leisure, and leisure is necessary for virtue" (Nussbaum 1988, 156). Nussbaum maintains that *Politics* VII is a "more primitive stage in Aristotle's thinking

on these issues"; *Politics* II–III represent his mature view (160). For a critique of Nussbaum's position, see Charles (1988).

10. Unless otherwise stated, all references to Confucius are from *The Analects of Confucius*, Roger Ames and Henry Rosemont, Jr., trans. (New York: Ballantine, 1998). For discussions of how filial piety forms the core of all human relationships in Confucius, see King (1985, 58); Hsu (1986, 33); and Jordan (1986, 82–94).

11. As Jean Elshtain puts it: "Women, slaves, and children did not partake in the full realization of goodness and rationality that defined co-equal participants in the perfect association. There was an 'essential' difference between the greater (free, male) and lesser (unfree, female) persons" (1982, 52).

12. See Yack (1993, 53–55) for a good discussion of the differences between citizens and family members, as well as the differences between political friendship and the amity that characterizes familial relations.

13. I discuss three senses of *yi* in Sim (2001, 458–59, n.14).

14. As Mulgan puts it, Aristotle "equates the common interest with absolute justice, by which he probably means justice in the wider or 'universal' sense, that is complete social virtue" (1977, 61). See also Barker's (1958, 113, nv) for the same point. Yack (1993) rightly equates Aristotle's political justice with his discussion of general justice, or complete virtue in the *Nicomachean Ethics*. As Yack puts it, "Justice, he suggests, is the 'political virtue' that seeks the common advantage, the virtue from which 'all the other virtues necessarily follow' (*Politics* 1283a38), a description that corresponds to Aristotle's similar characterization of general justice as the 'complete virtue' that involves the exercise of all the other moral virtues (*NE* 1129b26)" (159). These authors also reiterate the fact that regimes are just, for Aristotle, only if they pursue the common advantage of their state.

15. The Western Zhou (1122–771 B.C.E.) succeeded the Shang (1700–1122 B.C.E., the first dynasty with written records). The Eastern Zhou succeeded the Western Zhou and lasted till 221 B.C.E. By Confucius's time (551–479 B.C.E.), the states with allegiance to the Zhou dynasty had been warring for more than two centuries. Because of the escalating violence and related cultural changes, Confucius looks back to the Western Zhou as an ideal.

16. *The Book of Songs* contains about three hundred poems (see *Analects* 3.5), some of which originated in the Shang dynasty, but mostly from the Zhou. Together with *The Book of Changes*, *The Book of History*, *The Book of Rites*, and the *Spring and Autumn* (chronicle of events 722–481 B.C.E.), *The Book of Songs* make up the five canonical texts. As James Legge puts it, " 'The five *Ching*' are the five canonical Works, containing the truth upon the highest subjects.

17. I defend this interpretation in Sim (2004c and 2002).

18. Plato's disillusionment with the more intuitive personalist approach may help explain this.

19. Aristotle applies similar reasoning to the various forms of oligarchy. For instance, in a moderate oligarchy where most of the citizens have property but in moderate amounts, the generality have what we would call constitutional rights. But because they neither have so much wealth as to excuse them from all business, nor so little that they need to be supported by the state, the rule of law works better for them than rule by their own assemblies. Other forms of oligarchy are also ruled by laws, but for a different reason. In their case, it is a lack of power over the majority that makes them resort to the rule of law. Only in the most extreme form of oligarchy,

where the few own large properties and possess leisure and power, can they exercise rule directly (1293a30–34).

20. Children and wives can exhibit essentially the same kind of virtue as political subjects. I bracket the blatant paternalism of the Confucian way for the purposes of this chapter. A rectified Confucianism, such as I recommend elsewhere and gesture toward at the conclusion of this chapter, can avoid the paternalism but would still—if it is to be Confucian at all—have it that political virtues and familial virtues are essentially the same in kind.

21. See Sim's (2003) for an account of how a minimal sense of substance is required by Confucius's claims about the cultivation of virtue and how dialogue with Aristotle could help elucidate such a position.

22. See Sim (2004c) for a more elaborate discussion of this matter.

23. Such cooperation between the king and his associates is not alien to the Confucian tradition. I discuss this in Sim (2002). See also *Analects* 13.3 for a more positive attitude toward laws.

24. As David Hall and Roger Ames put it, "(a) fundamental problem with rights-based understandings of democracy is that they have few mechanisms preventing individuals from becoming alienated from communities since the rights serving as the fundamental signs and rewards of a just society are so often enjoyed in private. Such rights do not prevent individuals from joining together in communities or social unions, but neither do they enjoin or stimulate community building" (1999, 108). Strauss (1953) and MacIntyre (1981) argue that rights talk is alien to Aristotle. Miller (1995, 111), on the other hand, finds that Aristotle is already using " 'rights' locutions" and hence finds in Aristotle the concept of rights (cf. his chapter in the present volume). Cooper (1996) supports Miller's thesis for the most part, as long as one distances Aristotle's concerns from the modern and contemporary theorists' valuation of "subjective freedom." Kraut acknowledges similarities between Aristotle's concepts of justice and the concepts of rights held by philosophers with "full scale theories of natural rights" (1996, 774). But he is doubtful that the similarities are strong enough to say definitively that Aristotle has a concept of rights. Kraut's position (with which I'm sympathetic) is based in part on the fact that Aristotle makes very little use of rights talk (1996, 773). Brown isn't convinced by Miller's thesis. She thinks that Miller has not shown what he claimed—namely, that "political rights of a Hohfeldian kind are employed in Aristotle's *Politics* and *Nicomachean Ethics*" (2001, 271). This chapter does not attempt a full appraisal of Miller's thesis. My aim in this section is simply to argue that we can develop out of Aristotle's politics support for the promotion of moral rights.

25. See Sim (2004a), where I argue that a virtue theorist should accept and promote the rights of every human being to the necessary conditions of virtue.

26. This does not at all imply complete political or social autonomy, or a right to be left alone. After all, part of what I am claiming here is that an argument can and should ensue, an argument in which each tradition should try to persuade the other that it has advantageous features to offer and in which it might come to recognize shortcomings in itself that might not appear outside of a confrontation with an alien tradition of virtue.

27. At this point, it is legitimate to ask, as my good friend Lenn Goodman, does, if my claim that alternative virtue traditions will recognize and tolerate each other might not be an overstatement. Lenn offers warrior ethics as an example of a vision of

virtue that might not be widely accepted. A distinction between two forms of pluralism is helpful in addressing Lenn's question. One form of pluralism is that which can be readily handled by dialogue, where one tradition can learn from the resources of the other. This is exemplified by my comparison between the Aristotelian and Confucian traditions of virtue in this chapter. The other form of pluralism is more troubling as it involves the recognition of rival traditions of virtue and disagreements about the visions of virtue among the rivals. This is a legitimate problem even though it is not relevant to my focus here, and I will have to address it elsewhere.

28. For the extensive and constructive editorial comments Lenn Goodman made on an earlier version of this essay, I am truly grateful. Thanks are also due to the National Endowment for the Humanities Summer Stipend Award (2004), which supported my research on Confucian rights.

5

THE MORALITY OF NATIONS: AN ARISTOTELIAN APPROACH

Lloyd P. Gerson

ristotle has very little to say about what we would today call international relations. Nevertheless, I think that Aristotle does provide
us with the conceptual tools for making some sense of the philosophical issues surrounding and saturating the global village. The principal
insight gleaned from Aristotle in this regard is that much if not all of the
discussion of international relations today rests on a serious mistake. The
mistake is to suppose that nations are moral agents. If one supposes this, then
whatever theory of morality one wishes to defend, one will assume that that
theory applies to nations. Thus, if one, say, defends a version of utilitarianism or some sort of deontological theory, one will then go on to claim its
applicability to nations, treating them as if they were moral agents. I think
Aristotle can help us see that this is a mistake, whatever moral theory one
happens to hold. So much for the negative. But if nations are not moral
agents, what are they? Again, Aristotle can help us to see that they are
agents, although not moral agents, and that understanding the peculiar type
of agent that a nation is helps us to see how the real moral agents that
comprise nations ought to direct their nations on the international stage.

NATIONS AND PERSONS

In his groundbreaking book *The Gutenberg Galaxy*, written in 1962, Marshall
McLuhan coined the now famous phrase "the global village."[1] It hardly needs
arguing that over the last forty years the understanding of international
affairs, broadly speaking, has fed on this metaphor. There are two competing
or interlocking ideas here. The first is that individuals are, or can be, or
ought to be connected in various ways to the rest of humanity. Obviously,
technology is the engine that pulls *this* train. The second is that nations or

states are, or can be, or ought to be connected analogously to the way that individual members of a village are. I am fairly certain that McLuhan was focused on the first idea. But it does seem clear that the second idea builds on the first. If we are all members of a global village, then international relations ought to reflect that new reality. Of course, the idea of international relations antedates the "global village." Perhaps a convenient date for its origin is the Treaty of Westphalia of 1648. It seems, however, that in the last decades, theorizing about international relations has in fact intersected with the global village idea. Unquestionably, the idea of a normative basis for international relations draws heavily on the global village metaphor and others like it.

The incorporation of such metaphors into theorizing about the normative basis of international relations has actually been so complete that hardly anyone who engages in such theory regards it as problematic. I mean that it is simply assumed that the appropriate normative basis at the international level is carried over from its origin in theory concerned with morality among individuals. Thus, if we have a good idea about how human beings ought to act toward each other, we can simply apply that idea to matters regarding how nations ought to act toward each other. We can treat nations as moral agents on a par with individuals. In other words, the scope of a moral theory includes nations as well as individuals. The assumption that moral theory indifferently (or almost so) covers nations as well as individuals is so pervasive that the inferences from a moral prescription at the individual level to an identical moral prescription at the national level are taken as being practically immediate. Such thinking is facilitated by a raft of additional metaphors such as "the family of nations" and the "community of nations."

Occasionally, one discovers a passing acknowledgment that the application of moral prescriptions to nations and individuals indifferently is a fiction, albeit with the additional stipulation that it is a necessary or inevitable or desirable one. Here, we find reliance on the analogous term "legal fiction" as used in law. But it is far from obvious that a legal fiction is translatable into the basis for the ascription of moral agency. For example, one can hardly infer from the patent legal fiction that an errant military guard dog could be made subject to court martial to a conclusion that dogs are moral agents. So, one wonders why the legal fiction of moral agency in nations is necessary or even desirable, unless what is really going on is that one is thus better placed to amplify the potential consequences for others of accepting one's own moral theory.

In fact, it frequently appears that the proposal of employing the fiction of moral agency when talking about nations is itself based upon moral considerations. It is supposed that the fiction is a legitimate facilitator for connecting the moral prescriptions devolving upon individuals with *other* individuals belonging to other nations. The fiction has a kind of negative effect. That is, there is nothing about a nation that prevents the internationalization of morality. On the contrary, nations are just delivery systems for the actions flowing from moral prescriptions.

In this regard, the use of the first person plural 'we' in discussions of the normative basis for international relations is ubiquitous. It is also, of course, ambiguous. It can mean "each and every one of us" ought to do such and such. In that case, the nation does not come into the picture. But that "we" ought to do such and such can also be taken to be equivalent to a prescription aimed at our nation. It is assumed that there is nothing about a nation that prevents the "sum" of individual obligations from being concocted into a national obligation. In this case, the fiction of national moral agency is just a shorthand way of indicating this concoction.

The fiction is painfully in need of an argument. Granted there is a difference between a sum and a whole, one wants to know why in the present case the sum of moral agents and their moral obligations or responsibilities can justifiably be treated as a whole, as, in effect, an additional moral agent. It may seem that the argument is obvious. Nations are themselves fictions or "constructs." So, there could be nothing about them that would restrict or block the flow through of obligation from the sum to the whole.

This seems to me to be a very bad argument, indeed. Unless it can be established that nations are moral agents over and above the moral agents that comprise them, the very idea of a normative basis for international relations is unintelligible. It bears emphasizing that the accusation of unintelligibility should not be watered down into a rejection of one particular moral theory in favor of another. The point I am making is not that, say, utilitarianism is wrong whereas some deontological theory is right. Nor am I making the point that the correct moral theory at the international level is different from the correct one at the individual level. The problem I see is more radical than that of sorting out the pros and cons of moral theories. The problem is that *no* moral theory makes any sense unless we can understand what a moral agent is. If nations are not moral agents, then the application of moral theory to international relations hardly makes more sense than it does as applied to the jungle.

One might think to make short work of this problem by trimming one's moral theory to fit the fiction of moral agency applied to nations. One might argue that the expansion of the scope of moral theory is a fundamental property of human progress. This expansion can occur in two ways. According to one, we allow that human beings hitherto deemed inferior for one reason or another are on a par with others for purposes of moral theory. According to the other, we expand the scope of moral theory to include agents other than moral agents, for example, to primates or other animal groups. So, we might hold either that nations are moral agents like individuals or that moral agency is not necessary for inclusion in the scope of a moral theory. In the latter case, we might, for example, suppose it sufficient for inclusion that a nation has interests. In the former, we might hold that moral agency is not a property of individual organisms. The things that nations do or do not do indicate all that is necessary for moral agency. So, we might suppose that a sufficient condition for being a moral agent is having purposes or goals, something that nations can be reasonably assumed to possess.

I shall start by making a distinction among agents, that is, a distinction between a moral agent and a nonmoral agent. What I aim to show is that all and only persons are moral agents and that nations are not persons. By 'agent' I mean, roughly, something that causes a change in something else. The word "something" here can, if you like, be defined purely functionally, so an agent is just the cause of an array of possible effects, all of which are changes. Thus, viruses, hurricanes, raccoons, and industrial robots are all nonmoral agents, but the sixteenth century and the color green are not agents of any sort. Persons can, of course, also be nonmoral agents in those cases where they are not acting as moral agents. This occurs, for instance, in the case of someone who is drugged, or brainwashed, or sleepwalking, or, more interestingly, when the person is being considered *merely* as a body or organism. We typically and rightly distinguish nonmoral agents, which are responsible for what they do, although not morally responsible, from moral agents who are morally responsible, except when they are acting merely as nonmoral agents. The errant attack dog that is tried by the military for mauling its handler is, presumably, responsible but not morally responsible for its deed. Analogously, we may maintain that persons are responsible for damages they inflict but not morally responsible when no criminal intent is manifest.

If nations are not moral agents, then it is a sort of category mistake to suppose that nations have moral obligations or rights or duties, or that they can bear moral guilt or blame. Many people who would concede this claim strictly conceived would maintain that, nevertheless, it is desirable or even inevitable that we adopt the fiction that allows us to make moral judgments about the "citizens" of the community of nations. I suppose that this fiction is not entirely insidious, so long as it is agreed that all the claims about moral duties, obligations, rights, and so forth, made in regard to nations are fictions, too.[2] Thus, for example, to claim that one nation has an obligation to ameliorate the circumstances of another nation (or its members) is to implicate oneself in a fiction. The truth of this assertion is not, so far as I can see, affected by the hypothetical truth of another assertion; namely, that each and every human being has an obligation to ameliorate the circumstances of every other human being insofar as possible. It is not affected even if we concede that nations, like other groups, can have interests. If, for example, one acknowledges in oneself an obligation to serve the interests of the Jewish people, it does not follow from this that one's own nation has an obligation to support Israel. Indeed, more to the point, in my view the latter claim is unintelligible.[3]

If nations are not moral agents, then I take it that the notion of collective or group responsibility is nonsense, except insofar as the group is considered to be just the sum of responsible individuals (Lewis 1948). A similar point can be made about institutional responsibility, although in this case the obvious fact that institutions can be nonmorally responsible for consequences held to be deleterious sometimes leads to the attribution of moral responsibility.

Now the question is, What is it exactly that differentiates a nonmoral agent from a moral agent? The answers to this question in the literature usually reflect a prior commitment to the inclusion or exclusion of groups among the class of moral agents or persons. One of the most influential answers that what distinguishes moral agents from nonmoral agents is that the former have and the latter do not have the property of intentionality. And since this answer has historically been given by thinkers who want to argue for the inclusion of nations (and corporations, especially) in the class of moral agents, the term "intentionality" has mutated into the more rhetorically apt "intentional systems," which sounds a lot more plausible if it is going to be applied to groups in general as well as individuals.

The property of intentionality is best understood as the "aboutness" or "directedness" of mental states. Thus, I can think about things, I can desire them or dream about them or hope for them. These things are the so-called intentional objects of intentional states. Not all mental states are intentional states, however. Feeling cold or depressed are not cases where one has cold or depression as an intentional object. A peculiarity of the things that I can have as intentional objects is that they do not necessarily exist at all or in the way that ordinary things do. Thus, a child can long for the arrival of Santa Claus without our supposing that the sort of relationship that this sets up is the relationship between two separately existing things, the child and Santa Claus. And my dreams have a sort of existence only in my head. But cold and depression are not things to which I am related intentionally.

Here is how the line of thinking goes that wants to claim that nations are moral agents or persons. All and only moral agents have intentional states. There are many good examples of intentional states from the political sphere, for example, deliberating and voting on policy, planning, and proposing goals, entering into agreements with other nations, and so on. A nation declares war or enters into a trade agreement or enacts a law all on the basis of the intentional states of the representative legislative body. Nations, in their deliberative bodies and in their legitimate representatives certainly express intentionality in all these ways. So, nations, it seems, have the property required for being a moral agent.

First, let me say what part of this line of thinking I agree with. I agree that a nation, in doing the above, is some sort of an agent distinct from the moral agents who are the persons who make up the deliberative or legislative body. I have no wish to contest the existence of group dynamics or collective action or agency. I agree that a nation is an agent when it votes in an international assembly. After all, since a nation can, for example, declare war when some of the members of the legislative body are opposed to such a declaration, we can hardly maintain that there is no difference between the agency of the legislative body and that of the individuals who comprise it. Similarly, I have no ontological scruples about holding that, say, Germany (*not* Germans) can defeat Italy (*not* Italians) in football.

Having said this, I still think that the argument that seeks to include nations within the class of moral agents on the basis of intentionality is a weak one. Here is why. There is an ambiguity in the term "intentionality" that this argument exploits. In the sense in which nations have intentionality, the attribution of moral agency does not follow. In the sense of intentionality according to which moral agency does follow, this argument does not show that nations have that. Intentionality in the first sense can characterize any goal-directed behavior and can also be applied to any behavior that is understandable in the light of that goal. For example, it is perfectly reasonable to say that a squirrel is gathering nuts for the purpose of eating through the winter, or that the rattle of the snake's tail shows that it intends to strike, or that the field mouse is trying to get into the house in the autumn in order to keep warm, or that the chess-playing robot is trying to pin down my knight. But the sense of intentionality that applies to such goal-directed behavior by agents obviously does not indicate *moral* agency.

Intentionality in the second sense, the sense according to which its applicability *does* imply moral agency, is something else. In this sense, intentionality refers first and foremost to the self-awareness of the presence of the purpose and the self-awareness of the mental states leading to its realization. That is, of course, precisely why we refrain from claiming that someone is responsible for her actions when she is *unaware* of what she is doing, especially when she could not have been aware. The acknowledgment of self-awareness is necessary for the attribution of moral agency. I would in fact argue that all and only nondefective human beings have this ability to be self-aware. But that is not my point here. There *may* be agents other than human beings that are moral agents. My present point is that a *group* of human beings, such as the group that comprise a nation, cannot be self-aware in this way and therefore cannot be a moral agent.

Another way of making my point is to employ the well-known distinction that originates with the philosopher Harry Frankfurt, the distinction between first- and second-order desires (Frankfurt 1971). As Frankfurt shows, it is the ability to have desires about one's own desires that distinguishes persons from nonpersons. That these desires belong to the *same* person is, of course, necessary for the individuation of the person. For example, one can have a desire to take drugs, but also a desire either to have that desire be effective in action or a desire not to have that desire. In either case, our willingness to assign responsibility or blame to persons who follow their first-order desires rests upon our assumption that persons can formulate second-order desires in relation to these. In the case of nations, however, even if we assume that they have first-order desires to engage in actions, first-order desires whose existence is inferred from their behavior, they cannot have second-order desires. For the putative second-order desires could *only* be those of the individual members of the deliberative body whose decisions resulted in the nation's initiating an action. Thus, one member of the deliberative body might be opposed to the action and the putative desire to engage in it, or else she might herself endorse it. But in either case, that person is not the nation, which itself does not have the requisite equipment for having both first- and second-order desires in the same agent.[4]

Both of the above ways of understanding the intentionality of moral agents rest upon Aristotle's account of a moral agent as one that acts *meta logou*, or "with reason." Acting with reason is not equivalent to acting *kata logon*, or "according to reason."[5] A nonmoral agent can act in that way. To act with reason is to be able to conceptualize an occurent desire and fit that concept into a reasoning process which concludes with an intention or self-injunction to act. For one to act with reason, one must be aware of the *conceptualized* desire and incorporate it into a reasoning process of which one is simultaneously aware. Acting with reason, moreover, means being able to have conceptualized desires about one's own conceptualized desires. By contrast, acting according to reason is nothing more than rule-following motion or behavior. *Any* machine or *any* living thing acts according to reason if it submits input to a rule on behalf of achieving an output. I am just going to assume for the present that we have no inclination to recruit thermostats and paramecia into the ranks of moral agents. I do, however, acknowledge the need to show that the line between nonmoral and moral agents is not merely stipulative. For if this cannot be shown, there might well be a compelling argument to the effect that the drawing of such a line would properly place some groups of moral agents, for example, nations, among the moral agents themselves.

The obvious objection to my claim about the necessary condition for moral agency is that group deliberation and group action is action that is fully or robustly self-aware. When all of the members of a group are self-aware of what they are doing, then the group is self-aware. This is what happens when there is, say, a debate on policy, when everyone participates, and when a vote is taken. But here the defender of the position I am attacking is tripped up by his own insistence that group agency is distinct from the agency of the individuals that comprise the group. For if he is right about that—and I have agreed that he is—then, the group's presumed self-awareness is distinct from the self-awareness of any member of that group. As a member of the group, I can deliberate about whether my nation should declare war, and I can decide for or against that proposition. But whatever I (and my colleagues) each decide to do, there is not *another* decision that arises from another intentional act of deliberation by the nation. True, there is another action. I mean that, say, the declaration of war is an action over and above my voting for or against it. But that declaration of war is not a declaration by a self-aware agent, the nation. Naturally, we can, if we like, treat it as such. Nevertheless, all the metaphorical language habitually employed to describe nations as persons, such as calling them "members of a family of nations" does not constitute grounds for ascribing moral agency to nations. For such ascription, in order to be more than merely metaphorical, depends upon the possession of intentionality in the second, not the first, sense. And *that* nations cannot have. We may find it convenient, in Daniel Dennett's felicitous phrase, to take up the "intentional stance" in describing what they do, but this has no moral relevance whatsoever, since we can just as legitimately do this with regard to clearly nonmoral agents like squirrels and snakes and mice and chess-playing robots (Dennett 1976, 175–96, 176–78; Dennett 1987, 15–22). The fact that nations, unlike these agents, are comprised of persons makes no difference in itself. Thus, it literally makes no sense to say that a nation is morally responsible for an action, although it makes perfectly good sense to say that all those persons who contributed to the action's coming about are morally responsible.

Another way to look at this point is to consider that in cases of genuine self-awareness, the subject who has the intentional object, say, a purpose, must be identical with the subject who is aware of having that intentional object. But when the nation has a purpose, as expressed, say, in a resolution of a governing body, it is not the nation that is self-aware but the persons who comprise it. And that self-awareness is not of each individual's own purpose, since one's own purposes may be in conflict with those of the nation. Even if they are not in conflict, that is, even if there is 100 percent support for a motion, the awareness of the nation's purpose as expressed in the motion occurs in the individual persons and not in the nation. Unless you can put purpose and self-awareness of purpose in the identical subject, you cannot have a moral agent. And in the case of group action, you can never have the identical subject that both has the purpose and is self-aware of having it. Knowing that my nation has declared war is different from the act of declaring war and occurs in a different subject. Indeed, the nation or the nonmoral agent that declares war *cannot* know that it declares war anymore than the chess-playing robot can know that it won (Rovane 1994; Rovane 1998).

Here is another objection. Consider the smallest group of moral agents possible; namely a group of two. In particular, consider the group that consists of two parents. Could we not say that the parents, as a couple, have, say, obligations to their children over and above the obligations that each parent has? And these or some of these obligations may be indifferently assignable to each, so that if one parent fails or is unable to fulfill the obligation, then the other must—although we cannot know ahead of time which this is. Thus, it is the parent who has the obligation, but the parent in this case is not identifiable absolutely with either one. In that case, would not this group be a moral agent? I think the answer is fairly clearly no. For the obligations of each are easily and naturally expressed as including the hypothetical "if I don't do it, my partner ought to." There is no generic parent for an additional obligation to fall upon. I suggest that the burden of proof falls upon those who claim to discover an obligation for this group over and above the obligations that each member bears.

There is a great deal more that can be said about this particular topic. But I hope that I have said enough to lead you to consider that there may be reasonably good grounds for denying that nations are moral agents. That, however, leaves us with the obvious question of what nations are if they are not moral agents. If the answer that I am about to give to this question is plausible, it will I hope reinforce the above argument.

NATIONS AS ASSOCIATIONS

A nation is a kind of association. By "association" I follow Aristotle in referring to any group of persons or moral agents who unite voluntarily for some purpose.[6] The types of association are practically unlimited. They include cohabitation arrangements and marriage and family, clubs, business partnerships, teams, religions, service relationships like doctor-patient or teacher-student. They include all manner of political relationships from the local right up to the national level. People voluntarily enter into associations because they can thereby achieve something that they could not achieve on their own, although what each person achieves in the association may not be the same thing. That something that they do hope to achieve is thought by them to be either a constituent of their happiness or instrumental to it. For example, two people are fishing buddies, because that form of recreation is held by them to be part of a happy life. One person goes to a dentist and has what she hopes will be a brief association with that dentist, because she believes that this association is instrumental to a happy life. A nation, I shall argue, is in principle no different from such an association.

Although there can be associations larger than nations, for example, religions, a nation, as I understand Aristotle, has a self-sufficiency that other associations do not have (*Politics* III.1.1275b20–22). A nation is, as other associations are not, capable of providing all the conditions necessary for a good life as understood by its members, including those that are social, economic, political, legal, cultural, and so on. Nothing bigger than a nation is necessary, and nothing smaller than a nation will suffice, keeping in mind that a self-sufficient nation may actually be quite small. The point about self-sufficiency is especially important as we shall see in a moment.

But before I focus on nations, I would like to say a bit more about associations in general. The principal feature of associations that is important for my topic is that the purpose of an association is usually crystal clear both to its members and to outsiders. For, although the impetus to form associations is as natural as anything else in human beings, these associations are normally accompanied by practices and constructs whose instrumentality is transparent just because they are human artifacts. For example, it is easy to discover what a football is for and what the rules of football are and thereby to understand the association that consists in being on a football team.

Aristotle claims that the association that is a nation exists "according to nature." What this means is that it has a natural, not an artificial, purpose. The distinction between the natural and the artificial is not an Aristotelian throwaway grace note, but a core insight. For natural purposes are undercut if artificial ones are substituted for them.

If a nation is an association, then it is clear that its purpose is in general the happiness of the voluntary moral agents who are its members. A nation itself, as a nonmoral agent, does not have its own purpose except in a nonmoral way, that is, in the way described from the "intentional stance." I say "voluntary" because the nation's purpose is just the purpose of its members. And having a purpose in action is one way of defining what is voluntary. All of the artifacts that contribute to the association—here I mean laws, institutions, buildings, and so on—have to be understood as drawing their legitimacy, indeed, their very intelligibility, from their subservience to this fundamental purpose. The best criterion to employ in judging the value and effectiveness of the artifacts of a national association is how they contribute to the happiness of its members.

One of the things Aristotle says about things that exist by nature and their purposes that is frequently misunderstood is that these purposes are properties of kinds. That is, something that exists by nature has a defining purpose or function, as the term *ergon* is often misleadingly translated.[7] Among biological entities, the defining criterion is attained by specifying the life of the organism as that which necessarily follows from its unique organic structure. Among associations that exist by nature, the defining criterion is attained by specifying the unique role that the association serves in the achievement of happiness for those who comprise it. For example, two different sorts of competitive sports can have the same purpose—namely, recreation—and so they do not each have a unique purpose. By contrast, the recreational purpose *is* unique and is distinguishable from the purpose served by, say, marriage.

A nation, for Aristotle, is a self-sufficient association, meaning that like happiness itself, it is completely noninstrumental. That is, it is the second-order end constituted by all the activities and associations that are instrumental to this end. The unique purpose of the nation is secured by its being the uniquely self-sufficient association.

But this also means that the nation has nothing uniquely to contribute to the happiness of its members apart from providing the conditions for the virtuous activity that is happiness. If, indeed, there are necessary conditions for happiness-making activities, and those conditions cannot be provided by those who themselves engage in these activities, then ex hypothesi, as it were, the nation is uniquely placed to provide these. Unquestionably, there is room for debate over what these conditions might be. There might in fact be no one answer to the question, for nations vary in their circumstances. Still, we can say that on the Aristotelian approach a nation's functioning is absolutely exhausted by providing these conditions.

If we turn now to the arena of international relations, the role of a nation conceived as above can be nothing beyond contributing to the happiness of the members of that association. Remember here that we are assuming that the moral agents who direct the nation recognize that the nation itself is a nonmoral agent and not a moral agent and that it has no other purpose beyond that of contributing to the happiness of its members. The moral agents who comprise the nation may well enter into extranational associations that have extranational purposes. Persons who, say, belong to missionary societies, may decide to spread the good news to the most remote corners of the globe as a means of achieving their associative purpose. But that is neither here nor there. Whatever the association that is the nation can do must be justified as contributing to the happiness of its own members, since that is the only legitimate purpose of the association. International relations must be judged according to the criterion of the purpose of nations, which is, again, the happiness of its members.

Allow me to state an obvious and fundamental objection to this approach. One might begin this objection by pointing out that individual persons may belong to transnational associations. Why can we not suppose that persons may belong to the ultimate transnational association, which is the entire world, and that we are all in fact *cosmopolitans* or citizens of the world. In that case, although nations themselves, strictly speaking, are not persons and so personal morality does not apply to them, the persons who go to make up nations can be seen to have obligations to all the other cocitizens in the world. Nations themselves, whatever their status, cannot legitimately obstruct the "flow-through" from moral connectedness *within* nations to moral connectedness *among* nations, that is, among all the citizens of all the nations. On this view, the association that is humanity preempts, morally speaking, any other association. And in a weaker form, the objection insists that even if humanity does not preempt nationality absolutely, it can do so from time to time, in special circumstances.

The modern version of this objection finds its expression in the arguments on behalf of world government and, somewhat less grandiosely, in the UN Charter, especially its preamble. One might suppose that just as small associations can be embraced by the association that is a nation, so nations themselves can be embraced by a "world association." Watching the individual representatives of the 190 or so nations at the UN, each identified by their nations' names and not their own, debating the policies of that body, it is almost impossible not to think of these persons as the nations themselves doing exactly what the persons *within* a nation do when they debate national policies. But there is a fundamental and irremovable difference between the two.

A member of a national assembly would not get very far if she argued for a national policy purely out of self-interest. I do not suggest that this does not happen, only that it is not usually praised or encouraged. But at the UN, the entirety of the argument that occurs is based on perceived national self-interest as formulated by its government. The only time it is not done so directly and explicitly is when it is thought that other-regarding interests are at that moment instrumental to self-interest. A nation that intervenes to protect the interests of another does so because it holds that it is, for one reason or another, in its own interest to do so.

I am speaking now about what actually happens at the UN. But I think that this is what *ought* to happen, because it reflects the fact that nations are associations that exist for the good of their own members. So, an individual may, of course, regard himself as a citizen of the world and try to find other persons who are so inclined. He may opt to construct a protoworld government in his garage. But nobody actually cares unless that person comes into conflict with the laws of the real nation to which he belongs. Nothing follows from cosmopolitanism to tell us what a nation is and what its goal ought to be.

Another way of framing the objection is to insist that justice and human rights are transnational concepts and that the members of nations ought to promote these internationally through the instrumentality of their own nations. Nothing that I have already said contradicts the notion that on moral theories that include a concept of human rights, one might maintain that persons in nations other than one's own have had their rights violated. And nothing precludes the notion that the moral theory requires its adherents to take steps to ameliorate their condition. But if what I have said is true, then there is no logical connection between what is required of an individual person to do and what that person's nation should do. If it is said in reply that every decent nation must follow *some* moral theory as embodied in its constitution or laws, I would answer that even if that is so, and even if that moral theory includes a concept of rights, these have meaning only within that nation as part of the artificial apparatus instrumental to that nation's purpose.

Let me consider briefly an extreme form of a moral view that produces the above objection. It is the view that persons should act universally or globally to achieve egalitarian economic conditions. The only qualification of this claim is that one need not go so far as to act in such a way as to produce conditions that are, on balance, worse than they were before. So, one should give up one's own resources to the poor up to the level of equality but one need not do more than that, thereby simply reversing the original inequality. This globalistic form of utilitarianism is held by, among others,

Peter Singer as well as some of those who read the New Testament rather literally (Singer 1995). I have no intention here to challenge this view. My point is that *even if this view is correct*, it does not alter my case in regard to the morality of nations. Even if persons ought to act as Singer would have them act, it does not follow that nations ought to be directed so to act. It does not even follow that if a majority of those constituting the deliberative body of a nation agreed with Singer that they ought to make the nation act that way. Selling all that you have and giving it to the poor might be an admirable choice. But it seems to me less than admirable for Mr. A to sell Ms. B's possessions and to give them to the poor unless Ms. B did that voluntarily, in which case, of course, she would have already done it and Mr. A would have no opportunity to do it. And if Mr. A. is a Singerian *and* a legislator, his vote to follow his conscience by having his nation do what Singer advises, could *only* amount to forcing Ms. B to act nonvoluntarily.

THE MORAL FOUNDATION OF INTERNATIONAL RELATIONS

In this section, I would like to say briefly how I think we should view the moral dimension of international relations given that nations are not moral agents.[8] The key to the right approach, I believe, is to ask how moral agents—members of the association that is a nation—should direct that particular agent in relation to other nations. And we should ask this question in the light of the recognition that the unique and sole purpose or function of the nation is the happiness of its members. Thus, the moral consideration that ought to govern the interaction of nations is the instrumentality of this interaction to personal happiness. This moral consideration is *entirely* prudential, in the Aristotelian sense of the intellectual virtue that is just the perception of what is conducive to happiness.

Just as a corporation has one legitimate purpose only—namely, the benefits of its owners—so a nation exists for the benefit of *its* members. And just as corporations enter into contracts with other corporations to further this goal, so, too, nations ought to enter into contracts among themselves for the benefit of their members, to achieve benefits that could not otherwise be achieved. So, the moral theory governing the members of nations when they seek to have those nations act on the international stage is contractarian.[9] In Aristotelian terms, contractarianism among nations is like the type of friendship that is one of utility. Such friendships exist only for mutually agreed benefits.

The most obvious sorts of agreement that a nation thus conceived can enter into are those made in behalf of defense. The most obvious sorts of agreement that are thus prohibited are those intended exclusively to serve the interests of the members of other nations. Between these two extremes there are obviously areas in which a case might be made for the pursuit of international contractual arrangements. These seem to me all to flow from the exigencies of nationhood, that is, principally, territorial sovereignty and the monopoly of legitimate force. Examples of the relevant sort might include immigration and extradition treaties. And although the purpose of the nation precludes its involvement in the substantive matter of the production and distribution of goods and services, the nation might enter into contracts with other nations in order to facilitate international trade.

There are many disanalogies between contractarianism on the international level and contractarianism as a moral theory applied to moral agents within a nation or to moral agents acting independently of a nation. The principal difference is this: Whereas contracts within a nation—whether between corporations or between individuals or between corporations and individuals—operate under law and its explicit sanctions, contracts among nations do not.

In claiming this, am I not completely ignoring international law? In fact, I do not think that so-called international laws are laws at all, except in an equivocal sense. The tendency to deny this, in my view, is owing to the false analogy of a nation and a moral agent. For there to be a law, there has to be a sanction. A law without a sanction is nothing more than a prescription or an admonition ("Have a good day!" "Be careful!"). Even if one says, "Be careful . . . or you'll get hurt," that is not a sanction, but a suggested or implied inference. A sanction has to be a potential external constraint. That is why you cannot make laws in regard to your own behavior, even though you can, for example, make New Year's resolutions and metaresolutions about what you will do if you break the original ones. If a sanction is to be effective, indeed, if it is to be intelligible, it must be one that threatens to be applied regardless of your wishes. This is exactly what does *not* happen on the international level. Nations that agree to abide by impartial international court decisions and to accept imposed penalties are doing nothing more than making a cost-benefit calculation, one which includes as an option noncompliance with any putative sanction. It would probably be a good thing if nations abandoned the fiction of interacting under international law and instead employed other strategies (including risk management) for insuring contractual compliance.

I conclude by insisting on two things: (1) that a coherent theory of morality at the international level must start with the premise that a nation is not a moral agent and (2) that everything that a nation does at the international level must, if it is to be defensible, logically flow from the natural purpose of that nation, which is the happiness of its own members.

NOTES

1. "The new electronic interdependence recreates the world in the image of a global village" (McLuhan 1962, 31). McLuhan also coined the phrase "global tribe"

in the same work: "The electronic age" has sealed "the entire human family into a single global tribe" (1962, 8).

2. See Nardin, who says, "Perhaps the notion of collective conduct is always an abstraction or fiction, but if so it would seem to be an indispensable one for both moral and legal discourse" (1983, 234). The indispensability for legal discourse presumably follows for noncriminal law. It is not clear to me why the fiction is even relevant, much less necessary, for criminal law, hence, for morality.

3. For a contrasting view see Goodpaster: "It is appropriate not only to describe organizations (and their characteristics) by analogy with individuals, it is also appropriate *normatively* to look for and to foster moral attributes in organizations by analogy with those we look for and foster in individuals" (1984, 306).

4. Alternative ways of expressing intentionality can be found, e.g., in Moran (2001, esp. chaps. 3–4), who uses the technical term "avowal" to describe the fundamental feature of self-knowledge and rational agency. An avowal is a statement of one's belief when that belief is transparent to oneself. Also, see Fischer (1994, 132–34), who contrasts "guidance control" with "regulative control." The latter indicates that the agent "could have done otherwise." It is notable that in Fischer's account, the possession of guidance control and so of moral responsibility does not exclude causal determinism. Cf. 204–205. So, too, on the account of Frankfurt (1969).

5. See *Nicomachean Ethics* (IX.8.1069a1–2). Aristotle says that acting with reason is acting voluntarily. However, animals and children act voluntarily, although they do not act with reason. The additional factor is the awareness of having done something oneself, that is, having done something voluntarily.

6. See the first line of Aristotle's *Politics* (1252a1) for the identification of the polis as a type of association (*koinonia*). That association consists of joint action for the sake of some good. All action in the strict sense arises from "choice" (*prohairesis*). See *Nicomachean Ethics* (VI.2.1139a31). On the voluntary nature of actions done for the sake of some good, see *Nicomachean Ethics* (II.1.1110a12ff).

7. On the "function" of human beings, see *Nicomachean Ethics* I.6.

8. It is a widely, although not universally, assumed among theoreticians of the normative bases of international relations that nations as such can be included in the scope of whatever moral theory happens to be favored. See, e.g., French (1984); Goodin (1989); Brown (1992); Wendt (1994); Frost (1996); Reus-Smit (1999); Graham (2002).

9. See, especially, Gauthier (1986); also Gauthier and Sugden (1993); and Vallentyne (1991).

6

THE REVOLT OF THE JUST
Eugene Garver

Isn't democracy's insatiable desire for what it defines as the good also what destroys it?

—*Republic* (VIII.562b)

Goodness is not given to recrimination (*hē arete anegklētos*). . . . It is not natural for good men to go to law.

—*Eudemian Ethics* (VII.10.1243a3–11)

*P*olitics V is a frustrating book. Whatever Aristotle's concerns are, they seem at best oblique to the really important questions he ought to be talking about. The book fails to address a whole series of clearly urgent ethical questions about constitutional change. Does virtue play a role in the politics of constitutional change? Does the goodness of the constitution play a role? I'd like *Politics* V to offer me something equivalent to just-war theory, an account of when revolution is ethically justified. I want some guidance in knowing what the good person is to do when he finds himself living under an inferior constitution. Plato seems obsessed with these questions, so it isn't simply historical accident that prevents Aristotle from raising them. *Politics* V doesn't contain anything close. Because it ignores these crucial ethical issues, it seems fair to conclude that it must be an immoral book.[1]

Because book V works obliquely to the moral questions we naturally bring to it, Aristotle seems confused and contradictory on at least three crucial ethical axes of discussion: (1) The virtuous it seems don't revolt, yet in fact they do. (2) Some constitutional changes are just, and others unjust, yet change is always bad and stability always a worthy goal for the statesman. (3) Revolution is inevitable because of the imperfections of constitutions, and yet revolution comes about because of some more specific mistake, and so at least most of them can be avoided.

To increase our frustration, Aristotle's most direct remarks on the three issues I just mentioned are offhand:

(1) Those who excel in virtue would form a faction with the most justice of anyone (though they do this least of all), for it is most reasonable to regard as unequal without qualification these alone. (1.1301a40)

Those who excel in virtue do not cause faction, generally speaking; for they are few against many. (4.1304b4–5)

(2) It is possible to desire [equality and inequality] justly or again unjustly. (2.1302a28–29)

Both when men are themselves dishonored and when they see others honored, they form a faction. Factions occur unjustly when certain men are either honored or dishonored contrary to their worth, but justly when according to their worth (3.1302b11–14).

It is because of profit and honor that men are incited against one another . . . because they see others (some justly and some unjustly) getting more. (2.1302a39–1302b1)

Men are stirred up against one another by profit and by honor—not in order to acquire them for themselves . . . but because they see others aggrandizing themselves (whether justly or unjustly) with respect to these things. (2.1302a36–38)

(3) Many constitutions come into existence because, although every-one agrees about justice . . . , they are mistaken about it. . . . When one [group] or another does not participate in the constitution in accor-dance with their supposition (hypothesis) [about equality], they start faction. (1.1301a25–39)

Politics V has an amoral appearance—if not an amoral reality—because in the program laid out in IV.1 Aristotle says that a complete art of politics has to include the ability to preserve any given constitution.

If someone wants only a lower grade of fitness either of his body or of his knowledge, insufficient for actual competition, it is no less the busi-ness of the coach and trainer to produce this capacity too. (1288b17–19)

So it is clear that, with regard to the constitution, it belongs to the same science to study . . . the constitution based on a supposition (hypothesis)—for any given constitution should be studied [with a view to determining both how it might arise initially and in what manner it might be preserved for the longest time once in existence. (I am speaking of the case where a city happens neither to be governed by the best constitution—and is not equipped even with the things necessary for it—nor to be governed by the constitution that is [the best] possible among existing ones, but one that is poorer. (1288b21–33)

We must attempt to describe the sources of destruction and preservation [N.B.: "destruction and preservation"; improvement is not mentioned] of constitutions both in general and in the case of each separately. (IV.2.1289b23–25)

But trouble is already nascent in book III, and so not confined to this peculiar inquiry into what IV.1 calls hypothetically best. In configuring the relation between the good man and the good citizen, Aristotle concluded that only for the rulers of the best state are the good man and the good citizen identical. Nothing in the argument leading to that conclusion implied that there could be good men who were not good citizens, only that there could be good citizens who were not good men. Citizenship simply carries a lower standard than virtue, a thesis that returns in an especially interesting form in V.9 where sometimes we should trade off some virtue in a ruler for greater philia or ability (V.9.1309a33–36; see too III.11.1281b1–8). Virtuous activity and the good life are possible only for citizens, and for citizens acting as citizens. There is never a conflict between the good man and the good citizen. Under such a configuration of the relation of good man and good citizen, Aristotle cannot even conceive of my initial questions about what the good man is to do under a bad constitution. We will have to see whether this limitation on Aristotle's part has a countervailing payoff.

Book V's concerns with the politics of faction, then, are a particularly crucial place to see in action Aristotle's radical thesis that one can act virtuously only by acting as a citizen. One cannot become virtuous except through civic participation and education; one cannot act virtuously except by acting politically. Trying to overthrow the constitution can never be the action of a citizen. Those theses are especially hard to swallow—and have especially severe consequences—in situations of stasis and constitutional change.

If we learn in book III that virtuous action must be civic action, what is the good man to do in a world of imperfect constitutions, factions, and constitutional change? Or—more radically—are there no such good men, because ethical virtue comes only from participating in a good state? Does our dependence on the state—man is a political animal—mean that no one, neither ruler nor insurgent, can be better than the constitution he lives under? Are the statesmen who can do something about existing democracies and oligarchies themselves so corrupt that preservation is the only end they can aim at? Or are the states that Aristotle describes in book V states in which at least some people can live virtuous and happy lives? Is there a flexibility and an escape from social determinism so that people can be better than their constitutions? What of the claim that "the three things that make someone good and excellent are nature, habit, and reason" (VII.13.1332a38)?

Even if we are eventually entitled to the milder or less cynical answers to these last questions, that is, even if virtuous people can exist within imperfect constitutions, it remains true for Aristotle that no one can be ethically good without being a good citizen. If being a good citizen is a necessary condition of being a virtuous person, then revolt by the virtuous is ruled out, as is a virtuous withdrawal in a corrupt state so as to live as well as possible by finding fulfillment in nonpolitical ways. One cannot act virtuously except by acting as a citizen, and in revolting, one is not acting as a citizen. Is this the moral basis of Aristotle's apparently one-sided attitude that preservation is always good and revolution always bad?

It would seem that the virtuous outsider with his individual moral conscience doesn't exist for Aristotle. Still, the wise statesman is central, and he too confronts the problems that Aristotle's seemingly one-sided conservatism provokes. Does the good citizen defend whatever constitution he finds himself living under, regardless of its moral quality, and regardless of his own judgments of that quality? Are virtuous citizens ethically fulfilled in an imperfect state? Can someone live nobly and happily in a democracy or an oligarchy? How can someone aim at virtue under a constitution that aims at wealth or honor?

These seemingly theoretical or third-person questions about the possibilities for virtue in a corrupt state have a counterpart in more practical questions: If I know that I could act more virtuously if I lived in a better polis, should I, or may I, try to make my polis into a better one? Can I do so as a ruler, or only as a rebel? Can I make the same improvements that a rebel would? Must I suspend my own judgments in the name of loyalty or stability? If my polis restricts my moral development or my moral activities, should I be less engaged politically than I would be if the polis were better? Can the good man be a revolutionary, or must he always uphold an existing constitution, regardless of how just or unjust it is by higher standards? These seem a series of obvious and urgent practical questions. We have to ask why Aristotle isn't interested.

When, in IV.1, Aristotle announces the program for books IV through VIII, and speaks of the specific task of book V, he says that "to reform (*epanorthōsai*) a constitution is no less a task than to frame one from the beginning" (1289a3–4). Yet at the beginning of book V, he presents the destruction and the preservation of constitutions as an exhaustive pair, just as he does at the end of the *Ethics*: "Let us observe what sorts of things preserve and destroy cities" (X.9.1181b19). The statesman has to understand the causes of destruction and has to act to preserve the constitution.

> We must examine (1) the sources of change in constitutions and how many they are and of what sort; (2) what things destroy each constitution; and (3) from what sort and into what sort they are mostly transformed; further (4) what things preserve constitutions in general and each constitution in particular; and, finally (5) the means by which each constitution may best be preserved. (V.1.1301a20–25)

Some of the means Aristotle presents for resisting faction do in fact make the constitution better. But Aristotle never says that the statesman's task is anything but preservation. He seems intentionally to denigrate the statesman's task by calling it preservation when he could have ennobled it by talking about perfecting or improving given constitutions.

At this point we can already explain why Aristotle does not talk about what the good man is to do in a bad state. Identifying a good man living in a bad state requires some moral standards independent of the given constitution. Relying on such standards would prohibit the development of a conception of the good life proper to book V. Instead, the statesman should concentrate fully on stability and should not be distracted by his own conception of the good life. Even if he has a better understanding of the good life than that embodied in the constitution, he is not better off acting on that conception. Deliberation must be concerned with what is best to do in a given situation, not what is best in the abstract. Indeed, Aristotle thinks that injustice and *pleonexia*—taking more than one's share—amount to elevating considerations of what is best over what is best in a situation and what is best for the agent.[2]

All this, though, depends on the ethical plausibility of making preservation of an existing constitution into an end worth aiming at. How, then, can stability be such an overriding goal? Why should the statesman regard all constitutions—and the initial limitation to democracy and oligarchy means that all the constitutions he considers are imperfect—as worth preserving? The statesman is entitled to ignore antecedent moral considerations only if his own end of stability has sufficient moral value of its own.

It's one thing to focus attention on justice relative to a constitution rather than absolute justice, but the stability of any given constitution seems a much more arbitrary value. Justice relative to a constitution is still a form of justice, albeit imperfect. Aristotle is no legal positivist. But stability seems ethically neutral in a way that justice relative to a constitution is not. If stability is a value by itself, the best state on a supposition might be "best" in the way that someone could be a "perfect fool" or a "consummate anti-Semite." "If someone wants only a lower grade of fitness either of his body or of his knowledge, insufficient for actual competition, it is no less the business of the coach and trainer to produce this capacity too" (IV.1.1288b16). But not everything should be preserved for as long as possible. Shouldn't the statesman rather withdraw from public life than assist a state whose ambitions resemble those of the person who "wants only a lower grade of fitness either of his body or of his knowledge"? Even worse, something could be best in a purely comparative way, like the "best relief pitcher on the Minnesota Twins," who may not, by any other standard, be any good at all. Wouldn't "the good tyrant" fall into such a category?

At this point the amorality of Aristotle's argument in *Politics* V is reminiscent of another example of Aristotelian amorality. The statesman trying to resist faction in any state looks like the orator trying to defend any thesis, regardless of its truth. Is the preservation of the constitution worth any more than that sort of performance? *Politics* V looks vulnerable to the same moral challenge as the *Rhetoric*.

And yet that similarity between the statesman's task and the rhetorician's, far from indicting the statesman through guilt by association, exonerates both. The artful rhetorician must be able to argue both sides of any question. The statesman must defend whatever constitution he is given. Just as the rhetorician can argue either side of a question, in situations of faction and constitutional change, attack and defense are the only alternatives. The orator is not in a position to decide which alternative is really best, or to think that out of the clash of arguments a greater grasp of the truth will emerge.[3] Nor can the statesman afford to think about such things.

The statesman must be amoral in trying to preserve any constitution he is given. *Politics* V follows the *Rhetoric* in another regard too, and here making preservation a goal finds a deeper defense than the role morality that that last comparison relied on. When he considers the nature of different audiences in *Rhetoric* II.12–17, showing how differently to appeal to young and old, rich and poor, the one difference among people that he does not consider is the difference between good and bad. The ethical qualities of audiences are irrelevant to the art of rhetoric. Virtue is rhetorically impotent. Similarly in *Politics* V the causes of faction and conservation rarely require treating good and bad people differently, despite the fact that "the greatest division perhaps is virtue and vice, then wealth and poverty, and so on, one being greater than another" (V.3.1303b15–17, see IV.3.1290a1; IV.4.1291b2–13). Although virtue versus vice might be the greatest division, it's not one that characterizes faction. It is not a consideration for either ruler or ruled in confronting factions. The moral quality of the audience is irrelevant for rhetoric, and the moral qualities of both the constitution and the agents fighting for control of the state are irrelevant for defending the state against factions. Aristotle eliminates moral considerations from the treatment of factions not in order to be a value-free social scientist or social engineer, but in order to develop his own ethical purpose of making stability into a noble end.

The means of achieving stability center around distinguishing between living democratically or oligarchically, doing as one likes, as that is defined by the constitution, and ruling democratically or oligarchically. "Many of the things that are held to be democratic destroy democracies, and many that are held to be oligarchic destroy oligarchies. But those who think that the virtues most prominent and seemingly most effectual in their particular society are the only kind of virtue push the constitution to extremes" (V.9.1309b19–24). Living democratically means doing as one likes; living oligarchically means organizing one's life around wealth and honor. Ruling democratically or oligarchically means aiming at the preservation of the democratic or oligarchic constitution, and subordinating—not suppressing—one's other goals, of freedom, wealth, or honor.

The difference between living democratically or oligarchically and ruling democratically or oligarchically is parallel to the difference between persuading and finding the available means of persuasion in the *Rhetoric*.[4] Only the latter can be the subject of an art; similarly only ruling democratically or oligarchically can be part of political knowledge. Not all the effective ways of persuading an audience fall within the art of rhetoric—persuading through sexual charm may work, and yet it is not part of the art of rhetoric. In the same way, there are no doubt means of preserving a state that don't involve ruling constitutionally—massive intimidation often does work, and nursing grievances against a common enemy can make people forget their troubles and their differences—but these are literally unknowable, not accessible by Aristotle's practical sciences. Only ruling democratically or oligarchically, as opposed to living democratically or oligarchically, can be part of political science and therefore part of living well.

"One should not think it slavery to live in harmony with the constitution, but safety" (V.9.1310a34–36, see *Metaphysics* I.2.982b25–26; XII.10. 1075a18–23). Living in harmony with the constitution may feel like constraint to someone who wants to do just as he pleases. Such a person experiences living in harmony with any constitution as slavery. But even democratic constitutions demand doing something other than whatever one likes. "To be educated relative to the constitution is not to do the things enjoyed by oligarchs or proponents of democracy, but rather to do the things that will enable the rulers, respectively, to govern in an oligarchic or democratic way" (V.9.1310a19–22). This is book V's definition of the good life. Acting politically is a good life of justice and friendship. The ruler who aims at life alone aims at domination or living as he likes, whereas the good life is a political life of mutuality and reciprocity. In stable poleis, citizens act as political animals. Making man's political nature dominate other aspects of human nature is the key to stability.

Those who want "to do the things enjoyed by oligarchs or proponents of democracy" see the constitution as an instrument toward that enjoyment. So they rule for the sake of mere life, organized around goals like pleasure, honor, or profit—for their own gratification and not the good of the whole. But, for those who want "to do the things that will enable them . . . to govern in an oligarchic or democratic way," ruling and acting politically is of intrinsic worth. It is not a means to some ulterior end. Such governing, aiming at the preservation of the constitution, is rule for the sake of living well, just because it is its own end.

In deviant states, people "think it slavery to live in harmony with the constitution," but their rulers, seeking to avoid such slavery, end up ruling despotically. Constitutions that aim at the benefit of the rulers alone eliminate the possibility of friendship. Natural slaves may be better off when ruled by someone with more intelligence and virtue than they, but the fact that they are benefited doesn't make despotic rule into rule for the sake of anyone but the masters. Incidental benefits are not the same as a purpose.

> It is clear then that those constitutions that aim at the common advantage are in effect rightly framed in accordance with absolute justice (*to haplōs dikaion*), while those that aim only at the rulers' own advantage are faulty, and all of them are deviations from the right constitutions; for they have an element of despotism, whereas a city is a partnership of free men. (1279a17–22)

"The most important of all the things that have been mentioned for the endurance of constitutions, which all men now make light of, is to be educated in harmony with the constitution" (V.9.1310a12–14). Education in harmony with a constitution is education in moderation, in becoming a moderate democrat or oligarch. This education orients the citizen toward ruling democratically or oligarchically, instead of living democratically or oligarchically. So education in harmony with the constitution means becoming a fully political being. Stability and moderation are ways in which people become political animals in difficult circumstances. "All men now make light of" such education, because they prefer living democratically or oligarchically to ruling democratically or oligarchically. Even if man is by nature a political animal, living politically is demanding, and people will resist fulfilling their nature. Constitutions become stable when rulers fully realize their nature as political animals. If the *Ethics* is about how to be happy, the *Politics* is about how to be a political animal. Being a political animal is as much a full-time job as being virtuous is, whether one is a ruler or a nonruling citizen. In book V at least, one cannot often live politically except by living democratically or oligarchically. One can certainly never live politically except by living under some particular constitution.[5]

The constitutional ethos—the ethos of living politically—should dominate the more particular democratic or oligarchic ethos, because such domination rationally achieves security. "The character peculiar to each constitution usually safeguards it as well as establishes it initially (for example, the democratic character, a democracy; and the oligarchic one, an oligarchy), and a better character is always the cause of a better constitution" (VIII.1.1337a14–18). To rule constitutionally is to let the law rule, instead of a rule of men. Living as a political animal means finding fulfillment in alternately ruling and being ruled, rejecting the easier choices of despotism or withdrawal as a free rider. When the constitutional ethos dominates, the constitution has become a correct constitution, one that aims at the good of the whole, while remaining a democracy or an oligarchy, a rule of the few or the many, poor or rich. The statesman must convince his fellow citizens, through such education in harmony with the constitution and thus in moderation, to reject living democratically or oligarchically in favor of ruling democratically or oligarchically.

The distinctions Aristotle uses in book III to distinguish correct (*orthos*) from deviant constitutions are made more determinate in the specific inquiry of Book V. Rule of law, as opposed to rule of men, is the domination of ruling according to the constitution, over living according to the ends of the constitution. Ruling for the good of the whole, as opposed to ruling for the rulers' own benefit, becomes rule according to the constitutional ethos. Even more radically, the distinction from book III (and book I) between living and living well is now made determinate as the distinction between living and ruling according to the constitution. In the same way, the taxonomy of six constitutions functions differently in book V, and the other more determinate inquiries of IV through VIII, causing no end of troubles for commentators. In book III there is a clear distinction between three correct—monarchy, aristocracy, and polity—and three corresponding deviant constitutions—tyranny, oligarchy, and democracy. All six constitutions appear in book V, but they play different roles in the argument. Aristotle does not say that his more stable democracies and oligarchies will really be polities and aristocracies without knowing it, as though the statesman hides his political wisdom and induces the masses to act for their own good. Instead, as the treatment of polities and aristocracies in V.7—and indeed the treatment of monarchy and tyranny in V.10–11—show, the correct/deviant distinction is not at work in the politics of stasis of book V. Constitutions become stable by becoming constitutions first of all, and democracies or oligarchies secondarily. When rulers and other citizens act by the constitutional ethos, they will transform all constitutions into polities, the name Aristotle uses both for the general name for constitution in general and for the correct counterpart of democracy.

Therefore, in spite of the amoral surface to book V, Aristotle shows that preserving a constitution can be a noble action. Even if I can imagine better worlds in which being a moderate democrat would not be a virtue, in the world defined by faction, being a moderate democrat is an appropriate form of virtue.

For Aristotle to succeed at demonstrating the unlikely truth that stability and progress come about through the development of the constitutional ethos of mutuality, he has to marginalize the very limited role that more direct moral considerations play in destroying and preserving constitutions, even partially effacing the difference between monarchy and tyranny, which otherwise are the constitutions at the greatest distance from each other. To figure out what is within the scope of political deliberation, considerations of moral quality have to be mostly irrelevant, as the moral qualities of rhetorical audiences were in the *Rhetoric*. Consider, for just one example, the parenthesis: "Men are stirred up against one another by profit and by honor—not in order to acquire them for themselves . . . but because they see others aggrandizing themselves (whether justly or unjustly) with respect to these things" (V.2.1302a36–38). The power of the politics of envy and righteous indignation is independent of the validity of the accusations. It doesn't matter whether others are getting ahead justly or not. *Politics* V has its own moral purpose, to demonstrate people's political nature through an orientation to stability and moderation. To explore how the moral qualities of particular actors within political struggles affect their behavior would distract from his own moral project.

In both the *Rhetoric* and *Politics* V Aristotle suspends the moral in one sense to make room for it in another. Aristotle's own moral project can succeed only by muting other moral considerations. The rhetorician cannot be concerned with the virtue of his audience. The rhetorician must, though, persuade the audience of his own moral character, not for the sake of ethical honesty but for the lower reason that ethos persuades. He has to know enough about the ethos of his audience to show them that his ethos resembles theirs. But the art of rhetoric is not an art of appearance in which the rhetorician gathers up polling data to decide how to look like his audience. His ethos is primarily the ethos of a persuader, an ethos that is fully a function of his reasoning. His ethos, while it may be the ethos of a democracy or an oligarchy, is in the first place the ethos of a reasoner and a persuader. The rhetorician must present a character that is fully a function of his art and only in that way a matter of appearance (I.2.1356a8–13).

In precisely the same way the reformed constitution's ethos will primarily be a constitutional ethos. The differences among the constitutional forms mostly recede to the background in book V, as we learn in chapters 5 through 7 that most problems of preservation are generic and not specific to a particular kind of constitution. To put this turn of arguments in its most radical form: In book V all stable constitutions become *politeiai*. While the statesman in circumstances of faction must similarly worry about appearances, "one must not put one's trust in things that are concocted for the sake of chicanery toward the mass; for they are refuted by the facts" (V.8.1307b40–1308a2).

By limiting the rhetorician's means to argument alone, Aristotle shows how to construct rational connections between speaker and hearer. The art of rhetoric establishes relations of justice and friendship between speaker and hearer, even in adversarial situations, and even when the friendship extends no further than the act of persuasion itself. The limitation on the means of persuasion creates its own ethics. A speaker who tried to rely on his own antecedent, "real," moral qualities would depend on something other than argument and the rational relations between speaker and hearer. Antecedent morality can be an obstacle to the emergent morality of these rational connections.

Politics V does something analogous at every point. The rhetorician pays no attention to the virtue of his audience. The rhetorician must, though, persuade the audience of his own moral character. Similarly here, the statesman ignores the virtue of his fellow rulers and of the insurgents in order to fortify a constitution that both rules for the benefit of the whole and appears to do so. He doesn't reorient the constitution toward the good life because of some moral impulse, but simply in the name of stability.

Next, the rhetorician has to know enough about the ethos of his audience to show them that his ethos resembles theirs. The statesman has to create a correct constitution out of the democracy or oligarchy he starts with. He thereby establishes connections of *philia* between all the citizens and the constitution and therefore among the citizens themselves. The right way to distinguish correct from deviant constitutions in this context is not by saying that deviant constitutions aim at honor or profit, while correct constitutions aim at the good life. For the purposes of book V, all constitutions and all constitutional actors aim at honor and profit. The difference between correct and deviant constitutions is the difference between friendships of utility, revolving around the goods of honor and profit, and the more purely commercial or impersonal relations that also aim at honor or profit. Just as in the *Ethics* there is no imperative that obliges us to convert all friendships into virtue friendships, here we have no duty to aim at a life of virtue by denigrating the ends of honor and profit. Insurgents aim at honor and profit, while those preserving the state aim at perfecting actions organized around honor and profit into the best kinds of actions they can be. Friendships of utility really are friendships, and it is possible to live well aiming at honor or profit.

Masters can have personal friendships with their slaves, but not as masters and slaves. The rulers in good constitutions are friendly toward each other and even toward those outside the constitution, not as human beings in abstraction from their political offices, but as rulers engaged in ruling. Revolution cannot be an act of friendship. *Philia* limits the means of preservation.

The *Rhetoric* showed how to construct rational connections, and, because rational, relations of justice and friendship between speaker and hearer. In V.9 the means of preserving states move from avoiding injustice to establishing common bonds among the citizens, culminating in education in harmony with the constitution. Limiting the means of preservation creates its own ethics. The statesman who tried to rely on his own antecedent, "real," moral qualities would depend on something other than argument and the rational relations between ruler and ruled. Any such virtue existing outside the rhetorical situation inevitably becomes a form of force within the rhetorical situation. My past heroic exploits and my history of self-sacrifice, if not connected to any arguments I can make now, might silence my opponents or make the audience defer to me, but by themselves they do not contribute to a rational or friendly relation between us. Antecedent morality can be an obstacle to the emerging morality of these rational connections.

Constitutional stability and a constitution that consequently aims at the good life is its own ethical project. The world of faction is a world in which democrats and oligarchs struggle against each other, and the virtuous line up with one party or the other. Declarations that one is not a democrat or an oligarch but acting for virtue alone would, probably rightly, be regarded as mere partisanship. Disinterested virtue may have its place in the more limited justice of the judge, but the good citizen and the good statesman are, by definition, partisans, and partisans who act in the name of impartial justice are no less partisans for that. The virtuous play no distinctive role in this sort of politics.

By refusing to recognize any special role for antecedent virtue or for justice as due deference to merit, Aristotle clears the way for his own kind of moral politics. The constitutional ethos of friendship allows the goal of stability to be its own way of aiming at the good life. In one sense, Aristotle lowers his ambitions to the best life one can have. That is the price of starting with the material the statesman is given: what counts here as living well might, by other standards and in other contexts, fall short of the best life. In another way, though, making such a life a good life is a thoroughly ambitious project, one which makes moderation noble. This statesmanship sets its sights at the right height, aiming at stability and through stability at its own form of the good life. It persuades its followers and opponents that moderation is a political virtue, and that the ethos of acting politically should dominate the ethos of any particular constitution.

The orator, and the dialectician, will uphold whatever position he is assigned. Such a person can't limit his trade to noble causes. However, in the process of defending the given cause, he will restrict himself to making arguments, not corrupting the audience through emotional appeals, bribes, or sophistical tricks. Rhetoric and dialectic, then, develop their own ethics of argument, appreciating the value of rational argument over other means of victory. Such an ethical development is possible only if the speaker ignores antecedent morality, which would only be a distraction, both for himself, in making ethical choices, and for the audience, who must see external moral claims as irrational appeals to authority.

Similarly, the statesman will defend against faction the constitution he is given. However, in the process of defending the given constitution, he will restrict himself to those means of securing stability that do more than counter the causes of faction. He will concentrate on those means that make the state stable by embodying the constitutional ethos, ruling democratically or oligarchically rather than living democratically or oligarchically. The person of political wisdom chooses the right means for achieving stability. The right means are those that improve the state. There are no restrictions on the causes that may lead to the formation of factions or to their being success-ful—like the sophist, insurgents can do anything, and force and fraud are typical of the means insurgents use (1304b5–7). But preserving the state requires more restricted means. They are limited to the constitutional ethos. While Aristotle does recommend some institutional devices that will help achieve stability, the fundamental means of preserving constitutions is ethi-cal, not institutional.

I want to close by looking briefly at two specific places which exclude reference to antecedent moral considerations in addressing problems of con-stitutional change. First, book V opens by articulating the four causes of factions, and we can ask where the virtuous belong in each of the causes. In each case Aristotle's analysis will be amoral, but each is amoral in a different sense, and each uses this amorality as a way of furthering the moral purpose of making stability into a noble end. V.1 identifies the formal cause of con-stitutional change, the inevitably partial definitions of justice that constitute democracy and oligarchy. The fact that partisans aim only at partial justice could cut both ways: One virtuous person could be on the side of the con-stitution by seeing the justice in partial justice, while another could enlist against the existing constitution by seeing the injustice of partiality. If the virtuous can find themselves on either side, the formal cause of faction seems amoral.

V.2 sets out the other three causes, "the disposition of those who form factions, for the sake of what, and the origins of political tumults and of factions against one another" (V.2.1302a50–22). The disposition is the material cause. A desire for equality or inequality, could include the virtuous, but the analysis is amoral in that the virtuous have no special place.

The final cause is the aim or goal of rebellion. This, Aristotle says, is limited to honor and profit (V.2.1302a31–33). If so, revolt is always for the sake of living, not living well. It is always for the sake of goods of possession, not the goods of activity. Being outside the constitution puts one in a po-sition of necessarily aiming at these lower goods. Even if the virtuous should revolt, they would do so not for the sake of virtue but to secure honor and profit, either because of injury or insult, or for the nobler reason that honor and profit allow them or others to act virtuously. This aspect of Aristotle's causal treatment is amoral again, but in a different sense. It excludes moral agents from the picture. I might have an ultimate moral motive in rebelling, but the rebellion itself can only aim at honor and profit. While in books I and III Aristotle told us that states differ from other associations in aiming at the indefinite good of living well as opposed to more determinate goods, constitutional change aims only at those more limited goods, honor and profit. Good men, as such, can't be revolutionaries.[6]

That difference between the ends of constitutions and the ends of constitutional change explains why all constitutional change is for the worse.

Rebellion always aims at honor and profit, even when undertaken by the just. But preservation can be either for the sake of life or for the good life. Rulers can act to preserve their prerogatives and property; or they can try to maintain the state in order to rule for the common good and for living well. Aristotle has a good reason, which I wish he had made explicit, for thinking that all constitutional change is for the worse and that therefore all faction should be resisted.

The last cause Aristotle considers, the efficient cause, presents a different sort of ethical challenge. As Aristotle ticks off his list of such causes, they become increasingly distant from the constitution and eventually even from factions. As they become more and more external forces, they become amoral in the way that the weather is morally indifferent, raining equally on the just and the unjust. Yet, as I argued above, the moving causes that insurgents use are unlimited, while preservationists are restricted in their choice of means.[7]

Now for my second example. If my questions about whether virtuous people behave differently concerning factions are at best only obliquely addressed in V.1–6, V.7 explicitly raises and answers questions as to whether problems of stability and overthrow are different for aristocratic and political constitutions concerned with virtue than for democracy and oligarchy. V 1 said that all states—or all states Aristotle will consider, or all states when they are considered for the purpose of understanding factions—are democratic or oligarchic, but V.7 is about factions in aristocracies and polities. (Chapters 10–12 stray even farther from the initial dictum of Book V, by treating of factions in monarchies and tyrannies.) Those looking forward to the triumph of virtue will be disappointed in chapter 7. For the most part, aristocracies and polities are no different from oligarchies and democracies. "An aristocracy is an oligarchy in a way" (1306b24). People engaged in faction and in resisting it find no significant differences between aristocracy and oligarchy or between polity and democracy.

V.7 finds one difference between factions in aristocracies or polities and those already analyzed in a democracy or oligarchy. It is a small difference, not important to Aristotle but illuminating for my purpose. Justice according to virtue can make these states more unstable than democracy or oligarchy, because it gives outsiders yet another reason to revolt. Aristotle lists three causes of faction unique to aristocracies. The first reason aristocracies fall is because "there are a number of men who are swollen with pride on the ground of being equal in virtue" (1306b27). Such men destabilize aristocracy more than democracy or oligarchy. The second is the disparity between the rich and the poor. All states contain such a difference, but in an aristocracy it is easier for the poor to make arguments from desert as well as need, since merit is supposed to be the principle of justice (1307a2). The poor man has nothing to complain about when told that justice is proportional to wealth, but anyone might feel injured by being excluded on the basis of virtue. Finally, "if someone is great and capable of being still greater, he may stir up faction in order to rule alone" (1307a3–4). Virtue can be a cause of instability, especially in constitutions that promise justice proportioned to virtue. In all these respects, aristocracy's commitment to justice proportioned to merit makes things worse.[8]

If the purpose of Politics V is to encourage statesmen to transform democracies and oligarchies into their correct counterparts, polity and aristocracy, then showing that for the purposes of confronting factions, polity and aristocracy are not much different from democracy and oligarchy helps to smooth the way. The smaller the difference between correct and corrupt kinds of constitutions, the more plausible it is to demand that the statesman establish a constitutional ethos. The rest of chapter 7 considers both aristocracies and polities. It treats them as variants of oligarchy and democracy, with no special problems of their own. Since aristocracies mix democracy, oligarchy, and virtue, "some are less and some are more enduring" (7.1304a16). Their stability comes solely from their relation to the many and the wealthy, and not to how much virtue the constitution embodies. Polities and aristocracies have no moral exemption from faction.

Suppressing one kind of morality in order to advance another explains, finally, why Aristotle offers preservation and destruction as the sole alternatives, and doesn't show the statesman the way to reform. This is not a secret teaching of improvement beneath the surface meaning of stability. The statesman should aim at stability, not progress. Aiming at stability and choosing the ethically appropriate means, he will achieve progress. To aim directly at progress would substitute his own moral standards for those of the constitution, making him exempt from politics. He should instead aim at stability and come to recognize, and to show the other citizens, the full implications of the project of stability.

NOTES

1. Robinson (1995, 14), speaking of III.4: "Aristotle's difficulty here appears to be different from any of ours. We often worry whether the State's orders conflict with our conscience, or whether our duty to the State conflicts with our duty to our family, or whether a politician can be an honest man. None of these questions occurs to Aristotle."

2. "Since the unjust person is greedy, he will be concerned with goods—not with all goods, but only with those involved in good and bad fortune, goods which are, [considered] unconditionally, always good, but for this or that person not always good. Though human beings pray for these and pursue them, they are wrong; the right thing is to pray that what is good unconditionally will also be good for us, but to choose [only] what is good for us" (V.1.1129b1–7; see V.9.1137a26–30). "The absolutely good is absolutely desirable but what is good for oneself is desirable for oneself; and the two ought to come into agreement. This is effected by virtue; and

the purpose of politics is to bring it about in cases where it does not yet exist. And one who is a human being is well adapted to things and on the way to it (for by nature things that are absolutely good are good to him) . . . but the road is through pleasure—it is necessary that fine things should be pleasant. When there is discord between them, a man is not yet perfectly good; for it is possible for unrestraint to be engendered in him, as unrestraint is caused by discord between the good and the pleasant in the emotions" (*Eudemian Ethics* 1236b38–1237a3).

The virtuous man does not revolt because that would be choosing the best *haplōs* rather than the best in the circumstances. Such a choice is unjust. Choosing absolute justice rather than the justice appropriate to the given constitution is unjust.

3. Aristotle does not try to justify the existence of disputation by faith in the emergence of truth from debate or from a right of all parties to be heard in their own defense. "Rhetoric is useful because the true and the just are by nature stronger than their opposites, so that if judgments are not made in the right way [the true and the just] are necessarily defeated. And this is worthy of censure. Further, even if we had the most exact knowledge, it would not be very easy for us in speaking to use it to persuade some audiences (I.1.1355a21–25).

4. For details, see *Aristotle's Rhetoric: An Art of Character*, University of Chicago Press, 1994.

5. Of course there are complications because in V.7 he considers the special problems of faction in polities and aristocracies, and in the last three chapters he looks at monarchy and tyranny.

6. In both cases, the limitation of constitutions to democracy and oligarchy and the limitation of the ends of revolt to honor and profit, one could argue that I have it backwards, that it is only because Aristotle makes empirical generalizations and nothing formally complete that he has restricted his subject to democracy and oligarchy and to the ends of honor and profit. The amorality of the inquiry then comes from the way we live now and not from anything deeper. I don't think that line of reasoning will work. Aristotle doesn't view the central phenomena for his inquiries as accidental. See too *Nicomachean Ethics* (VIII.12.1162b5–8): "Accusations and complaints arise in friendship for usefulness—either in this friendship alone or especially so, with good reason. For friends on account of virtue are eager to treat each other well (this being characteristic of virtue and friendship), and when that is what people are contending for, there cannot be recriminations or conflicts."

7. For more details, see my "Factions and the Paradox of Aristotelian Practical Science."

8. See too IV.4.1291b5–6: "All men claim to possess virtue and think they are worthy to fill most public offices."

7

ARISTOTLE'S REGIME OF THE AMERICANS
Peter L. P. Simpson

INTRODUCTION

The discovery of ancient texts once thought to have been irretrievably lost is a rare event. But it does happen. The discovery a few years ago of the works of Posidippus is a case in point. As far as the texts of Aristotle are concerned, the most dramatic event in modern times was the discovery, in the nineteenth century, of his *Athenaion Politeia*, or *Regime of the Athenians*. Not less dramatic is the text that follows and that I offer here for the first time both in the original Greek and in accompanying English translation. How the text came into my hands is a complex story that would take too long to explain, so let me just say that it involves a shadowy Hittite book dealer near ancient Scepsis in the Troad. The text's title of *Amerikanon Politeia*, taken from the opening words, is Aristotelian enough and, as will immediately appear, so is much of its content. Indeed several sentences and paragraphs can easily be paralleled in Aristotle's *Politics*. This gives us, accordingly, some reason to regard the text as his or at least as preserving genuinely Aristotelian thought.

What will give us pause, of course, is the seeming anachronism of the subject matter. The regime of the Americans seems an unlikely, nay, an impossible topic for Aristotle to have written about. Did he not die millennia before the regime came into existence? This question, however, betrays an anachronism of its own. According to Aristotle himself, as we learn from texts undoubtedly his, the world is eternal and experiences periodic cataclysms during which human civilization is reduced to primitive savagery whence it slowly rises, recovering all that was previously lost, until the next cataclysm destroys everything again. Consequently the regime of the Americans, or something like it, has already existed many times in the past. Our current views about the age and origin of the cosmos are not as definite or as complete as altogether to rule out Aristotle's speculations. If so, there is no compelling reason to deny that he could have come to learn about an American-style regime from ancient tales or records. There is also, therefore, no compelling reason to deny that he could have described and assessed that regime in the same way as he did the regimes of the Athenians and Spartans. At all events, one should judge the text that follows, not by its anachronism (for it has none), but by its content. And that content seems Aristotelian enough. To aid the understanding of the content, therefore, I have divided the text into numbered paragraphs and also marked, in the translation, where the author passes from description to criticism.

ΑΡΙΣΤΟΤΕΛΟΥΣ ΑΜΕΡΙΚΑΝΩΝ ΠΟΛΙΤΕΙΑ

1. ἡ δὲ Ἀμερικανῶν πολιτεία, ἣν σχεδὸν ἐν πάσαις ταῖς πόλεσιν ἔχονται καὶ ἐν τῇ συμμαχίᾳ τῇ πρὸς ἀλλήλους, εἰς εἴδη ἀρχῶν μάλιστα τρία διανέμεται· ὧν δὲ πλείστας μὲν ὁ δῆμος αἱρεῖται, αἱ δὲ τοῦ τρίτου μέγισται ὑπὸ τῶν ἄλλων ἀρχῶν καθίστανται. λέγω δὲ τρία τὴν μὲν μοναρχίαν, τοὺς δὲ γέροντάς τε καὶ τὴν ἐκκλησίαν, καὶ τρίτον δὲ τὰ δικαστήρια. καίπερ μὲν γὰρ τὸν μόναρχον τῆς αὐτῶν μητροπόλεως διὰ πολέμου ἐκβαλόντες ὡς ὄντα τύραννον, ὅμως δὲ τὴν μοναρχικὴν ἀρχὴν σφόδρα φιλοῦσιν οἱ Ἀμερικανοὶ καὶ μεγάλας ἀρχὰς μόνας μὲν ὄντας κυρίας δὲ πολλῶν τῶν κοινῶν κατέστησαν πανταχοῦ. καλοῦσι δὲ προέδρους ἢ κυβερνήτας ἢ καὶ δημάρχους. οὓς καὶ ἐν ἀρχῇ διαμένειν ἐῶσιν ἔτη πολλὰ καὶ εἰς τὴν αὐτὴν τοὺς αὐτοὺς πολλάκις αἱροῦνται· οὐ μὴν ἀλλ' ἐνίοτε τὸν αὐτὸν εἰς τὴν αὐτὴν βαδίζειν οὐκ ἐῶσιν πλὴν ἅπαξ ἢ δίς. πρὸς δὲ τούτοις περὶ καταστάσεις ἄλλων ἀρχῶν ποιοῦσι πολλῶν τοιούτους μὲν κυρίους εἶναι, τῷ δὲ δήμῳ τοῦ ταύτας αἱρεῖσθαι ἀρχὰς ἐξουσίαν οὐ διδόντες οὐδεμίαν.

2. μετὰ δὲ τὴν μοναρχίαν εἰσὶ δ' αὐτοῖς ἡ τῶν γερόντων ἀρχὴ καὶ ἡ τῆς ἐκκλησίας, ὥσπερ ἐχθρὰς πρὸς τοὺς μονάρχους καὶ ἑτέραν πρὸς ἑτέραν κατέστησαν· οἱ γὰρ Ἀμερικανοὶ τοῖς μονάρχοις καὶ πᾶσι τοῖς ἐν ἀρχῇ μάλιστα φθονοῦσι καὶ ὡς οὐκ οὖσιν ἱκανῶς ἀγαθοῖς ἀνδράσιν ἀπιστοῦσιν· εἰ καὶ γὰρ δύναμιν αὐτοῖς διδόασι μεγίστην, ἀεὶ θέλουσιν αὐτοὺς ὑπ' ἄλλων κατὰ τὴν βούλησιν κατέχεσθαι. ἔτι δὲ τοὺς γέροντας καὶ τοὺς ἐκκλησιαστὰς αἱροῦνται πάντες οἱ πολῖται, ὅπερ δημοκρατικὸν μέν ἐστι καὶ τοῖς Ἀμερικανοῖς αἰτία τοῦ τὴν αὐτῶν πολιτείαν καλεῖσθαι δημοκρατίαν· ὅμως δὲ ταύτας τὰς ἀρχὰς ποιοῦσι πολυχρονιωτέρας κατὰ δύα ἢ τέτταρα ἢ καὶ ἓξ ἔτη, τοὺς αὐτοὺς εἰς τὴν αὐτὴν αἱρούμενοι πολλάκις, ὅπερ λίαν ὀλιγαρχικόν. ἔτι δ' οὐκ ἐκ πάντων ἀλλ' ἐξ ἑταιριῶν τινῶν ἢ μερίδων πολιτικῶν (ὡς καλοῦσιν) ὑπερπλουσίων οὐσῶν αἱροῦνται μόνον· ἐκεῖναι δ' ἑταιρίαι δημαγωγοῦσιν καὶ τὰς ἐριθείας ἵν' αἱρεθῶνται ποιοῦσιν, ὅπερ δαπάνης δεῖται πολλῆς.

TRANSLATION OF ARISTOTLE'S REGIME OF THE AMERICANS

Description of the Regime

1. The regime of the Americans, which they have in almost all their cities and in their alliance with each other, is divided into three kinds of office in particular, most of which are elected by the populace though the most important ones among the third kind are appointed by the other offices. The three offices I mean are the monarchy, the senate and assembly, and the courts third. For though the Americans overthrew the monarch of their mother country, whom they accused of tyranny and fought a war against, yet they have an especial love for the office of monarch and have established powerful offices everywhere that are held by one man and are possessed of control over many matters of common concern. These monarchs they call presidents or governors or mayors. Moreover they allow them to hold office for many years and they elect the same men to the same office many times, though in some cases they do not allow the same man to hold the same office more than once or twice. In addition they put such monarchs in control of appointing many other offices where the populace are given no power to do any electing at all.

2. After the monarchy they have the office of senate and assembly, which they have set up as hostile rivals to the monarchs as well as to each other. For the Americans are very jealous of their monarchs and of all those who hold office and do not trust them as being good men, for even though they give them great power they want them always to be checked in their will by others. The senates and assemblies are elected by all the citizens, which is democratic and which is why the American regime is called a democracy. But they give these offices rather long terms, up to two or four or even six years, and they elect the same people to the same office many times over, which is extremely oligarchic. In addition they do not elect from among everyone but only from among certain overly rich clubs or political parties, as they are called, and in order to get elected these clubs engage in demagoguery and competing for votes, which involve great expense.

3. αἱ μὲν οὖν τῆς αἱρέσεως στρατεῖαι (τὰς γὰρ ἐριθείας οὕτως καλοῦσιν οἱ Ἀμερικανοί) πολλοὺς μῆνους ἢ καὶ ἐνιαυτὸν ὅλον διατείνονται, ἐν αἷς αἱ ἑταιρίαι πολιτικαὶ πρὸς ἑαυτὰς στασιάζουσιν· καὶ τοὺς μονάρχους ὁμοίως αἱροῦνται στασιάζοντες. ὁ δὲ δῆμος τῇ ὀλιγαρχίᾳ τοιαύτῃ οὐ δυσχεραίνει διὰ τὸ μετέχειν μὲν ἐξεῖναι τῶν ἑταιριῶν καὶ τῶν μεγάλων ἀρχῶν, μάλιστα δὲ διὰ τὸ τὰς ἀρχὰς αὐτὸς αἱρεῖσθαι· οὕτως γὰρ τῆς τῶν ἑταιριῶν στάσεως διαιτητής ἐστιν ὁ δῆμος καὶ δεσπότης τῶν εὐτυχημάτων πολιτικῶν· διὰ δὴ τοῦτ' ἀεὶ ὑπὸ τῶν πλουσίων καὶ δυνατῶν κολακεύεται τῶν τὰς ψήφους ὅπως ἄρχωσιν θηρευόντων.

4. λοιπὸν δὲ τῶν τριῶν εἰπεῖν τὸ δικαστικόν· ἐπὶ δὲ καὶ τούτῳ μόναρχον ἄλλον καθίστανται, τὸν καλούμενον κριτὴν ἢ δικαιοῦντα, πλείους δὲ τοιούτους ἐνίοτ' ἐν τῷ αὐτῷ δικαστηρίῳ ποιοῦσιν. ἀλλ' οὐκ ἐῶσιν αὐτοὺς καίπερ δυνατοὺς ὄντας κατὰ πάντα κυρίους εἶναι. ἐπικαλοῦσι γὰρ καὶ τὸν δῆμον τῶν δικαστηρίων κοινωνεῖν, οὐχ ἅμα πάντ' ἀλλὰ κατὰ μέρος ἐκ καταλόγου συλλεχθέντα. οὕτως δὴ τῶν κρίσεων ὁ δῆμος σχεδὸν πασῶν μετέχει, μάλιστα δὲ τῶν μεγίστων (λέγω δὲ τὰς μεγίστας τὰς περὶ θανάτου καὶ ζωῆς καὶ δημεύσεως καὶ ὅσων εἰς τὴν πολιτείαν φέρουσιν). οὐ μὴν ἀλλὰ κρίνει μόνον μὲν εἰ ἔνοχος ὁ φεύγων, τὴν δὲ ζημίαν καὶ τὴν τοῦ νόμου ἑρμηνείαν τοῖς μονάρχοις ἀφείς. τούτων δὲ μοναρχῶν οἵ γε πλεῖστοι οὐχ ὑπὸ τοῦ δήμου αἱροῦνται, εἰ μὴ ὀλίγοι τὰ μικρὰ κύριοι ὄντες, ἀλλ' ὑπὸ τῶν ἄλλων ἀρχόντων τῶν τε μοναρχῶν καὶ γερόντων. ἔτι δὲ διὰ βίου κύριοι μένουσιν εἰ μή τι κακίστως δράσαντες ὑπὸ τῶν αὐτοὺς καταστησάντων κρι— θῶσι καὶ ἐκβάλωνται.

5. αὗται μὲν οὖν εἰσιν ἀρχαὶ τῆς πολιτείας τοῖς Ἀμερικανοῖς αἱ μέγισται, ἣν δημοκρατίαν ὡς εἰρήκαμεν καλοῦσιν. ὅτι δ' ἐν αὐτῇ πολλὰ τῶν ὀλιγαρχικῶν ὑπάρχει καὶ τούτων ἔνια τῆς ἐσχάτης ὀλιγαρχίας παρεκβάσεις δῆλον. ἀλλὰ καλὸν τοῦτο νομίζουσιν εἶναι καὶ τρόπον τινὰ τοῦ σώζειν τὴν δημοκρατίαν. ἡ γὰρ δὴ πολιτεία κατὰ δύο μάλιστα τρόπους δημοκρατικῶς ἔχει, καθ' ἕνα μὲν τὸ πάντα τὸν δῆμον τοὺς μονάρχους καὶ γέροντας καὶ ἐκκλησιαστὰς αἱρεῖσθαι, καθ' ἕτερον δὲ τὴν αὐτῶν δίαιταν. ζῇ γὰρ σχεδὸν ἕκαστος τῶν Ἀμερικανῶν ὡς βούλεται καὶ 'εἰς τὸ χρῇζον', ὡς φησιν Εὐριπίδης· χρηματιζόμενοι δ' οὖν διατελοῦσι διὰ τὸ δεῖσθαι χορηγίας ἀφθόνου τὸ ζῆν οὕτως· ἔτι δὲ σφόδρα τοιούτους τιμῶσιν οἷοι τὴν χρηματιστικὴν ἐπιτετυχη— κασι ποιοῦντες ἢ καὶ κατανοήματα τοῦ πανταχῇ πλουτεῖν ἐπεξευρήκασι καινά. ὡς γὰρ καί τις τῶν μοναρχῶν αὐτῶν ποτ' εἶπεν, 'χρηματιστικὴ χρῆμα τοῖς Ἀμερικανοῖς'.

6. τοσοῦτο δὴ οὖν φιλοῦσι τὸν χρηματισμὸν ὥστε καὶ τὰς ἀρχὰς ποιεῖσθαι ὠνητὰς μέν (οὐδενὶ γὰρ ἔξεστιν αἱρεῖσθαι ἄρχοντι ᾧ μὴ πολλὰ χρήματ' ἢ καὶ φίλοι πλούσιοι ἢ καὶ ἑταιρία τις), μισθαρνικὰς δέ· πάντες γὰρ οἱ ἄρχοντες μισθὸν ἐξ ἀρχῆς φέρουσι καὶ χρηματίζουσι

3. Now these election campaigns, as the Americans call such competing for votes, also last many months and even a whole year, in which the political clubs engage in factional fighting with each other. Their monarchs are chosen in the same factional way. But the populace are not displeased at this sort of oligarchy both because it is open to them to join the political clubs and to occupy high office themselves, and most of all because it is they who elect the offices. For thus they are arbiters of the factions between the clubs and of these clubs' political fortunes. Hence it is that the populace are always being flattered by the rich and powerful in their pursuit of votes to win office.

4. The remaining of the three offices to speak about is the judiciary, over which they also set up another monarch, whom they call judge or justice, though sometimes they set up several monarchs in the same court. But they do not allow them, despite their power, to have total control. For they also require the populace to take part in the courts, not all in a mass but according to a selection by turns from the citizen rolls. Thus the populace are involved in the deciding of almost all court cases and especially of the most important ones (I mean those concerning life and death, fines, and anything to do with the regime), save that they are only allowed to decide the question of guilt, while the matter of punishment as well as the interpreting of the law they leave to the monarchs alone. And about these monarchs, they are for the most part not elected by the populace, or only a few with small powers are, but they are appointed instead by the other offices, by the monarchs and the senators. Furthermore they retain control throughout life, unless they commit some serious wrong, in which case those who appointed them can try them and remove them.

5. These then are the chief offices in the regime of the Americans, which, as we said, they call a democracy. That it has nevertheless many oligarchic features, with some of these deviating to extreme oligarchy, is clear. But they think this to be a noble thing and even a way of preserving the democracy. For the regime is democratic in two ways in particular, in the electing of the monarchs and senates and assemblies by all the populace, and also in their way of life. For pretty well all the Americans live each as he likes or, as Euripides says, "with a view to what he craves." So, since living as they like requires abundance of resources, they spend their lives in getting money, and they especially admire those who have been successful in business and have invented new devices for everywhere acquiring wealth. As even one of their monarchs once said, "the business of America is business."

6. So great indeed is their love of making money that they both put political office up for sale (for no one can get elected to office who does not have much money himself, or rich friends, or belongs to one of the political clubs), and use it as a source of income. For all office holders receive wages

δι᾽ ἀρχῆς πολλαχῶς, οἷον δὴ δῶρα ἀπὸ τῶν εὐπόρων λαβόντες τῶν χάριτας θελόντων σφίσιν αὐτοῖς νέμεσθαι πολιτικάς· ἔτι δὲ προσόδων ἐκ εἰσφορᾶς κύριοι μεγάλων εἰσὶ παρ᾽ ὧν φυλαττομένων τοῖς φίλοις καὶ τοῖς ἐκ τοῦ δήμου διαλαβομένοις μερίζονται· ὥστ᾽ ἀεὶ πάντα ῥεῖ τὰ χρήματα ἄνω τε καὶ κάτω, τὰ μὲν ἴδια πρὸς τοὺς ἄρχοντας ἀπὸ τῶν φίλων καὶ τοῦ δήμου, τὰ δ᾽ ἀπ᾽ ἐκείνων πρὸς τούτους κοινά.

7. ἀλλὰ τὰ χρήματα οὐ λάθρα μὲν παρ᾽ ἑαυτοῖς σωρεύουσιν καθάπερ οἱ Λακεδαιμόνιοι, φανερῶς δὲ δαπανᾶσθαι νομίζουσι δεῖν εἰς εὐημερίαν· ὥστε σφόδρα φιλαγοράζονται, μηδ᾽ ἂν εὕροι τις οἰκίαν ἐν ὅλῃ τῇ χώρᾳ μηδεμίαν ὅπου μὴ πλήθει ὄργανα δαπανηρὰ καὶ χρήσιμα. κτήμασι γὰρ δὴ πάντα ὑπερέχουσι τὰ ἔθνη τῷ θ᾽ εὑρεῖν μηχανήματα πρὸς τὸ ποιεῖσθαι καὶ πωλεῖν καὶ πρίασθαι πολλὰ χρήσιμα καὶ ἡδέα. ταῦτα γὰρ διωκοῦσι καὶ οἱ πένητες, ὥσθ᾽ οὗτοι μὲν διὰ χρηματιστικῆς παντοίας ἀεὶ εὔποροι γίγνονται, πλούσιοι δὲ διὰ τυχῆς ἢ τοῦ ζῆν ἀσελγῶς ἄποροι. οὕτως γὰρ δὴ πάντες ἴσοι λέγουσιν εἶναι, τῷ πᾶσιν ἐξεῖναι χρηματίζειν καὶ μεγίστας ἀρχὰς ἄρχειν εἰ βούλονται καὶ φιλοπονῶσιν, ἐναντίως δὲ εἰ μή.

8. πολλὰ δὲ καὶ τῶν ἔθνων περὶ ἱδρυμένων ταῦτα νομίζει τοῖς Ἀμερικανοῖς καὶ ταῦτα βούλεται κτᾶσθαι, ὥστ᾽ ἂν εἴποι τις τούτους ζηλωτοτάτους καὶ μιμητοτάτους γεγονέναι πάντων τῶν ἐν τῇ οἰκουμένῃ. δοκεῖ δὲ ἡ χώρα αὐτῶν καὶ πρὸς τὴν ἀρχὴν τὴν κοσμικὴν πεφυκέναι καὶ κεῖσθαι καλῶς· δυοῖν γὰρ ἐπίκειται ταῖς Εὐρώπης τε καὶ τῆς Ἀσίας ἠπείροις, τῶν ἔθνων σχεδὸν πάντων ἐν ταύταις ἱδρυμένων. ἀλλὰ διὰ τὴν τῆς χρηματιστικῆς χρῆσίν τε καὶ ἔρωτα μᾶλλον ἢ διὰ τὰ ὅπλα καὶ πολεμοῦντες ἀρχὴν κέκτηνται οἱ Ἀμερικανοὶ τῆς γῆς· προσέρχονται γὰρ πρὸς πάντα τὰ ἔθνη χρηματισόμενοι καὶ καπηλευσόμενοι, συζευγνύασί τ᾽ αὐτὰ σὺν ἑαυτοῖς διὰ φιλαυτίαν ἀμφοτέρωθι. ἔτι δ᾽ ἄλλοι πάντες, ὡς εἴπομεν, τοὺς Ἀμερικανοὺς ζηλοῦσιν τοῦ πλούτου καὶ κτημάτων, ὅμοιοί τε γενέσθαι ἐπιθυμοῦσιν· ὥστ᾽ ἐκείνους μιμεῖσθαι τῷ τε πρὸς τῇ χρηματιστικῇ προσέχειν τὸν νοῦν καὶ τῷ τὰς ἀρχὰς αἱρετὰς ποιεῖσθαι καὶ τὰς ὀλιγαρχικὰς προσδέχεσθαι ἑταιρίας. πᾶσι γὰρ δοκεῖ, λέγουσί τ᾽ αὐτοὶ οἱ Ἀμερικανοί, οὐχ οἷόν τε χρηματιζομένους ἐπιτύχειν ἄνευ τοιαύτης τῇ πολιτείᾳ τάξεως.

9. ἐπιτιμήσειεν δ᾽ ἄν τις ἐν ταύτῃ τῇ πολιτείᾳ πρῶτον μὲν τὸ νομίζειν αὐτὴν δεῖν πρὸς τὴν χρηματιστικὴν τάττεσθαι. μέρος γὰρ μόνον ἡ χρηματιστικὴ τῆς οἰκονομικῆς καὶ πολιτικῆς, ὡς εἴπομεν, καὶ ὄργανον μὲν τοῦ ἔργου τῆς πόλεως καὶ οἰκίας, αὐτὸ δὲ τὸ ἔργον οὔκ· ἀρετὴ γὰρ ἐστι τοῦτο τὸ ἔργον καὶ οὐ χρηματιστική. οὐ μὴν ἀλλὰ χρήσιμον μὲν γνωρίζειν τὰ χρηματιστικὰ καὶ τοῖς πολιτικοῖς· πολλαῖς γὰρ πόλεσι δεῖ χρηματισμοῦ καὶ τοιούτων πόρων, ὥσπερ οἰκίᾳ, μᾶλλον δέ. διόπερ τινὲς καὶ πολιτεύονται τῶν πολιτευομένων ταῦτα μόνον, καὶ μάλιστα

for being in office, and holding office enables them to make money in many ways, as especially in receiving gifts from those of the rich who want political favors to be handed out to them. Further these office holders have control of large public funds from taxes, which they guard and hand out to their friends and followers among the populace. The result is that money is in perpetual flux in both directions: private funds coming from friends and populace to the office holders and public funds going from office holders to friends and populace.

7. But the Americans do not, like the Spartans, hoard their money in secret; rather they think money is for enjoyment in being spent openly. So they are in love with shopping and one cannot find a single household in the whole land which is not full of useful and expensive things. For in fact they exceed all other nations in their possessions as well as in discovering inventive ways of making and selling and buying a multitude of things both useful and pleasant. For even the poor adopt the same pursuit and are, through many forms of business, forever becoming well off just as some of the rich through chance or riotous living are forever becoming needy. For this, they say, is how they all are equal, that all may make money and hold high office if they want to and if they work hard, but the opposite if they do not.

8. Many of the nations lying round about agree with the Americans in this and want to have the same as the Americans have, so that one may say that the Americans have become the most envied and most imitated people of all on earth. The land of the Americans seems, in fact, to be naturally fitted and nobly situated for world empire, since it lies opposite the two continents of Europe and Asia where all nations, pretty much, are settled. But it is more through their practice and love of business than through arms and wars that the Americans have won empire over the earth. For they travel to all nations to do business and to engage in trade, binding these nations to themselves by self-interest on both sides. Moreover, as we said, all others envy the Americans for their wealth and their possessions and wish to be like them. So these others imitate them by also putting their energies into business and by adopting the practice of elections and oligarchic clubs, for all think, and the Americans themselves say, that great success in business is not possible without such a way of arranging the regime.

Criticisms of the Regime

9. The first thing one might criticize in the regime of the Americans is this supposition they have that the regime should be arranged for business. For, as we say, business is only a part of the city and of household management and is an instrument for doing the work of the city and household and is not itself that work. This work is virtue and not the making of money. Of course it is useful for political rulers to know about these things, for many cities have need of business practices and suchlike revenues, just as households do, only more so. Hence some politicians even focus all their political

τῶν Ἀμερικανῶν. ἀλλ' ἄτοπον νομίζειν τοὺς ἀνθρώπους εἰς τὴν πολιτικὴν κοινωνίαν τοῦ ζῆν ἕνεκεν συνέρχεσθαι καὶ μὴ μᾶλλον τοῦ εὖ ζῆν. τί δὲ λέγομεν τὸ εὖ ζῆν καὶ ὅπως πρὸς αὐτὸ καλῶς ἂν ἡ πολιτεία καθισταῖτο, ὕστερον ἐροῦμεν.

10. εἶτα δὲ τὰ περὶ τῶν ἀρχῶν ψέγοι τις ἄν, καὶ πρῶτον μὲν ἣν ποιοῦνται τῶν τριῶν ἀρχῶν διαίρεσιν, τῆς μοναρχίας καὶ τῆς τε γερουσίας καὶ ἐκκλησίας καὶ τρίτον τοῦ δικαστηρίου. σχίζουσι γὰρ ταύτας ἀπ' ἀλλήλων, τοῦτο 'τὸν τῶν δυνάμεων χωρισμὸν' καλοῦντες· λέγουσι δὲ καὶ πλείους ἢ μίαν τούτων μὴ δεῖν ἅμα τὸν αὐτὸν ἄρχειν, ὅπερ καλὸν μέν· ἓν γὰρ ὑφ' ἑνὸς ἔργον ἄριστ' ἀποτελεῖται. δεῖ δ' ὅπως γίνηται τοῦθ' ὁρᾶν τὸν νομοθέτην, καὶ μὴ προστάττειν τὸν αὐτὸν αὐλεῖν καὶ σκυτοτομεῖν. ὥστε πολιτικώτερον πλείονας μετέχειν τῶν ἀρχῶν, καὶ δημοτικώτερον· κοινότερόν τε γὰρ καὶ κάλλιον ἕκαστον ἀποτελεῖται τῶν αὐτῶν καὶ θᾶττον. δῆλον δὲ τοῦτο ἐπὶ τῶν πολεμικῶν καὶ τῶν ναυτικῶν· ἐν τούτοις γὰρ ἀμφοτέροις διὰ πάντων ὡς εἰπεῖν διελήλυθε τὸ ἄρχειν καὶ τὸ ἄρχεσθαι. τοῦτο δὴ καλὸν μὲν νομιστέον, τὸν δὲ τῶν Ἀμερικανῶν τρόπον μή. τοὺς γὰρ ἐν ταὐτῷ τῆς πόλεως μέρει καὶ τάξει ἐῶσιν ἅμ' ἄρχειν πάσας τὰς ἀρχάς, ὥσθ' ἓν μέρος ἐν τῇ πόλει μόνον ἀεὶ ἄρχειν ἄλλα δὲ μήποτε. λέγομεν δὲ μέρος ἓν μὲν τοὺς πλουσίους ἄλλο δὲ τοὺς πένητες ἔτι δ' ἄλλο τοὺς σπουδαίους· φαμὲν δὲ καὶ πολιτείαν ἄλλην εἶναι τούτων, οἷον ὀλιγαρχίαν μὲν τῶν πλουσίων κυρίων ὄντων, δημοκρατίαν δὲ τῶν ἀπόρων, ἀριστοκρατίαν δ' ἢ πολιτείαν τῶν σπουδαίων.

11. τὸ μὲν οὖν ἐν τῇ τῶν Ἀμερικανῶν πολιτείᾳ τοὺς πλουσίους καὶ τοὺς ἐκ τῶν ἑταιριῶν ἐᾶν τὰς ἀρχὰς ἅμ' ἄρχειν πάσας φαῦλον· τὸ δὲ τοὺς ἐκ τῆς αὐτῆς καὶ μίας ἑταιρίας οὕτως ἄρχειν ἐᾶν (τοῦτο γὰρ συμβαίνει ἂν ἑταιρία τις δυνατωτέρα εἴη τῶν ἄλλων) ἔτι φαυλότερον. παρεκβάσεις γὰρ ἄμφω μὲν εἰς ὀλιγαρχίαν, αὕτη δὲ μάλιστα· καὶ δὴ καὶ τὸν τῶν δυνάμεων χωρισμὸν ὀλιγαρχικὸν νομιστέον εἶναι σόφισμα τῶν εὐπόρων τῶν δι' αὐτῶν τὴν πολιτείαν βουλομένων εἶναι. πείθουσι μὲν γὰρ τὸν δῆμον τούτου δεῖσθαι τοῦ χωρισμοῦ ἵνα μὴ δυνατώτερος ἄρχων τις γένηται καὶ τυραννίδα κατασκευάσῃ· τὸ δὲ πάσας ἅμα κέκτησθαι ἀρχὰς αὐτοί τε καὶ οἱ ἑαυτῶν φίλοι κρύπτουσιν. τούτου δ' ἄκος τὸ διαιρεῖσθαι τὰς ἀρχὰς μὴ μόνον ἀπ' ἀλλήλων ἀλλὰ καὶ εἰς τὰ τῆς πόλεως μέρη, ὥστε μετέχειν αὐτῶν καὶ τοὺς μὴ πλουσίους καὶ τοὺς μὴ ἐν ταῖς ἑταιρίαις. ἤδη γὰρ κατὰ τὰ δικαστήρια τοιαύτην ποιοῦνται τάξιν, τὸν δῆμον ἀεὶ κοινωνεῖν ἀναγκάζοντες. ταὐτὸ δεῖ ποιεῖσθαι καὶ κατὰ τὰς ἄλλας ἀρχάς, οἷον κατὰ τὴν μοναρχίαν ἣν πολλοὶ συνιόντες συνάρχειν ἀνθ' ἑνὸς δύναιντ' ἄν. ὅπου γὰρ συνέστηκεν ἐξ ὁμοίων καὶ ἴσων ἡ πόλις, οὐ δίκαιον τοὺς μὲν ἄρχειν ἀεὶ τοὺς δὲ μήποτε, ἀλλ' ἀνὰ μέρος ἄρχεσθαι καὶ ἄρχειν πάντας. νῦν δὲ σύμπασαι αἱ ἀρχαὶ δι' εὐπόρων μέν εἰσιν, διὰ δὲ δήμου οὐδεμία.

activity on these matters alone, and among the Americans most of all. Yet it is absurd to suppose that people come together in political communities for life alone and not rather for good life. But what is meant by the good life and how the regime should be best arranged to secure it we will discuss later.

10. The matter of the offices is the next thing one might criticize, and first concerning the division the Americans make of all their offices into the three of the monarchy, the senate and assembly, and third the judiciary. They divide up these offices from each other, calling this the "separation of powers," and say that the same persons should not hold more than one of these offices at the same time, which is a fine thing, for one man completes one work best, and bringing that about is what the legislator should look to and not bid the same man both to play the pipes and be a shoemaker. Accordingly it is more political and more popular if more take part in office since it is more communal like this and the same things get completed in a nobler and quicker way. This is clear in armies and navies, for in both of these everyone, so to say, is involved in ruling and being ruled. But while this practice must be deemed noble, the way the Americans do it must not be. For they allow persons from the same part or class in the city to occupy all these offices at the same time, so that one part alone in the city is always ruling while the other parts never do. By a part in the city we mean the rich as one part and the poor as another, and also the virtuous as yet another; and we say that there is a different regime in each case, as that there is oligarchy if the rich are in control, democracy if the poor are, aristocracy or polity if the virtuous are.

11. Now it is a base thing that in the regime of the Americans they allow the rich and those from the political clubs to occupy all the offices at once. But it is baser still to allow people from one and the same political club to occupy them all at once (as does happen if one club is more influential than the rest). For these are both deviations toward oligarchy, and the latter especially so. The separation of powers, in fact, must be deemed an oligarchic sophistry of the rich wanting to keep the regime to themselves. For while they impress upon the populace that this separation of powers is needed to prevent any office holder becoming too powerful and setting up a tyranny, they hide the fact that all these offices are together in the hands of themselves and their friends. A remedy for this would be to divide the offices, not only from each other, but also among the different parts in the city, so that those who are not rich nor members of the clubs also take part in them. For the Americans already adopt this arrangement in their courts where they require the populace always to take part. They should do the same in the other offices as well, as for instance in their monarchies, since these could be occupied by many together ruling jointly instead of by one man. For where all are similar and equal, justice requires, not that some always rule and others never, but that all take turns in ruling and being ruled. As things stand now, however, the offices are all in the control of the rich and the poor are excluded.

12. ἔστι δ' ἐπιτίμησις ἑτέρα κατὰ τὸν τῶν δυνάμεων χωρισμόν, ὅτι ὁ νομοθέτης αἰτίαν στάσεως κατεσκεύασεν αὐτόν· ἐκ γὰρ τούτου δῆλον ὡς οὐδ' αὐτὸς οἴεται δύνασθαι ποιεῖν καλοὺς κἀγαθοὺς τοὺς ἄρχοντας, ἀλλὰ σωτηρίαν νομίζει τῇ πόλει εἶναι τὸ στασιάζειν πρὸς ἀλλήλους· τὰς γοῦν τρεῖς ἀρχὰς καθέστηκεν ἀνταγωνιστάς. εἰώθασι δὲ καὶ οἱ δυνατοί, εἴτ' ἐν ἀρχῇ ὄντες εἴτε μή, τὸν δῆμον καὶ τοὺς φίλους διαλαμβάνοντες μοναρχίαν ποιεῖν καὶ στασιάζειν καὶ μάχεσθαι πρὸς ἀλλήλους· καίτοι τί διαφέρει τὸ τοιοῦτον ἢ διά τινος χρόνου μηκέτι πόλιν εἶναι τὴν τοιαύτην ἀλλὰ λύεσθαι τὴν πολιτικὴν κοινωνίαν; ἔστι δ' ἐπικίνδυνος οὕτως ἔχουσα πόλις, τῶν βουλομένων ἐπιτίθεσθαι καὶ δυναμένων. ἀλλὰ σώζεται τῶν Ἀμερικανῶν πολιτεία διὰ τὸ πληθύειν ἀνθρώπων, καθάπερ ἔλεγεν καὶ τῶν μονάρχων τις· διὰ γὰρ τοῦτ' εἰσὶν ἐν αὐτοῖς ἀεὶ στάσεις πολλαί· καὶ διαλαμβάνειν μὲν ἀεὶ τὸν δῆμον ἅμ' ὅλον οὐ δύναται ἑταιρία οὐδεμία, συγχωρεῖν δὲ δεῖ πάσας συμβόλαιά τε σὺν ἀλλήλαις καὶ συμμαχίαν ποιεῖσθαι. σώζεται δὲ καὶ διὰ τὸν τόπον ἡ Ἀμερική· ξενηλασίας γὰρ τὸ πόρρω πεποίηκεν καὶ τοὺς ἂν ἐπιόντας πλείστους ἀποτέτραφεν.

13. τὸ μὲν οὖν τοῖς αὐτοῖς ἐξεῖναι τὰς αὐτὰς ἀρχὰς πολλ' ἔτη ἄρχειν (πολυχρονιώτεραι γάρ εἰσι καὶ δύναται ὁ αὐτὸς ἐφεξῆς ἐφαιρεῖσθαι) φαῦλόν ἐστιν· τὴν γὰρ πολιτείαν ποιεῖ ὀλιγαρχικήν, ὡς εἴρηται πρότερον. ἔτι δὲ καὶ τὴν κακουργίαν ἐπαυξάνει· οὐ γὰρ ὁμοίως ῥᾴδιον κακουργῆσαι ὀλίγον χρόνον ἄρχοντας καὶ πολύν. φαίνονται δέ γε καταδωροδοκούμενοι καὶ καταχαριζόμενοι πολλὰ τῶν κοινῶν τοῖς φίλοις τε καὶ ἑταίροις οἱ κεκοινωνηκότες τῶν ἀρχῶν. τὸ γὰρ πολὺν χρόνον ἄρχειν μεῖζόν ἐστι γέρας τῆς ἀξίας αὐτοῖς, καὶ τὸ μὴ κατὰ γράμματα ἄρχειν ἀλλὰ πολλ' αὐτογνώμονας ἐπισφαλές. μάλιστα δ' ἐπικίνδυνον τὸ ἐξεῖναι αὐτοῖς ἀρχὰς ἄλλας καὶ μεγάλας κατὰ βούλησιν καθιστάναι· οὐ γὰρ κατ' ἀρετὴν ἢ ἀξίαν τῶν καθεσταμένων τοῦτο δρῶσιν, ἀλλὰ κατὰ φιλίαν· τοῖς γὰρ ἑταίροις ὡς νίκης ἆθλον ταύτας τὰς ἀρχὰς ἀποδιδόασι καὶ ὡς ἀνταπόδοσιν τῆς τ' ὠφελίας καὶ τῶν χρημάτων ἀπ' ἐκείνων πρὸς τὴν ἐριθείαν ληφθέντων· πρεσβευτὰς γε πολλοὺς καὶ κριτὰς οὕτως καθίστανται. ταῦτα δὴ πάντα βέλτιον γίνεσθαι κατὰ νόμον ἢ κατ' ἀνθρώπων βούλησιν· οὐ γὰρ ἀσφαλὴς ὁ κανών.

14. βέλτιον δὲ καὶ τοὺς ἄρχοντας μὴ ἀνευθύνους εἶναι· νῦν δ' εἰσίν. δεῖ δ' οὖν αὐτοὺς εὐθύνας διδόναι κατὰ νόμον τεταγμένας παντὸς ἐνώπιον τοῦ δήμου. τοῦτό τοι ποιείσθω ὁπόταν ἐκ τῶν ἀρχῶν ἐξέρχωνται καὶ πρὶν εἰς τὰς ἀρχὰς βαδίζειν. τοῦ δὲ μὴ κλέπτεσθαι τὰ κοινὰ ἡ παράδοσις γιγνέσθω τῶν χρημάτων παρόντων πάντων τῶν πολιτῶν, καὶ τοῦ δὲ ἀκερδῶς ἄρχειν τιμὰς εἶναι δεῖ νενομοθετημένας τοῖς εὐδοκιμοῦσιν. τὸ γὰρ ἐπανακρεμᾶσθαι καὶ μὴ πᾶν ἐξεῖναι ποιεῖν ὅ τι ἂν δόξῃ συμφέρον ἐστίν· ἡ γὰρ ἐξουσία τοῦ πράττειν ὅ τι ἂν ἐθέλῃ τις οὐ δύναται φυλάττειν τὸ ἐν ἑκάστῳ τῶν ἀνθρώπων φαῦλον.

12. Another complaint one might raise about the separation of powers is that the legislator designed it to be a cause of faction. For from this it is clear that he does not think he can make the rulers into gentlemen. Instead he thinks it safety for the regime if they are engaged in factional disputes with each other, for he has set up the three offices as rivals. Moreover, the habit of the powerful, whether in or out of office, is to create rival followings among the populace and their friends, to set up monarchies, to form factions and fight against each other. Yet what is the difference between such behavior and the city periodically ceasing to exist and the political community being destroyed? A city in this condition is in great danger because those who have the desire to attack it will also be able to. But the regime of the Americans is saved by their great numbers, as even one of their monarchs said, for thus it is that there are always many factions among them and no club can always win over the whole populace together to its side but they must all make compromises and form deals and alliances with each other. America is also saved by its position because its distance has acted to keep foreigners out and to deter most who would invade.

13. Now, that the same individuals can occupy the same office for many years (because the terms themselves are rather long and the same individual can be reelected many times in succession) is a base thing, since it makes the regime oligarchic, as was said earlier. But it also increases crime. For criminal activity is not as easy for those who rule a short time as it is for those who rule a long time. At any rate, as regards many matters of common concern those in office have been conspicuous in taking bribes and showing favoritism to friends and followers. Serving for long periods is a greater privilege than they deserve and their exercising rule in many respects by their own discretion and not by written rules is not safe. It is particularly dangerous that they should be able to appoint other and powerful offices as they wish. For they do not do this on the basis of virtue or worth in those they appoint but on the basis of friendship, since they hand over these offices as a prize of victory to their companions in the political clubs and in repayment for the money or help these companions gave them for their election campaign. Many ambassadors and judges, at any rate, are appointed in this way. It would be better if all such things took place according to law and not human wish, which is no safe standard.

14. It would also be better for the offices not to go unaudited. Now they are, however. They should, then, be subjected to regular audits according to law and in the presence of all the populace. So let this be done at the term of any office and before anyone takes up office. And to ensure there is no theft of common funds let the handing over of monies be done in the presence of all the citizens, and to ensure that rule brings no profit legislation has to have been passed giving honors to those of good repute. For it is of advantage to be kept always responsible to others and not to be able to do whatever one thinks good. The license or right to do whatever one wishes is incapable of providing defense against the base element in each man.

15. ἀναγκαιότατον μὲν οὖν ἐν τῇ τῶν ᾿Αμερικανῶν πολιτείᾳ τὸ τοὺς ἄρξοντας εὐπορεῖν· οὐδεὶς γὰρ οἷός τ᾿ ἄρχων γίγνεσθαι εἰ μὴ σχολάζει καὶ τῷ δήμῳ χαρίζει ψηφοφορίαν μνηστεύων. ἀλλ᾿ οὐκ ἔστιν ἱκανὸν τοῖς εὖ ἄρξουσιν εὐπορίαν ἔχειν· εὐπορία γὲ δὴ τοιούτοις ἐμπόδιός ἐστιν ὑπερβάλλουσα. τὸ γὰρ ὑπέρκαλον δὲ ἢ ὑπερίσχυρον ἢ ὑπερευγενῆ ἢ ὑπερπλούσιον χαλεπὸν τῷ λόγῳ ἀκολουθεῖν· γίγνονται γὰρ ὑβρισταὶ καὶ μεγαλοπόνηροι μᾶλλον. πρὸς δὲ τούτοις οἱ ἐν ὑπεροχαῖς εὐτυχημάτων ὄντες (ἰσχυος καὶ πλούτου καὶ φίλων καὶ τῶν ἄλλων τῶν τοιούτων) ἄρχεσθαι οὔτε βούλονται οὔτε ἐπίστανται, καὶ τοῦτ᾿ εὐθὺς οἴκοθεν ὑπάρχει παισὶν οὖσιν· διὰ γὰρ τὴν τρυφὴν οὐδ᾿ ἐν τοῖς διδασκαλείοις ἄρχεσθαι σύνηθες αὐτοῖς. ὥστ᾿ ἄρχειν μὲν ἐπίστανται μόνον δεσποτικὴν ἀρχήν, κατὰ μέρος δ᾿ ἄρχεσθαι καὶ ἄρχειν ὡς ἴσοι μή. τὸ δὲ δεόμενον τοῖς ἄρχουσιν, μάλιστα τοῖς ἐν ταῖς μεγίσταις ἀρχαῖς, ἀρετὴ πολιτική· ἐξ ἀρχῆς οὖν τοῦθ᾿ ὁρᾶν ἐστι τῶν ἀναγκαιοτάτων, ὅπως οἱ βέλτιστοι δύνωνται σχολάζειν καὶ μηδὲν ἀσχημονεῖν, μὴ μόνον ἄρχοντες ἀλλὰ μηδ᾿ ἰδιωτεύοντες. εἰ δὲ δεῖ βλέπειν καὶ πρὸς εὐπορίαν χάριν σχολῆς, φαῦλον τὸ τὰς μεγίστας ὠνητὰς εἶναι τῶν ἀρχῶν, τάς τε προέδρων καὶ κυβερνητῶν. ἔντιμον γὰρ ὁ νόμος οὗτος ποιεῖ τὸν πλοῦτον μᾶλλον τῆς ἀρετῆς, καὶ τὴν πόλιν ὅλην φιλοχρήματον. ὅ τι δ᾿ ἂν ὑπολάβῃ τίμιον εἶναι τὸ κύριον, ἀνάγκη καὶ τὴν τῶν ἄλλων πολιτῶν δόξαν ἀκολουθεῖν τούτοις. ὅπου δὲ μὴ μάλιστα ἀρετὴ τιμᾶται, ταύτην οὐχ οἷόν τε καλῶς ἔχειν τὴν πολιτείαν. ἐθίζεσθαι δ᾿ εὔλογον κερδαίνειν τοὺς ὠνουμένους, ὅταν δαπανήσαντες ἄρχωσιν· ἄτοπον γὰρ εἰ πένης μὲν ὢν ἐπιεικὴς δὲ βουλήσεται κερδαίνειν, φαυλότερος δ᾿ ὢν οὐ βουλήσεται δαπανήσας. διὸ δεῖ τοὺς δυναμένους ἄριστ᾿ ἄρχειν, τούτους ἄρχειν. νῦν δὲ μόναρχοι οὗτοι καὶ οἱ ἄλλοι ἄρχοντες μεγάλων κύριοι καθεστῶτες, ἂν εὐτελεῖς ὦσι καὶ μὴ σπουδαῖοι, μεγάλα βλάπτουσι καὶ ἔβλαψαν ἤδη τὴν πολιτείαν τὴν τῶν ᾿Αμερικανῶν.

16. ἔτι δ᾿ εἰ καὶ τάχ᾿ ἂν εἴπειέ τις συμφέρειν τῇ πόλει τὰς ἀρχὰς τὰς τῶν γερόντων καὶ ἐκκλησιαστῶν καὶ κριτῶν καὶ μοναρχῶν ἐπιεικῶν ὄντων καὶ πεπαιδευμένων ἱκανῶς πρὸς ἀνδραγαθίαν, καίτοι τό γε διὰ βίου κυρίους εἶναι τῶν μεγίστων (ἐὰν συμβῇ τοὺς αὐτοὺς ἐφεξῆς ἐφαιρεῖσθαι) ἀμφισβητήσιμον· ἔστι γάρ, ὥσπερ καὶ σώματος, καὶ διανοίας γῆρας.

17. ἔχει δὲ καὶ τὰ περὶ τὴν τῶν ἀρχῶν αἵρεσιν φαύλως. ὀλιγαρχικὰ γάρ ἐστι διὰ τὰς ἐριθείας. μόνον γοῦν οἱ ὑπερβάλλοντες πῶς τοῦ ὄχλου καὶ ἐμφανεῖς ὄντες οἷοί τε ψήφους πολλὰς κτᾶσθαι, ὅπερ πλουσίοις μὲν καὶ γνωρίμοις ῥάδιον, ἀπόροις δὲ χαλεπὸν ἢ καὶ νὴ Δί᾿ ἀδύνατον. βέλτιον ἄρ᾿ ἂν εἴη καὶ τῷ κλήρῳ χρῆσθαι καὶ μὴ αἱρέσει μόνον. καλῶς δ᾿ ἔχει μιμεῖσθαι τὰ Ταραντίνων. ἐκεῖνοι γὰρ τὰς ἀρχὰς

15. A very necessary thing in the regime of the Americans is that anyone who is going to rule must be well off. For no one can gain office if he does not have leisure and can bestow favors on the populace while soliciting their votes. But, if one is to rule well, being well off is not enough. An excess of means is even an impediment to good rule. For whatever is exceedingly beautiful or strong or well born or wealthy finds it hard to follow reason. Such as these grow rather insolent and wicked in great matters. In addition those who are surrounded by an excess of good fortune (strength, wealth, friends, and other things of the sort) neither wish nor know how to be ruled, and this is something that begins immediately at home when they are still children. For, because of the luxury they live in, being ruled is not something they get used to, even at school. So they only know how to rule like masters over inferiors and not to rule and be ruled in turn like equals. What is most needed by those who are to rule, especially in the greatest offices, is political virtue. Hence one of the most important matters right from the beginning is to see to it that the best are able to be at leisure and can avoid doing anything unseemly not only when in office but also when out of it. For even if the need for leisure when it comes to office requires one to pay attention also to prosperity, still it is a base thing to put the greatest offices, president and governor, up for sale. This law makes wealth rather than virtue to be the object of honor; that is, it makes the whole city to be in love with money. For the opinion that those in control have about what is honorable will inevitably be followed in the thinking of the other citizens as well, and a regime in which virtue is not held in highest honor cannot be ruled nobly. One can reasonably expect that those who buy office will get accustomed to making a profit out of it, since it is by having spent money that they are in office. For if someone respectable but poor is going to want to make a profit, it would be strange if a baser man, already out of pocket, is not going to. That is why those should rule who have the ability to do it best. But as it is, these monarchs and other offices, being set in control of important matters, cause much damage when they are not virtuous but of a low sort, which is what they have already done in the regime of the Americans.

16. In addition, while one might say that the senates and assemblies, as well as the judgeships and monarchs, would be of advantage to the Americans if their members were decent men and adequately educated in manly goodness, yet even so, allowing them to have control over the greatest matters throughout life (if the same individuals happen to keep getting reelected) is a debatable practice. There is an old age of thought as well as of the body.

17. The way the offices are elected is also in a base condition, for election campaigns make the thing oligarchic. At any rate only those who are conspicuous and stand out from the crowd in some way are able to win many votes, and this is easy for the rich and notables but hard or even, by Zeus, impossible for the needy. It would be better therefore if the Americans also used the device of the lot and not just that of election. A noble thing

πάσας ἐποίησαν διττάς, τὰς μὲν αἱρετὰς τὰς δὲ κληρωτάς, τὰς μὲν κληρωτὰς ὅπως ὁ δῆμος αὐτῶν μετέχῃ, τὰς δ᾽ αἱρετὰς ἵνα πολιτεύωνται βέλτιον. ἔστι δὲ τοῦτο ποιῆσαι καὶ τῆς αὐτῆς ἀρχῆς μερίζοντας, τοὺς μὲν κληρωτὰς τοὺς δ᾽ αἱρετούς. τούτῳ δὴ τρόπῳ καὶ τοῖς πένησιν τοῖς τ᾽ ἐπιεικέσι μὲν ἀπόροις δ᾽ ἔξεστιν ἄρχειν.

18. ἀλλὰ μὴν καὶ τὰ περὶ τὰς βουλάς, ἃς ἐπιτροπὰς καλοῦσιν, οὐκ ἔχει καλῶς, καὶ μάλιστα τὰ περὶ τὸν τούτων πρόεδρον· αὗται μὲν γὰρ τῇ γερουσίᾳ καὶ τῇ ἐκκλησίᾳ προβουλεύουσι τίνα δεῖ εἰσφέρειν ἢ μή, ὅπερ ἔργον ἐστὶ μέγιστον· ὁ δὲ πρόεδρος τούτων κυριεύει κατὰ τὸν Ἀμερικανὸν τρόπον ὡς μόναρχος. φαῦλον οὖν τοῦτον καὶ τοὺς βουλευτὰς κατὰ τὴν δύναμιν καὶ τὴν ἡλικίαν αἱρεῖσθαι· λέγω δὲ δύναμιν μὲν ὁπόσους γέροντας ἢ ἐκκλησιαστὰς ἔχει τις φίλους, ἡλικίαν δ᾽ ὁπόσ᾽ ἔτη τις ἐν ἀρχῇ διαμεμένηκεν. βούλαι γὰρ αὗται, δυνατωτέρως ἤδη ἔχουσαι καὶ ὡς ὀλιγαρχία ἐν τῇ ὀλιγαρχίᾳ, ἔτι ὀλιγαρχικώτεραι τῷδε τῷ τρόπῳ γίγνονται· ὥστε πρῶτον μὲν λίαν ὀλίγοι κύριοι ὄντες ἐπὶ τοῖς ἄλλοις ἐπικρατοῦσι τοῖς ἐν τῇ γερουσίᾳ καὶ τῇ ἐκκλησίᾳ, δεύτερον δὲ ἐπ᾽ ἐκείνοις δεσποτεύει ὁ εἷς. τούτου δ᾽ ἄκος ἢ τὸ μὴ τοιαύτας βούλας ἔχειν, ἢ ἔχειν μέν, εἴπερ δέον, κυρίας δὲ μήτε τοσοῦτον εἶναι μήτε τοὺς βουλευτὰς καὶ τὸν πρόεδρον αἱρετούς· κληρωτοὶ δὲ μᾶλλον ἔστωσαν ἐκ πάντων ἀλλ᾽ οὐκ ἐξ ὀλίγων τῶν καθ᾽ ἡλικίαν ὑπερεχόντων ἢ δύναμιν.

19. ὀλιγαρχικὸν δ᾽ αὖ τὸ ἐξεῖναι μὲν πᾶσιν ψηφοφορεῖν ἀναγκαῖον δὲ μή, ὥστε τῶν μὲν εὐπόρων καὶ τῶν ἑταίρων πλείστους μετέχειν, τοῦ δὲ δήμου ὀλίγους. τί γὰρ διαφέρει τὸ ἐξεῖναι μὲν μὴ ἐνεργεῖν δὲ καὶ τὸ μὴ ἐξεῖναι; ταὐτὸ γὲ δὴ συμβαίνει. βέλτιον οὖν ἂν εἴη τὸν δῆμον νόμοις ἀναγκάζεσθαι ψηφοφορεῖν ἢ καὶ μισθὸν πορίζειν. ἀλλὰ τοῦτ᾽ οὐκ ἀρέσκει τοῖς Ἀμερικανοῖς, οὐ μὴν οὐδὲ τῷ δήμῳ· τὴν γὰρ ἀνάγκην ὑπενάντιον εἶναι τῇ ἐλευθερίᾳ τῇ τοῦ ζῆν ὡς ἂν βούληταί τις· ὡσεὶ δήπου αἱρούμενοι μὲν τοὺς αὑτῶν ἄρχοντας εἶεν δοῦλοι, μὴ αἱρούμενοι δ᾽ ἐλεύθεροι. καίτοι οὐ δεῖ οἴεσθαι δουλείαν γὲ τὸ ζῆν πρὸς τὴν πολιτείαν, ἀλλὰ σωτηρίαν.

20. πρὸς δὲ τούτοις τὸ αὐτὸν αἰτεῖσθαι τὸν ἀξιωθησόμενον τῆς ἀρχῆς οὐκ ὀρθῶς ἔχει. νῦν δὲ δὴ τοῦτο εὐδοκιμεῖ παρὰ τοῖς Ἀμερικανοῖς. ἀναγκάζονται γὰρ τοὺς ἄρχειν θέλοντας πρῶτον μὲν ἑταιρίαν τινὰ προσποιεῖσθαι, εἶτα δ᾽ αἰτεῖσθαι τὴν ψῆφον τὸν δῆμον μνηστεύοντας. ἀλλὰ δεῖ καὶ βουλόμενον καὶ μὴ βουλόμενον ἄρχειν τὸν ἄξιον τῆς ἀρχῆς. οὐδεὶς γὰρ ἂν ἄρχειν αἰτήσαιτο μὴ φιλότιμος ὤν· καίτοι τῶν γ᾽ ἀδικημάτων ἑκουσίων τὰ πλεῖστα συμβαίνει σχεδὸν διὰ φιλοτιμίαν καὶ διὰ φιλοχρηματίαν τοῖς ἀνθρώποις.

21. εἰσὶ δὲ καὶ παρ᾽ αὐτοῖς αἱρέσεις διτταί· πρῶτον μὲν γὰρ πρόκρισιν ποιοῦνται αἱ ἑταιρίαι ἐν ᾗπερ ἑκάστη τὸν αὑτῆς ἀγωνιστὴν

is to imitate what the Tarentines do, for they have made all their offices double, one set is elected and the other chosen by lot, so that by means of the latter the populace get a share and by means of the former the government is carried on in a better way. But it is possible also to do this by dividing up the selfsame office and having some of the members elected and others chosen by lot. In this way the poor and the men of quality lacking means can also rule.

18. Moreover, their councils, which they call committees, are not in a noble condition and in particular as regards the chairman of them. For, on the one hand, these councils do the advance deliberating about what proposals are to be brought or not brought before the senate and assembly, which is a very important job; while, on the other hand, the chairman lords it over them in the American fashion as a monarch. So it is base for this chairman and the council members to be chosen according to power and seniority, I mean according to how many friends someone has in the senate or assembly and to how long he has remained in office. For in this way these councils, which are very powerful and already form a sort of oligarchy within the oligarchy, become more oligarchic still and the result is that, first, an extremely small number of people get control and dominate all the rest in the senate and assembly and, second, one man gets to dominate over them. A cure for this would be either to have no such councils or, if they are needed, to have them but not to make them so powerful nor to have their members and the chairman elected. Let them rather be chosen from all by lot and not from the few who excel in power and seniority.

19. Oligarchic, too, is that everyone is allowed to vote but not everyone is required to do so, whence it results that while most of the rich and of those in the clubs vote, few of the populace do. For what is the difference between being able to vote but not voting and not being able to vote? The same result follows. Accordingly it would be better to compel the populace to vote by law or even to pay them to do so. But this does not please the Americans, not even the populace, since they say compulsion is contrary to their freedom to live as they like—as if, I suppose, they were slaves when they choose their rulers and free when they do not. However, one ought not to think it slavery but safety to live according to the regime.

20. Moreover, it is not right that anyone who is going to be judged worthy of office should himself have to ask for it. Yet this practice is held in high repute among the Americans. They compel those who want to rule first to get the support of some political club and then go out soliciting the populace for their votes. But if a man is worthy of office he should rule whether he wants to or not. No one would ask to rule who was not in love with honor. Yet men commit most voluntary wrongs more or less from love of honor and money.

21. The Americans also have double electing. For the political clubs first have a primary election in which each chooses its candidate, and then

αἱρεῖται, δεύτερον δ' ἐκ τούτων τῶν ἀγωνιστῶν δεῖ τὸν ὄχλον τὸν ἄρξοντα αἱρεῖσθαι. ἀλλὰ τὸ ἐξ αἱρετῶν αἱρεῖσθαι ἐπικίνδυνον· τοῖς γὰρ ἑταίροις μάλιστ' ἢ καὶ μόνον ἔξεστι τὸν αὐτῶν αἱρεῖσθαι ἀγωνιστήν, ὥστ' ὀλίγοι τοὺς ἀγωνιστὰς αἱρεῖσθαι. τούτῳ γὲ δὴ τῷ τρόπῳ ὀλίγοις ἔστιν ἐξ ὀλίγων τὰς ἀρχὰς καθίστασθαι. εἰ μὲν γὰρ ἑταιρία τις παρὰ τῷ δήμῳ ἐστί που δυνατώτερα (τοῦτο δὲ δὴ πολλάκις συμβαίνει διὰ τὸ κυρίας εἶναι τὰς ἑταιρίας τῆς τοῦ δήμου εἰς φυλὰς ψηφοφόρους διανομῆς), ἀναγκαῖον ἀεὶ τὸν ταύτης ἀγωνιστὴν νικᾶν καὶ εἰς τὴν ἀρχὴν βαδίζειν. εἰ δ' ἰσόρροποι πᾶσαι, οὐδὲν ἧττον δεῖ τὸν δῆμον ἐκ τῶν προκρίτων αἱρεῖσθαι. ὥστ' εἰ συστῆναί τινες θέλουσι καὶ μέτριοι τὸ πλῆθος, αἰεὶ κατὰ τὴν τούτων αἱρεθήσονται βούλησιν ἄρχοντες.

22. ἄλλως τε καὶ ἐπιτιμήσειεν ἄν τις τὴν ἐν τῇ τῶν Ἀμερικανῶν πολιτείᾳ δημαγωγίαν. πάντας γὰρ τοὺς ἄρχειν σπουδάζοντας δεῖ τὸν ὄχλον δημαγωγεῖν, οἷον ἐν Λαρίσῃ οἱ πολιτοφύλακες ἐδημαγώγουν διὰ τὸ αἱρεῖσθαι αὐτοὺς τὸν ὄχλον. δημαγωγοῦσί γε δὴ ἐν ὅσαις πολιτείαις οὐχ οὗτοι αἱροῦνται τὰς ἀρχὰς ἐξ ὧν οἱ ἄρχοντές εἰσιν, ἀλλ' αἱ μὲν ἀρχαὶ ἐκ τιμημάτων μεγάλων εἰσὶν ἢ ἑταιριῶν, αἱροῦνται δ' οἱ μέσοι ἢ ὁ δῆμος, ὅπερ ἐν Ἀβύδῳ μὲν συνέβαινεν νῦν δὲ μάλιστ' ἐν Ἀμερικῇ.

23. ἔτι δὲ δημαγωγίαν αἱ διτταὶ αἱρέσεις ἐπαυξάνουσιν διὰ τὸ δεῖν τοὺς ἄρξειν θέλοντας τὸν δῆμον δὶς μνηστεύειν. τούτους γὲ χρὴ τὸν δῆμον παραγγέλοντας ἀεὶ περιιέναι καὶ τίνες εἰσὶν κηρύττειν καὶ τίνος ἑταιρίας καὶ πῶς ἐν ἀρχῇ ὄντες ὠφελήσουσιν· ὥστε μάχονται πάντες πρὸς ἀλλήλους τῷ δήμῳ χαρίζοντες. φιλόνεικοι δ' οὖν γίγνονται τῷ δήμῳ πολλ' ὑπισχνούμενοι. πρὸς δὲ τούτοις ἀλλήλων κατηγοροῦσιν καὶ μέμφονται εἴτ' ἀληθῶς εἴτε μή, ὅπερ καθ' αὐτὸ μὲν αἰσχρόν (τίς γὰρ ἐπιεικῆς τοιαῦτ' ἂν ἑκὼν δράσειεν;), τῇ δὲ πολιτείᾳ βλαβερόν.

24. καὶ δὴ καὶ τοὺς πλουσίους μνηστεύουσι νόμισμα αἰτησόμενοι πρὸς τὸ τίνειν τὰ δαπανήματα ἅπερ ὀφλισκάνουσι τὰς δόξας πανταχοῦ κηρύττοντες καὶ τὸν δῆμον ἀπ' ἄλλων πρὸς ἑαυτοὺς προτρέποντες· ἔτι δ' ἐκείνοις ἄρχοντές γ' ἀντωφελήσειν ὑπισχνοῦνται. ὥσθ' ἡ πολιτεία ἐπὶ τούτοις γίγνεται οἷς ἀναγκαῖον πρῶτον μὲν τὰς ἀρχὰς πωλεῖν ἵν' ἔπειτα πρίωνται· πῶς δ' ἂν τοιοῦτοι τοῦ ἄρχειν εἶεν ἄξιοι; εἰ καὶ ἤδη πλούτῳ ὑπερέχουσιν ἔνιοι ὥστε πρίασθαι τὰς ἀρχὰς ἄνευ τοῦ πρῶτον πωλεῖν (τοῦτο γὰρ ποιεῖν τινὲς δύνανται), πῶς ἐστὶ βέλτιον; οὐδὲν γὰρ ἧττον ὀλιγαρχία, καὶ τοσούτῳ χείρων ὅσῳ σπανιώτεροι καὶ πλουσιώτεροι οἱ ἄρχοντες. αἱ γοῦν πλεονεξίαι τῶν πλουσίων μᾶλλον ἀπολλύουσι τὴν πολιτείαν ἢ αἱ τοῦ δήμου.

25. ὀλιγαρχικῆς δ' οὔσης τῆς πολιτείας ἄριστα ἐκφεύγουσιν, ὡς εἴπομεν, τῷ τὸν δῆμον ἀεὶ πλουτεῖν δύνασθαι. οὐ γὰρ μόνον τὸ πλουτεῖν οἱ Ἀμερικανοὶ διώκουσιν τούς τ' ἄλλους ἐπ' αὐτὸ παρακαλοῦσιν (ὥστε μετάδοσις γίγνεται τῷ πλήθει τοῦ πολιτεύματος),

afterward the crowd elects from among these candidates which one will hold office. But it is dangerous to elect from those already elected. For those who elect the candidates for the clubs are mainly or even only those who belong to the clubs, and thus a few elect the candidates. In this way, indeed, the offices can be set up by a few people from a few people. For if one club somewhere has more influence among the populace (which happens often enough because the clubs have control over the division of the populace into their voting tribes), its candidate must always win and come to hold office. And if the clubs are all equal, nevertheless the populace must elect from those already elected. The result is that if even a few are willing to band together those elected to office will always be the ones they want.

22. Above all one might blame the demagoguery in the regime of the Americans. All those eager for office must become demagogues to the crowd, as the regime guardians used to do in Larissa, because it is the crowd that elects them. The same is true of all regimes where those who provide the rulers are not those who elect to office but the offices are filled from high property qualifications or from political clubs, and those possessed of moderate wealth or the populace do the electing. This used to happen in Abydos and happens now especially in America.

23. The double electing also increases the demagoguery, because those who want to be in office must solicit the populace twice. At any rate they must go out and about summoning the populace and telling them who they are and which club they belong to and what they will do for them if they are elected. So they must all fight each other for the favor of the populace. They compete, therefore, in multiplying promises to the populace. In addition they blame and accuse each other, whether truthfully or not, and this is both base in itself (for what decent man could willingly do such things?) and harmful to the regime.

24. They also solicit the rich for money to cover the costs they incur in advertising their opinions everywhere and in turning the populace away from others toward themselves. They then in addition make promises to these rich of what they will do for them when they possess office. The result is that the regime falls into the hands of those who must buy their office by first selling it, and how can such persons be fit to rule? Even if some already have an excess of wealth of their own and can buy office without first selling it (for there are certain people who can do this), how is that better? For it is oligarchy all the same and so much the worse an oligarchy the fewer and wealthier the office holders. The graspings of the rich, at any rate, do more to ruin the regime than those of the populace.

25. But though the regime is oligarchic, they have, as we said, a very good way of escaping the consequences by the populace always being able to get rich. For not only do the Americans pursue wealth and encourage others to do the same (so that the multitude are given a share in the regime), but

ἀλλὰ καὶ κοινωνεῖν τῶν ἑταιριῶν ἐῶσι τὸν τυχόντα τοῦ τ᾽ ἄρχειν ἀγωνιστὴν γίγνεσθαι θελόμενον καὶ δυνάμενον. ἔτι δ᾽ ὁμιλεῖν σὺν ἀλλήλοις σφόδρ᾽ ἐπιθυμοῦσιν ἄλλοι κατ᾽ ἄλλα (οἷον κατὰ τὰς γνώμας τὰς τῆς εὐσεβείας ἢ τῆς χρηματιστικῆς ἢ τῆς πολιτικῆς ἢ τῶν τοιούτων), καὶ ἑταιρίας καθίστασθαι πρὸς τὸ κοινὸν αὐτοῖς ἀγαθόν, ὃν ᾽ἴδιον συμφέρον᾽ καλοῦσιν. τοῦτο δὲ ποιεῖσθαι καὶ τοῖς ἀπόροις ἔξεστιν, οἳ συνελθόντες ἐνίοτε πλουσιώτεροι καὶ δυνατώτεροι τῶν εὐπόρων μὲν ὀλιγωτέρων δὲ γίγνονται. οὕτως γὲ δὴ συμβαίνει τοὺς πένητας ὡς πλουσίους πρὸς πλουσίους ἀνταγωνίζεσθαι καὶ τὰ τῆς πολιτείας ὀλιγαρχικὰ εἰς ἑαυτούς πως περιιστάναι.

26. καίπερ οὖν οὖσαν μάλιστ᾽ ὀλιγαρχικὴν τὴν πολιτείαν οὐκ ἐπὶ λίαν ὀλίγοις ἐπιτείνωσιν, ἀλλά τινων μὲν ἀπελθόντων εἰσέρχονται δ᾽ ἀεὶ ἄλλοι, ὥστε μηδένα ἀγανακτεῖν μὴ κοινωνοῦντα· γνωρίζει γὰρ ἕκαστος αὐτῷ θέλοντι κοινωνεῖν ἐξεῖναι καὶ πλοῦτον πρὸς τὸ τοῦτο δρᾶν κτᾶσθαι· δεῖ μὲν οὖν πᾶσιν ἐξεῖναι, ὥς φασί γε, πλουτεῖν καὶ ἄρχειν, μὴ μόνον δὲ τοῖς ἤδη πλουτοῦσιν ἢ γένων τινῶν ἢ οἰκιῶν γεγόνοσιν. τούτῳ γὰρ ἰῶνται καὶ ποιοῦσι μόνιμον τὴν πολιτείαν. ἀλλὰ τὸ τὴν Ἀμερικὴν χώραν εὐπορωτάτην εἶναι καὶ πρὸς τήν τε χρηματιστικὴν καὶ τὴν καπηλικὴν κεῖσθαι καλῶς τύχης ἐστὶν ἔργον, δεῖ δὲ ἀστασιάστους τοὺς πολλοὺς εἶναι διὰ τὸν νομοθέτην. νῦν δέ, ἂν ἀτυχία γένηταί τις καὶ τὸ πλῆθος ἀποστῇ τῶν ἀρχομένων, οὐδέν ἐστι φάρμακον διὰ τῶν νόμων τῆς ἡσυχίας.

27. περὶ μὲν οὖν τῆς Ἀμερικανῶν πολιτείας ἐπὶ τοσοῦτον εἰρη—᾽σθω· ταῦτα γάρ ἐστιν ἃ μάλιστ᾽ ἄν τις ἐπιτιμήσειεν.*

---

*My thanks to Harry Platanakis for help in transcribing the Greek.

they also allow anyone at all to join the political clubs and even, if he wants to and has the ability, to become a candidate for office. In addition they have a great love of forming associations with each other, some for this reason and others for that (as for example their opinions in religion or economics or politics or the like), and of setting up clubs to further their common good, which they term a "special interest." Even the poor can do this, and the poor, when united, may sometimes be richer and more powerful than a few who are well off. Hence it comes about, indeed, that the poor can compete as rich against rich and turn the oligarchic elements in the regime in some way to their own advantage.

26. Accordingly, although the regime is very oligarchic, yet the oligarchy is not narrow but people are forever entering it or leaving it. So no one is upset to be excluded for everyone knows he can share in it if he wishes, and accumulate wealth for this purpose too. For, as they say at any rate, everyone should have the right to become rich and hold office and not just those who are already rich or come from certain clans or families. In this way they effect a cure and give stability to the regime. But that America is a rich land and nobly adapted to business and trade is the work of chance, whereas the legislator should be the one responsible for making the many free of faction. As it is, if some misfortune happens and the multitude of the ruled revolt, there is no cure in the laws for restoring calm.

27. Let so much then be said about the regime of the Americans. For these are the things that one might most of all criticize.

8

ARISTOTLE'S POLITY TODAY

Lenn E. Goodman

I t's hard to say just how much philosophy is autobiographical. Surely
those philosophers who devote their lives to musing on the reality of
possible worlds or the unreality of time seem to survey an arid landscape.
Perhaps the territory they scan draws their gaze because of its remoteness
from the world they live in. But Aristotle's rich panorama of the world
beyond the mind offers tantalizing insights into his perspective too, not
confessions ala Rousseau or Augustine but vistas vividly colored by the values and insights of the viewing subject. Aristotle did not live to enjoy an
old age retired to some priesthood for study and reflection, emerging, perhaps, from time to time, with advice or instruction. But he does picture
such a retirement, wondering, perhaps, if it would suit.[1] Addressing child-
hood, more that of others than his own, he prescribes music in education—
not, heaven forfend, to make professional performers of one's offspring, but
to broaden their experience, enliven and enlarge their character, open up
their sensibilities to emotional potentials beyond what we might wish them
to know by direct experience (*Politics*, VIII.3–7).[2] The outlook is reveal-
ing—a professional intellectual praises liberal education and enriched experience, and not just for the young. Similarly, when Aristotle mentions
the chance for friendship between persons of disparate social standing,[3]
disparages *barbarians* for treating wives like slaves (*Politics* I.2.1252b5–6),
and glowingly paints the best of friendships as reliant not just on benefits
exchanged or pleasures shared but on mutual admiration and respect, he
might be describing a good marriage—although Greek conventions demar-
cating the public from the private make it awkward for him to say so.[4] He
does list friendship prominently among the factors that draw men and
women together as couples (*Nicomachean Ethics* VIII.12.1162a16–24;
Swanson 1992, 25.) And, unlike Plato, who projects equality for women
and men but never actually married, Aristotle did, after all, marry two
women in his life, a former princess and a former slave. He rescued the first

on the ruin of his patron's state and provided in his will for remarriage by the second, should she wish it—but in keeping with his own and not her former station.[5]

Aristotle lacks the sublimated radicalism of Plato's *Republic* and is all too ready, with an outsider's warmth, to affirm and rationalize what he beholds, whether it be the institution of slavery or the sequestration of (respectable) women. But his deference to the status quo makes his critiques all the more trenchant, whether arguing that some men are natural slaves, even if they and their peers have never noticed it, or insisting that women too need virtues, even if not the identical virtues that he would expect in a man (*Politics* I.13).

Clearly when Aristotle analyses life as a system of activities and among activities gives the highest rank to the life of the mind, finding it the most self-sufficient and the most fulfilling of what is best in us, he is sketching his own ideal. Likewise when he chides his students against squeamishness about their dissections, urging that if we admire art for virtuosic representations of nature, all the more should we admire the original, and recognize, with Heraclitus, that here too there are gods (*Parts of Animals* I.5.644b32–645a34). When Aristotle says that one who would live without friends and fellows must be either subhuman or superhuman, a beast or a god, he echoes a thought of Homer's and traces in it the course of his own reflections on society, without which human life would not be human in actuality at all.[6]

Aristotle's thesis that man is a social animal draws out and makes explicit a key premise of Plato's in the *Republic*. To show that the tyrant is indeed not the happiest but the most wretched of men, Plato must show not only that tyranny robs the tyrant of friendship and trust but also that in so doing it harms his well-being, by thwarting the social nature constitutive in every healthy human identity. The tyrant will be alienated not only from others but also from himself. He demonstrates what he imagines to be his power only through perversity, and his inner drives and urges are therefore at war with one another. His fragmented personality reflects and is reflected in the fragmentation of the state and society he thinks he rules. Given free rein, he will undermine and destroy himself as surely as he saps and destroys the society that is his victim or accomplice. Plato has witnessed this scenario at close range. So have we, in the lives of Hitler, Stalin, Mussolini, Ceaucescu, Pol Pot, Idi Amin, and Saddam. But it is Aristotle who supplies the middle term, to show why and how tyranny is destructive to the tyrant: It is because man's most basic needs—let alone his most distinctive—are not met without social collaboration, and because the trust that rests on fellowship is central among those needs.

Thought here outstrips experience, explaining what history and the newspapers can only report. For intelligence is the ready ability to grasp the middle term (*Posterior Analytics* I.34.89b10). When Aristotle puts that term in place to hold the thesis steady and transform Plato's dramatic scenario into theory, we catch a glimpse of Aristotle's mind: not just his quick intelligence but his values, and the way those values, far from being arbitrary personal choices or socially inscribed defaults, are anchored in thought: Friendship is precious not only in what it does for us but also in what it makes of us. It is part of what makes us what we are. Indeed, friendship of a certain sort grounds the viability of any society.

Aristotle was not the founder of political theory, but he was clearly the founder of political science. His survey of 158 constitutions and his book-length study of the Athenian constitution laid the empirical and historical basis for his general claims in the *Politics*. These claims were not militantly value free in the manner commended by Comte or Weber.[7] A fortiori does Aristotle eschew the opportunism of a Machiavelli or Metternich. In politics, as in rhetoric, on Aristotle's account, certain values can be assumed. Some, like stability, are all but constitutive to the enterprise. Others, like freedom and justice, reflect the aims and aspirations for whose sake societies are constructed and preserved. Observation gives Aristotle much to say about the diverse ways in which these values can be interpreted and pursued. His outlook, in this regard, is characteristically pluralistic. For he sees right and wrong ways to run a state of various kinds, whether the rule is by one or few or many.[8] The aim is not to discover which faction in the polis has the best slogan or manifesto. In this he differs strikingly from, say, Rawls, whose ideal is acutely localized in time and place. Aristotle's pluralism and his commitment to theory give his work far wider relevance—not in every way, certainly not in all that he says about slavery, or labor, or women, but in much that remains vitally useful, not just curious but valuable for our own political deliberations. My aim here is to note a few of Aristotle's political maxims that I think hold enduring value for our own political understanding, and enduring usefulness for our own political practice. Let me list them here and then discuss them individually.

1. Political authority is not the same as business acumen. A state is not the same sort of enterprise as a business—or a household. So the governance of human beings will not collapse into the administration of things.

2. Like organisms, societies have members whose sound functioning in their roles sustains the well-being of the whole, but states are not organisms and it's a grave error to treat them as such. It is not societies but their members who are individuals. The society exists for their sake, to make their lives more fully human. To be sure, the community is more precious than any one of its members—since its project supports all of theirs. So the state can ask sacrifices of its people in the common interest. States are able to do many things that their individual members cannot, and individuals can do many things through their membership in a society that they otherwise could not do at all or as well. But that only reminds us why communities exist—to humanize human lives.[9] We do not exist to serve the larger *whole*. For the community is not a whole in the way that an individual is, and the community

exists to preserve not just individuals but their individuality. Again there's a corollary: Community of property or of women is not a bastion of justice but a gimmick undermining the independence of the individuals whose dynamic interrelations do the work of society and thus frame the locus of justice or injustice.

3. Justice is the strength of a society, and injustice weakens it. Notions of justice may diverge, but human nature and the human telos set parameters for such diversity, and a society whose members find it unjust is seriously, perhaps fatally, ill.

4. Constitutionalism, the rule of law, is what makes any government healthy—monarchical, aristocratic, or democratic. Participation, in all these cases, is the key. Not only is it a mark of the rule of law as opposed to arbitrary authority, but it also cements the commitment of citizens to the common weal. Deliberation is a distinctively human activity, and public deliberation on matters of shared concern is a fitting use of freedom, allowing individuals not only to express but to fulfill their human nature. Some citizens, of course, can contribute little, but exclusion will only alienate them. In a healthy society most people will find plenty to occupy their interests and will not feel the need to obtrude themselves into political affairs, but those who feel so inclined can always put their oar in, and their insights may well prove welcome.

5. Education is the most vital function of a society.

1. A Polity Is Not a Business

"Some people," Aristotle writes, "think that the qualifications of a statesman, king, householder, and master are the same, and that they differ, not in kind but only in the number of their subjects." The notion is still with us, not only in the view that the skills of the statesman are essentially those of the businessman or home economist, but also in the Marxian notion that politics, the governance of people, can and one day will be replaced by the administration of things. What kind of argument does Aristotle offer that might help us see through such notions? His argument, based, he says, on his usual procedure, appeals to analysis (*Politics* I.1.1252a17–20). But, as with his biological dissections, the aim is not just to find the parts of the state but to identify its function. For if we hope to speak scientifically about politics, we must remember the rule we apply in biology, that "things are defined by their function and power" (*Politics* I.2.1253a23). So Aristotle will speak of families and households, men and women, slaves and beasts, but to argue that no such component of society is self-sufficient. The polis is a natural entity, prior by nature to the family and the individual, since human life is not perfected without it (*Politics* I.2.1253a19–40):

> Clearly a city is not simply a gathering together in order to avoid mutual wrong and exchange services. These are certainly necessary conditions, but they do not make a city. A city is a gathering together of houses and families in order to live well, in other words, to live a perfect and independent life. (*Politics* III.5.1280b)

The polis is not just an artificial structure of relations but a community of a particular kind. Every community serves some good, or individuals would not affiliate with it. But the state serves the highest good (*Politics* I.1.1252a1–6)— not necessarily the most elevated or edifying but the most general. Compare Lasky's notion of the irrelevance of sovereignty: The state, Aristotle is arguing, is not just another institution. It sets priorities, provides the court of last resort, laying down final determinations in matters of policy and cases of law. In this sense there will always be politics and states will always be necessary. Anarchy is not the withering away of the state but the dissolution of a coherent groundwork for decision making at the general, societal level.

The first-order skills of a householder, husbandman, or business person are particularistic, readily enunciated in terms of income and outgo. But the needs of a society are different, not just in scale but in kind. When a society's work is gauged in terms of a fiscal bottom line, perspectives have been narrowed and questions have been begged about value priorities and human needs, goods like risk and honor, nobility and discovery, discipline and faith. Such goods, as Plato saw, are often not commensurate. Yet they need to be accommodated to one another in appropriate relations of coordination, subordination, or superordination, in any functioning society.

One might run a business but one does not in the same sense run a society. In a key sense, truth be told, it is the householder or business person who needs to think and act more like a statesman, not the statesman who needs to behave more like a manager, as Plato shows in the *Republic* (I.342). Aristotle generalizes the point when he argues that "household management" is more a matter of dealing with (and living with) people than of sheer quest for gain (*Politics* I.13.1259b18). For before one deliberates about ways and means one needs to know one's proper and reachable goals. In Aristotle's homely analogy: The household manager is like a weaver, whose task is not to make wool but to use it, "and to know, too, what sort of wool is good and serviceable or bad and unserviceable" (*Politics* I.10.1258a25–28). Not just in making value judgments, then, but in working with and "ordering" the materials nature supplies, be it wool or human resources, the household manager's task is synthetic and multidimensional, not confined to getting and spending. But taking the manager's task as a foil, interpreting it as focused on ways and means, Aristotle can say that such a conception is far too narrow for the statesman. The statesman needs to know the proper aims and attainable hopes of human beings in general and those of the citizens in his own society, specifically, as they see them. He will look not just to the efficiency of the machinery of the state but will seek to optimize the goods constitutive in that state's achievement.

States do not define the human good. That, on Aristotle's account, depends on human nature. But states do make critical determinations about how the broad aims laid down by our nature are to be interpreted, as well as the means by which they are to be pursued. Nothing could be more critical to human well-being. By establishing the framework in which our goals are pursued and setting out the ground rules of the interactions through which we organize our diverse enterprises, the state becomes the vehicle for the achievement of our ends. That makes its work critical to the fulfillment of our humanity, as the matrix of our individuality and framework of the communities that nest within it. It is in this sense that the state is prior by nature to the individual, family, and household, and to the race, clan, or tribe—a fortiori, to the firm, party, union, class, or team. Like the living body, the state is presupposed in the adequate functioning of its members. Without it they could not exercise the functions that shape and express their identities (*Politics* I.1.1253a19–27). And yet the state is not an organism.

2. The State Is Not an Organism

Aristotle ascribes to Socrates an organic view of the state, which he blames for the communist error typified in projects for the abolition of private property and dissolution of private families. Community of women and of property, Aristotle argues, is impractical, ill conceived, and inadequately supported by the arguments Plato lays out in its behalf. The critique is borne out by history. The family as a biological and economic unit was never effaced by communism. Efforts in that direction in Russia and China were stark failures. The desires and loyalties to be thwarted were too strong to uproot, even for a regime that made totalitarian claims. Logically, there was a problem even beyond the moral one. For if the aim was to establish comradeship (and so strengthen the bonds of unity within the state), it remains unclear how that aim could be won by generating a nation of strangers. What force or worth was there in asking members of a community to see each other as brothers, unless there was some special force or worth to start with in brotherhood of a simpler sort?

I think Plato uses community of wives and property as an abstractive device, to call out the radical inappropriateness of the familiar warrants of political authority: birth, wealth, and gender. The Guardians, as a class, are divested of personal and familial wealth, and so, per hypothesi, of all dynastic interests, by their fictive sharing of property and ignorance of the identities of their offspring. It is when the code is broken and lineages are leaked that

Plato's meritocracy breaks down and declines into a timocracy, substituting repute for genuine leadership and insight.

Aristotle adopts Plato's fiction that Socrates is the author of the plan he criticizes. For the view held up to scrutiny is rather abstract and schematic, not a concrete proposal at all. But communistic notions have always had their appeal, and Plato's famous scheme gives Aristotle's critique a solid enough conceptual target, readily assimilated to the further projections of Plato's late views in the *Laws* (*Politics* II.6.1264b26–27). What troubles Aristotle is a diametric opposite to the dissolution of the state into a mere collection of individuals, a family, firm, or farm writ large. Now the individual is threatened. Aristotle seeks a mean between the two extremes of atomization and collapse:

> Unity there should be, both of the family and of the state, but only in some respects. For there is a point at which a state may reach such a degree of unity as to be no longer a state, or at which, without actually ceasing to exist, it will become an inferior state, like harmony passing into unison or rhythm reduced to a single foot (*Politics* II.5.1263b31–36).

The premise singled out for criticism in "Socrates' " argument is "that it is best for the state to be as unified as possible" (*Politics* II.2.1261a15). But that kind of extreme is self-defeating:

> Is it not obvious that a state may at length attain such a degree of unity as to be no longer a state?—since the nature of a state is to be a plurality, and in tending to greater unity, from being a state, it becomes a family, and from being a family, an individual . . . we ought not to attain this greatest unity even if we could, for it would be the destruction of the state. A state is not made up only of so many men, but of different kinds of men; for similars do not constitute a state. It is not like a military alliance, which depends on its quantity even where there is no difference in quality . . . the elements out of which a unity is to be formed differ in kind. That is why the principle of reciprocity, as I have already remarked in the *Ethics*, is the salvation of states. (*Politics* II.2.1261a16–31; see *Nicomachean Ethics* V.5)

The strength and value of the state is not in reducing us all to one person, or even one purpose, but in promoting our power to coordinate and concert our purposes. That value is vitiated and that strength trivialized if we all somehow acquire the same indistinguishable purpose and outlook. That would collapse our ability to collaborate into a quantitative measure, like just adding weight to the scale. But with different skills and strengths, we can achieve things that no mere mass of individuals could do, as if organized in villages (*Politics* II.2.1261a27–29).

Of course unity of purpose can be a desideratum, if taken broadly, by reference to shared goals. But when pressed to extremes, as the paramount political value, unity itself loses its appeal. For it loses the vigor of complementarity, and society loses the elasticity and equilibrium that give it its vitality. If there is any truth in the organic metaphor, it lies not in the subjection of the goals of all individuals to a single societal aim—as though society could have any legitimate purpose to the exclusion of the proper purposes of its members—but in the dynamism, the give and take, that makes for the life and health of any organism.

When Aristotle likens political unity to poetic rhythms and musical harmonies, he is insisting that the individual, not the state, is the ultimate beneficiary of political organization, the ultimate test of any social scheme, and the ultimate source of any power that such a scheme may manifest: A harmony works because it combines its elements while preserving their diverse values; likewise, a rhythmic cadence. To submerge those elements is not to perfect but to destroy the harmony and collapse the cadence. Aristotle assumes that the polis exists not just for its own good but for the good of its members, the ends they hope to achieve by enlisting one another's energies. If a common good emerges in that process, as it will, that good rests on and still comprises the good of those who make it possible. Which brings us to Aristotle's point about the strength of justice.

3. JUSTICE IS A PRINCIPLE OF STABILITY AND STRENGTH

Liberals, constitutionalists, democrats, and republicans like to speak, self-effacingly, about the weakness and inefficiency of the system they prize. Perhaps the cliche hides a trace of superstition, like Olan's worry in *The Good Earth* that praise of her daughter's beauty will rouse the envy of the gods. Or perhaps it means to excuse bureaucratic bungles by making them concomitants of principle, confounding extrinsic flaws with constitutive virtues. But Plato saw the risk in this kind of fatalism or romanticism, the kind that leads people to say that at least Mussolini made the trains run on time, or Stalin kept the people fed—even though he did not—or at least under Saddam, Baghdad was secure. Some of that is just hankering for the fleshpots of Egypt, glossing over yesterday's oppression in the heat of today's crisis. But some of it is much worse, a ready apology and open invitation to new oppression and usurpation. Locke saw the rule of law in civil society as a foundation of liberty. But Spinoza saw liberty as a principle of societal strength, recognizing, with Plato, that justice is the bastion of that strength. The idea was central to what Aristotle learned from Plato and what Plato framed as a universal thesis, culled from the talk and life of Socrates: Virtues, rightly understood, are strengths; vices, weaknesses. Thrasymachus had it backward when he called justice the interest of the stronger: Justice is not a fancy name for the truckling of the weak to the strong. On the contrary, real justice, adequately understood, serves the real interests of those who would be strong, and thus of society at large. Vices are not virtues, and virtues that bring weaknesses in train are not pure and perfect virtues. Hence the moral and intellectual bite of the catharsis in tragedy, in the recognition that it is not his strengths that bring down the tragic hero but the decline of those strengths into weaknesses when they grow distended by excess. As Plato saw and showed in the argument he fathers on Socrates, it is not by their vices that the band of thieves plunders successfully but by the (limited and narrow-gauge) virtues the thieves show toward one another (*Republic* I.351c). And it was the strength and worth of virtue, of justice in particular, that Aristotle hailed as Plato's great theme, calling him "the only man, or the first, to show clearly by his own life and the reasonings of his discourses, that to be happy is to be good."

Even slaves need virtues, Aristotle argued—albeit not quite the same virtues as their masters (*Politics* I.2). A fortiori, so do the free men and free women of a sound polity. So, just as the householder will converse with his slaves and hope they develop such virtues as fortitude, and just as he will pursue a common life for his whole household, women and children included, since their well-being is his concern, the wise statesman will seek the engagement of the citizenry in public concerns and will regard education fostering strong character as the state's highest aim and the chief means to its more specific goals.

Aristotle's innocence of our commitment to human existential equality and his dissent from Plato's view that men and women can or should share the same virtues make his stance all the more striking: A man rules his wife and children—but monarchically over the children, constitutionally over his wife (*Politics* I.12). A good father does govern his offspring, but in their interest. He chooses for them, paternalistically, as we say, substituting his judgment for theirs, yet fostering in them sound habits of independent judgment. A wise husband consults and deliberates with his wife. Aristotle's assumption that individuals differ in their capacity for rule highlights his more sagacious thesis, that there is not just one kind of rule. Political governance is not rule over slaves; and domination, most pointedly is not the same as constitutional rule (*Politics* I.7.1255b.16).[10] For in constitutional rule, as Aristotle understands it, authority would generally rotate among political equals, differentiated only by the forms and marks of office (*Politics* I.2.1259bll.1–8). An officer may in principle be replaced and find himself in the shoes of those he governed. But to despots subjects are chattels to exploit. Here is the link between political strength and justice: For liberty and law bring the power of reciprocity to a polity, and the lack of mutuality fragments a despotism.

Plato had seen the risks of alienation in despotism, whole societies riven by internal warfare, the tax base wrung dry by exactions, the poor wracked and excluded, the wealthy mulcted, productivity dried up and loyalty to any cause beyond greed and Hobbesian vanity, sapped by well-earned cynicism. We too have seen the effects of that kind of kleptocracy, in Liberia, Uganda, Iraq, the Congo. When Aristotle concedes that statecraft, like household management, has an economic base (I.3), he's talking about physical and fiscal survival. The basic facts of economics suffice to show that grasping is not a principle of strength.

And the same reasoning applies to broader ambitions. Even if it is the state and not just its ruler that seeks boundless acquisitions, the pursuit is both unnatural and perverse: unnatural, because the appetite has no limit; perverse, because the quest distracts from life's higher aims (*Politics* I.9–11).[11] Here Aristotle echoes Plato's charge that those who live to serve their appetites are trying to carry water in a sieve, their efforts inevitably frustrate, as desire expands to meet and exceed every new gain. Imperial expansion, whether military, economic, or confessional, derails the state from the pursuit of its real purpose and is thus inherently destabilizing. Just as an individual's chase after wealth for its own sake confuses means with ends, so does a society's quest for limitless wealth distract it from the achievable goal of humanizing human lives and sets it on a predictable course toward destruction in pursuit of an unreachable goal and the attempt to sate insatiable appetites.

4. CONSTITUTIONALISM AND PARTICIPATION

Aristotle distinguishes quite a variety of democratic, oligarchic, and monarchical forms, but less with a view to choosing among their rival partisans than to show how vital is the role of law in each. Among democracies, for example, he distinguishes those where governance is shared under the rule of law from those where the multitude rule by decree. Swayed by demagogues who appeal to their passions, the latter swamp the laws in arbitrary fiats. The suppression of constitutional principle blurs the very distinction of democracy from autarchy:

> For the people becomes a monarch. . . . This sort of democracy, now a monarchy, and no longer under the control of law, seeks to exercise monarchical sway, and grows into a despot. . . . This sort of democracy is to other democracies what tyranny is to other forms of monarchy. The spirit of both is the same, and they alike exercise a despotic rule over the better citizens. The decrees of the one correspond to the edicts of the tyrant, and the demagogue is to the one what the flatterer is to the other. . . . The demagogues make the decrees of the people override the laws, by referring all things to the popular assembly. So

they grow great, because the people have all things in their hands, and they hold in their hands the votes of the people, who obey them. Those who have any complaint to bring against the magistrates say, "Let the people be the judges"; the people are happy to accept the invitation; and so the authority of every office is undermined. Such a democracy is open to the objection that it is not a constitution at all; for where the laws have no authority there is no constitution. The law ought to be supreme over all, and the magistracies should judge of particulars, and only this should be considered a constitution. (*Politics* IV.4.1292b10–31)

So despotism has more than one form. Like Plato, Aristotle acknowledges the strengths of democracy. But, in keeping with his larger theme, he finds its strengths not simply in popular sovereignty but in the rule of law. A democracy crumbles and its appeal gutters when its principles of justice are undermined. The fault lies not in the idea of democracy or even in an excess of its application, as if any virtue were simply a matter of degree. In politics, as in ethics, numerous values need to be considered and coordinated if stability and strength are to be attained. But what counts most politically is respect for sound laws. For in a democracy that respects the laws, "the best citizens hold the first place" and the aims of sound governance will remain within reach (*Politics* IV.4.1292a 4–10).

Again with oligarchy, whether hereditary or dynastic, promulgated through wealth, perpetuated by cooptation, or grounded in the recognition of skill, wisdom, and merit, only the laws can preserve the values the scheme of governance is meant to serve. When the power of the few eclipses that of the law, the oligarchic counterpart of tyranny arises (*Politics* IV.5.1292b1–11). Much depends, therefore, on the political ethos—the qualities of character for which leaders are chosen, the values they serve and those which they and the citizens expect government to respect.

Even monarchies may be governed constitutionally. Indeed, the longest lived, Aristotle argues, are those in which royal powers are limited and not used arbitrarily. The Spartan kings may rule for life, but they do not wield absolute power. They do control religious matters. But only in the field do they hold a power of life and death over their subjects. In effect, they are generals with lifelong terms of office, perhaps a holdover from the heroic age, when kings were generals and judges, ruling by consent. But that informal pattern is overlaid with legal constraints (*Politics* III.14.1285b20–27) that make Sparta's monarchy, although hereditary, constitutional. Only compare the regimes that throttle and garrotte those "Asiatics," whom Aristotle blames as "too servile" to throw off an enslaving despotism. The counterpart of their servility survives in the plebiscites that modern dictators may use to bolster their imposture as tribunes of the people. The goosestepping and the spit-and-polish of ersatz discipline, the substitutes for real commitment, are visible markers of despotism. (In the Soviet state, before its fall, Party hacks were often afraid, we're told, to be the first to stop applauding at the appearance of some apparatchik gauleiter, lest their lack of zeal be noted down and used against them.) The prominence of pretorian guards in a less-than-constitutional state, Aristotle observes, are another sign of tyranny: "For kings rule according to law over voluntary subjects" and are "guarded by their fellow citizens." But tyrants must be protected from their unwilling subjects (*Politics* III.14.1285a17–29). Consent, for Aristotle, then, is marked not by oaths of allegiance but by open institutions and free interchange between the rulers and the ruled, who live and interact as fellow citizens and not herdsmen and herd.

Participation is the key. A citizen takes part in public life—particularly, in deliberations as to matters of policy, strategy, and direction, and centrally, in the administration of justice and the exercise of office (*Politics* III.1.1275a21; 1275b19–21). Minimally, as Aristotle allows, in one of his typical expressions of deference to the varieties of common usage, a citizen is one who can sue or be sued. Even mere residents of a polity or denizens of a certain tract of land are sometimes called its citizens. But with its proper force, the name applies to those who may take part in the affairs of a state. For even a corporation can be sued, and even bears and rats are denizens! Aristotle's point is about what we sometimes call the ownership of stakeholders. Hence his talk of people's tendency to identify the actions of a state with the acts of its leader, or its people. Accountability is part of what's in question here; but, more largely, the sense of belonging that leads individuals to take on responsibilities beyond their atomic interests. That works best, Aristotle finds, in a democracy; the notion of participation may well need to be adjusted to be applied in the context of more exclusionary states (*Politics* III.1.1275b5–16). But the great strength of democracies is in instilling a sense of belonging, identification, and commitment; and that entails a warning, to the people and the leaders of democracies, against any social trend or political movement that would sap that sense of belonging.

To apply Aristotle's point very concretely: Universal national service will strengthen a democracy. So will internships and merit-based scholarships, especially those with service requirements. (Compare the Athenian ephebate.) Music, stories, and chatter that foment discord between the genders or among the social, economic, ethnic, or linguistic groups of a society breed alienation from the shared purposes and common interests of its members, weakening the sense of participation. So does any form of political exclusion or civil disability. Hence the unwisdom of racial segregation, and the achilles heel of restraints on coeducation.

Just as some slaves do not deserve to be slaves (*Politics* I.5.1254b33) and some rulers are not fit to rule, so some citizens are not suited to their role (*Politics* III.2). A good citizen is judged by his contributions in the role the constitution gives him—and, more broadly, by his contributions to the commonweal. A seaman is judged by the part he plays as a crew member. All those aboard a ship, with all their diverse skills and responsibilities, have safe sailing as their common object. And all citizens, with their diverse strengths and interests, have a common interest in the preservation of the community—and its flourishing (*Politics* III.4.1276b20–29). What Aristotle recommends is an open door to a certain level of engagement. He relies on self-selection to weed out at least some of those whose contributions would be less than helpful. Exclusion of whole classes will only generate hostility. But a few busybodies, presumably, can be tolerated; and in a moderately successful society citizens will have plenty to occupy them in their private capacities, so the public spirited and energetic will be more likely to engage more actively in the affairs of state. That sort of ideal seems to have been instantiated in the remarkable group of men who came forward, at great personal risk, to write the American Declaration of Independence, and in those who went on to draft the Constitution and the Federalist Papers. But we can't ignore the other side of the coin: Bad conditions are a breeding ground for demagogues, opportunists, and flatterers. Even in a prosperous society litigiousness and greed can undermine the self-selection filter on which Aristotle seems to rely—especially when there are professional lobbyists to secrete private interests improperly into public debate, and when lawmakers and other spokesmen of the polity and its people become dependent on such interests for livelihood and office.

That quandary is not quite within the range of Aristotle's experience. But even here his thinking offers something in the way of counsel. For our natural response might be manipulative, to reach for mechanisms designed to bind elected representatives, staffers, bureaucrats, and administrators to the public interest and draw them back from the temptations arrayed before them.[12] But Aristotle's advice here, as with communism, rests on the principle he learned from Plato, that political mechanisms are only as effective as the ethos that underwrites them. Education of, therefore, is once again the sine qua non of justice.

Monarchy, oligarchy, and democracy, Aristotle holds, may well be suited to different circumstances—historical, cultural, even ethnic. Not that he finds no form of government any better or worse than any other. Aristotle is a pluralist, not a relativist; he does not deem all cultures to be of equal worth. Nor does he assume without qualification (or quantification) that change is good. The general bias of his method in the *Politics* is toward preservation of the existing social and political fabric. I don't think he would endorse the Burkean view that whatever has long endured deserves to be preserved. But, like Plato and many another theorist from Confucius to Spinoza and beyond, Aristotle adopts the perspective of the social order and couches his argument prudentially, as advice about the preservation of stability—a dialectical stance, designed to show the strengths of virtue to an audience who may well be skeptical of merely moral claims, perhaps finding them unrealistic, outmoded, soft, or utopian—or perhaps because they have too often seen bad or vicious policy wrapped in the cloak of moralism. What does matter to Aristotle is that constitutionalism is attainable in each of the familiarly contrasted types of states. He admires polities of a mixed type for their potential to hem in excesses of authority. And here, I think, our own society has embedded in it some genuine fragments of Aristotelian wisdom. For it is a mixed system. We call it a democracy, but our strong executive exercises many of the powers of a monarch, and the system profits from many of the strengths of monarchy, without sinking into the arbitrariness of despotism. Similarly with our republican form of government: There is at least the potential for selection on the grounds of merit, if the electorate does not confuse a warm smile with effective leadership, or powerful advertizing with well-concerted policy. Our checks and balances and constitutional guarantees have much in common with Aristotle's counsels as to the strengths of a mixed constitution. For constitutional rule is not compatible with absolutism.

Aristotle admires professionalism, for its expertise but also for the stability it imparts. But this stability, like that imparted by the rule of law and constraint of capricious edicts, is a product of reason—the Socratic admiration for the specialist's knowledge and the Platonic appeal to the wisdom of the just ruler, now brought down to cases and concrete legal principles—not rules for the sake of rules, or for the sake of uniformity, but rational laws set in place to institute and implement the goals for which a society exists. The workability of such rules will depend, always, on the virtue of the citizens. Such virtue too may vary, but not in every conceivable way. It depends for its content, stability, and flexibility of response, ultimately, on education of a special yet very familiar kind.

5. THE COMMUNITY AS TEACHER OF VIRTUE

Plato's defense of Socrates against the charge of misleading the youth rested in part on the insistence that Socrates was not a teacher at all, not a sophist promising, for a fee, to guide young men to happy and successful lives, winning friends and influencing people, but himself, in fact, a seeker. If the implicit charge, veiled by notional deference to the Law of Oblivion, was that Socrates was to blame for the character of Alcibiades, the mutilation of the hermae, profanation of the mysteries, and all the betrayals and decadence of which those events were emblematic, then Plato's riposte was that the Athenians themselves bore responsibility for Alcibiades' character, and their own. Society is responsible for the ethos of its members. The project of politics, accordingly, is to frame institutions that will allow practical wisdom to permeate the social ethos, so that individuals need not themselves have the minds of philosophers before they can learn to live wisely and well. This is what Aristotle means in urging, as a properly Socratic thesis, that it is education that should give unity to society, not by suppressing our natural and socially indispensable individuality but by allowing us to attain that modicum of fellowship which is necessary to the conduct of any social enterprise.

The real method and highest aim of legislation is to forge an ethos. That does not mean uniformity of thought or style. Still less does it demand homogeneity of roles or lockstep congruity of behavior. What it does ask is the inculcation of certain basic virtues, values, habits of mind, and dispositions of character that will enable citizens to live together, work together, fight together when necessary, and deliberate together about the means by which to optimize the quality of their lives.

Leaders, Aristotle argues, must be loyal to the constitution of their state, if it is to endure. But such loyalty must not be dogged or dogmatic. For, extremes are dangerous, ugly, as Aristotle puts it here: There's more than one good shape for a nose, but even a good shape can go too far. Even in an elitist society, leaders must be faithful to the people's interests, and even an ardent democrat must leave room for social differences (for incentives, as our contemporaries like to say, or, more broadly, for the reward of excellence and, critically, for the recognition of good judgment and effective service). That said, Aristotle goes on to voice his chief concern in the language of complaint:

> But of all the things I have mentioned what most contributes to the permanence of constitutions is the adaptation of education to the form of government. Yet in our own day this principle is universally neglected. The best laws, though sanctioned by every citizen of the state, will be of no avail unless the young are trained by habit and education in the spirit of the constitution: if the laws are democratic, democratically, or oligarchically if the laws are oligarchical. Now, to have been educated in the spirit of the constitution is not to perform the actions in which oligarchs or democrats delight, but those by which the existence of an oligarchy or a democracy is made possible. Whereas, among us the sons of the ruling class in an oligarchy live in luxury, but the sons of the poor are hardened by exercise and toil, and hence both more inclined and better able to make a revolution. And in democracies of the more extreme type there has arisen a false idea of freedom which is contradictory to the true interests of the state. For two principles are characteristic of democracy: the government of the majority and freedom. Men think that what is just is equal; and that equality is the supremacy of the popular will; and that freedom means doing what one likes. In such democracies everyone lives as he pleases, or in the words of Euripides, "according to his fancy." But this is all wrong; men should not think it slavery to live according to the rule of the constitution; for it is their salvation. (*Politics* V.9.1310a12–35)

Habit here is not conditioning, and spirit is not a seamless or unquestioned worldview. Both refer to the ethos, and specifically, to a shared commitment to the values on which a common life is predicated. Universal altruism or selflessness is not presumed or demanded. But every society is seen as reliant for its effective operations on key attitudinal pivot points. In our democracy, we assume that all citizens have equal standing before the law. In an elitist society, standing might be scaled to the claimant's status as a bearer of certain traits, real or ascriptive. Aristotle's openness about just which rules and fulcrums matter most might irritate us, but it's helpful too, since it makes his point applicable in quite a variety of settings.

We believe in equal pay for equal work, but not for unequal work. We don't think that those who slack off in their jobs deserve the same pay as those who faithfully perform them. We fight for equal opportunity, but we don't draw lots for skating in the Olympics. That kind of opportunity depends on demonstrated merit. We distinguish as *civil* rights those deserts whose defeasance requires pretty substantial demonstrated violations of core societal norms; and we single out, as basic or existential human rights, those residual deserts that survive even such a defeat. But in any context, the working of a social system demands a certain level of commitment. Aristotle's point is that failure to inculcate that kind of commitment erodes and undermines a society's effectiveness—cuts off its air and blood supply.

"No one will doubt," Aristotle writes, "that the lawmaker should direct his attention above all to the education of the youth. For the neglect of education does harm to the constitution. The citizen should be moulded to the form of government under which he lives" (*Politics* VIII.1.1337a10–13). What was a truism for Aristotle, and a dictum he could expect his hearers to accept without a qualm (despite their regretted tendency to honor it better in the breach than by their practice) has become *dubia causa* at best among us. But that renders the point all the more precious to us. Every constitution has its own culture and makes its demands on the character of those who will live in its jurisdiction. The embarrassment of parents about setting standards and creating incentives to attune the ethos of their offspring creates an ethical problem that many in our society have difficulty addressing. But the difficulty rises to a higher power when that embarrassment, the lack of tact that passes for tact and the lack of rapport that passes for affording space and privacy, is elevated to a societal plane and becomes a blanket condemnation of legislative concern with character, now condemned as paternalism, or even thought control. Notice the equivocation in the charge, hidden even in the imagery of molding that Aristotle uses. Characters grow and change. They are not fixed, let alone molded. And ethical traits, as Aristotle taught, are capacities to respond thoughtfully and appropriately to life's varied circumstances. The clearest mark of a character weakness is the mechanical, unmeasured, merely reactive response found in both the cowardly and the rash, the niggardly and the spendthrift. Bergson saw such mechanism as the key to comedy, when he traced laughter to the stilted and mechanical operations of the stage figure whose ineptitude manifests an incapacity for nuanced judgment and sensitive response to circumstance.

To educate for virtue, on Aristotle's account, is not to train or provoke approved responses but to instill thoughtful modes of judgment in situations whose particularities cannot be prefigured in any mere rule. That is the strength of virtue ethics, allowing it to penetrate into the fine recesses of ordinary life, where a rule-based deontology might yield only the crudest or most minimal, if not vacuous, imperatives.

A society with a specific kind of constitution, Aristotle is arguing, asks a specific sort of attunement of its citizens. Uniformity, as we have seen, was never the goal. Aristotle's citizens are not told what song to sing. But there is a certain kind of harmony that they ought to be adept at reaching (and so, of teaching) if their interactions are to be constructive. Failure to impart the skills and attitudes that promote such interactions will corrode the social institutions, which are not bronze cogs, after all, but modes of relationship among living, breathing human beings. Aristotle's characteristic pluralism prompts him to allow that reasonable patterns of interaction (like human noses) might take quite a variety of forms. But randomness here, as in music, will be jarring. Its yield is noise and not coherent pattern.

As in his ethics and his model of tragedy, so in his politics, Aristotle sees human strengths as collapsing into weaknesses if thoughtlessness and unresponsiveness are allowed to push them to an extreme. The strength that Aristotle sees in oligarchy would lie, presumably, in its cultivation of excellence, ideally expressed in a capacity for rule. That, as Plato urged, would mean judgment, but also self-discipline, and even self-sacrifice. Nobility, to be more than nominal, must yield noble actions. Privilege, the nasty exudate of oligarchy, yields not nobility but decadence in individuals and dissolution in the state. The inequalities meant to carry the humanization of human life to a peak, at least for some, have exacted their cost but choked on their profit, even for the chosen.

The dialectic of tragedy works just as fatally in a democracy that fails to instill its principles: Democracy should bring liberty and equality. But if equality means entitlements uncoupled from merit or desert, and liberty means following one's fancy, without regard for the dependence of liberty on the reign of law and on respect for privacy and decency, democracy inevitably will fail of its promise. The state, with its people demoralized, alienated from one another and cynical about its great values, now reduced to empty shells of rhetoric and scraps of bunting, spins into disillusion, its incandescent vows of progress and prosperity dimmed and doused. The fault, again, is not in the idea of democracy but in the delusions attached to it. The people expected their vanishing rights and goods to spring up from the ground. They have forgotten, or were never taught in any practical way, that law is the real source of civil freedom and that equality along with all else

that is enriching and empowering in a democracy stems from the commitment of each to all. In the kingdom of free riders, no one rides at all.

The limitations of Aristotle's approach are legion. Most serious, no doubt are
his acceptance of slavery and his ill-informed ideas about women. Even here
there is much that we can profit from. For despite his acceptance of the
institution of slavery, Aristotle, far better than many an abolitionist, articulates
the reason why slavery is morally abhorrent: It is because slaves are living tools,
as he puts it. Barred from choosing their own ends, they are denied the
subjecthood that is constitutive in the human telos. The reason God and
nature give them is thwarted, their personhood, their subjecthood, negated,
regardless of how "well" they are treated or cared for. Compounding Aristotle's
help to us on this score is his warning about "natural slaves." For the mere fact
of freedom does not suffice to impart actual freedom to any of us. Freedom is
won only when we actually can and do choose ends for ourselves, not slavishly
apprenticing ourselves to convention or emulation or indenturing ourselves to
externals. It is only when we learn to act thoughtfully and creatively in the
situations we encounter, neither ignoring nor rejecting, nor passively accepting
them, that we can say that we actually deserve and earn and use the freedom
that the fortunes of history have accorded us.

   As for women, Aristotle pays a price for his realism and accommodation to the mores of his society. Gone is Plato's radicalism. For Aristotle does
not believe that sheer intuition of the Form of the Good would give us
concrete enough knowledge of the doable good to guide us in particular
situations. His empiricist sense that we need something much more thickly
contextual pushes him toward an acceptance of the status quo that is in some
measure a product of his social status as a metic, and that is complemented
and seconded by his pluralist open mindedness. We, of course, stand at much
greater distance from the givens that Aristotle labored to accommodate, and
we have no more need to accept his views about the capabilities of women
than we have to follow him in his rationalization of slavery as an institution.
But his view that friendship is possible even with slaves, and his view that
consultation and shared deliberation, "constitutional rule," are what is needed
between a man and a woman, give us a line of argument that would not
readily be expressed in our more egalitarian language or rhetoric: that even
if women do differ from men, whether for social or intellectual or even
biological reasons, they are not therefore to be tyrannized. Difference, even
when conceded, does not entail or permit moral invidiousness. It would be
strange if Aristotle, living over a hundred generations ago did not convey at
least some of the biases and limitations of the culture he swam in, just as any
writing of ours would carry the markings and the DNA of our ideas, personal
and shared. We do not need to accept Aristotle's conventional attitudes
about infanticide. We should recoil from these in horror. And the idea that
slavery can be a source of civilization to the benighted smacks too broadly

of rationalization to be credited as a warrant for anything, and least of all for warfare. Nor do we need to accept the prejudice against workers and merchants that Aristotle breathes—although his warnings about those who mix up means and ends and his cautions about the dehumanizing effects of certain kinds of work retain their bite. Leisure too, we must acknowledge, can also be dehumanizing. But stereotypes, even those that may once have served as homiletic foils, afford no sure footing to philosophic reasoning. Of course merchants can be vulgar babbitts. But not every businessman or trader fits the caricature. The ruins at Pompeii yield evidence of both vulgarity and thoughtfulness, art and philosophy, sport, and piety, among the ashes, all growing from the soil of the same wealth.

Aristotle will not give us the humanism of the Judeo-Christian tradition, the Sabbath, which opens leisure, spiritualized and intellectualized, even to the enslaved, in ways that Aristotle never conceived. Nor will his philosophy yield the discomfort with blood sports that many think essential to ethics, the rejection of infanticide and abortion that is so central in the monotheistic versions of ethics. Our own culture is still at work in the effort to determine how much of such an ethos can be integrated to the culture of a large and pluralistic society. But in such a society deliberative participation remains critical, and what Aristotle has to teach us about the centrality of such participation to human aims and ends, and to the means by which those ends are to be achieved, remains critically apposite.

A community—family, tribe, or nation—is governed by roles not rules. But a society—a firm, union, foundation, or state—needs formal rules. Where the intimacy of a community can invoke interpersonal bonds sometimes more powerful than those of a society, the formal rules of a society allow for expansion of the social enterprise beyond the nest of intimacy. Laws can structure and define, regulate and regularize, the diffuse yet powerful sense of fellowship that links the members of a tribe, clan, or nation. Despite their impersonality, or in a curious way because of it, they can help forge a populace into a state, by making norms explicit that were typically left unstated in a closeknit community or a large but amorphous population. Constitutions can go further, by spelling out matters of principle in larger, logically more basic laws that gain a privileged standing, taking the higher-order posture of laws about laws (Goodman 1991, 15–16, 22–23, and 28–42).

Modern constitutions are typically seen as bastions of rights. Aristotle is not a champion of rights in the sense of universal entitlements or absolute guarantees against intrusions by the state. Yet the idea of rights is not foreign to him. The core of that idea must be very ancient, perhaps as old as any notion of justified claims, powers or immunities—that is, as old as politics, and so, by Aristotle's standards, as old as humanity itself (Miller 1995). But just as Aristotle's virtue ethics is an ethics of tendency, lacking quite the strong sense of sin and wrong that marks the Judeo-Christian synthesis, so his politics tends to avoid setting down absolute boundaries. And yet he does voice a clear a sense of what despotism would be, and is, and a repugnance for the arbitrary exercise of authority. Guiding and accompanying that sense is a realist's recognition of the variable but real parameters of public outrage and expectation. Justice, on Aristotle's account, will be rooted in laws, and laws in turn, in social practices, above all, in reciprocity, recognized among its participants and recognizable to outsiders, anchored in the culture and history of a place, but by no means irrelevant or incomprehensible elsewhere, and by no means immune to an outsider's critique.[13]

Notes

1. Aristotle criticizes Socrates in the *Republic* for confining his attention to classes whose activities are a stark necessity "as if a state were established merely to supply the necessities of life, rather than for the sake of the good." Among those whose contributions are left out of account here he enumerates warriors (who are added in the *Republic* only after the society has grown wealthy). Also necessary to the full functioning of the state are those who administer and dispense justice, those who deliberate, and those who serve by providing wealth (*Politics* IV.4.1291a12). The same individual in real life, he adds (although this defeats the analytic purposes of Plato's model in the *Republic*), may play multiple roles. Among those needed further, if the function of the state is to enhance human life and not just to allow some notion of survival, Aristotle adds a priestly class of diverse functions (*Politics* VI.8.1322b18–29). And these, he thinks, should be chosen from the ranks of the citizenry, to offer fitting honor to the gods, affording a well-deserved rest in their elderly years to those who have served actively when younger (*Politics* VII.9.1329a30–34).

2. Seeking sense in Plato's rationale for the traditional role of music in Greek education, Aristotle writes: "music is pursued, not only as an alleviation of past toil, but also as providing recreation. And who can say whether, having this use, it may not also have a nobler one? In addition to this common pleasure, felt and shared by all (for the pleasure given in music is natural, and therefore adapted to all ages and characters), may it not have also some influence over the character of the soul? It must have such an influence if characters are affected by it. And that they are so affected is proved in many ways, and not least by the power which the songs of Olympus exercise; for beyond question they inspire enthusiasm, and enthusiasm is an emotion of the character of the soul. Besides, when men hear imitations, even apart from the rhythms and tunes themselves, their feelings move in sympathy. Since then music is a pleasure, and virtue consists in rejoicing and loving and hating rightly, there is clearly nothing which we are so much concerned to acquire and to cultivate as the power of forming right judgments, and of taking delight in good dispositions and noble actions. Rhythm and melody supply imitations of anger and gentleness, and also of courage and temperance, and of all the qualities contrary to these, and of the other qualities of character, which hardly fall short of the actual affections, as we know from our own experience, for in listening to such strains our souls undergo a change. The habit of feeling pleasure or pain at mere representations is not far removed from the same feeling about realities. . . . The objects of no other sense, such as taste or touch, have any resemblance to moral qualities; in visible objects there is

only a little. . . . On the other hand, even in mere melodies there is an imitation of character. . . . The whole subject has been well treated by philosophical writers on this branch of education, and they confirm their arguments by facts. . . . Enough has been said to show that music has a power of forming the character and should therefore be introduced into the education of the young. The study is suited to the stage of youth, for young persons will not, if they can help, endure anything which is not sweetened by pleasure, and music has a natural sweetness" (*Politics* VIII.5.1339b40–1340b16; cf. Lord 1982, 97–98; Swanson 1992, 151–54).

3. *Nicomachean Ethics* (VIII.9.1158b11–19; cf. 11.1161a3–1161b10); *Politics* (I.6.1255b14–15).

4. Citing Slater (1971), Littman (1974, 17–21) ascribes much of the narcissism of ancient Greek culture to an ambivalence expressed in the sequestration of women but rooted in a deep fear of female power. Bruce Thornton in *Greek Ways* (2000) softens the blow, noting that despite women's many disadvantages in ancient Greece, the Greek ideals of liberty and inquiry had a liberating effect in the long term, on both women and men, by opening human social institutions and ameliorating the human condition through the rise of technology and science. For Aristotle's deference to Greek social strictures, see Elshtain (1981, 44–53).

5. *Diogenes Laertius* V.13.16, where Aristotle also provides for his burial beside the bones of Pythias, *in keeping with her own instructions.* Judith Swanson (1992, 52) treats Aristotle's remarks (*Nicomachean Ethics* IX.12.1172a10–14) on how marriage partners complement each other's strengths and correct each other's weaknesses.

6. Aristotle (*Politics* I.2) cites Homer (*Iliad* IX.63) in laying out his thesis that man is a social animal. Austin (1975, 135–70) explicates in detail Homer's thematic development of what will become Aristotele's thesis. Scylla, Charybdis, Proteus, Aeolus, the cattle of Helios, and Polyphemus, the spells of Circe and the groves of Calypso, so strikingly contrasted with the orchards of the Phaeacians, set out the parameters of the Homeric contrast of civil life with its alternatives. Clearly Aristotle knows these episodes well; and, as Austin notes, Aristotle read Homer as a connected narrative and no mere collection of disparate stories (see *Metaphysics* Zeta, 1030b9). So the work would have thematic unities for him and lend itself to the same unpacking of its dramatic imagery that Aristotle applied to the mythopoeisis of Plato. Aristotle's remarks about myth makers as protophilosophers (*Metaphysics* Alpha, 982b11–982b28) address not simply cosmology in the manner of Hesiod, then, but politics and the insights of Homer.

7. That Comte pushed values of his own into his social analysis is pretty obvious; and that freeing such analysis from value judgments is itself a project that rests on value judgments is again pretty obvious—not only in the trivial sense that objectivity is a value but also in the subtler sense that values are needed to discriminate between extraneous and pertinent values in descriptive as well as interpretive work. But they tell me that Weber fudged on the basic data (about the *Gymnasium* and *Realschule*) that grounded his famous thesis about Protestantism and the rise of capitalism. That in a way is a more serious charge, since the data are rarely presented when the thesis is restated, and the distortions (in this case about the role of ideologies) are much harder to allow for than are the outspoken biases, say, of Comte.

8. Unlike Plato, Aristotle does not offer a single ideal scheme; and, unlike Plato, he does not think pure intuitions into the form of the Good will be of much use to the statesman, since such intuitions, even for those privileged to grasp them,

are too general to specify *the doable good* in concrete circumstances. Experience is more relevant—in part because one does not typically start with a political blank slate but with an existing polity, people, and history. Aristotle is deferential to these. Yet he is no mere apologist of whatever may be the status quo. Here again there would need to be some specifics. Aristotle lacks the profound and early sense of alienation that makes Plato a radical thinker—about women's status, for example. But he is enough of an outsider at Athens and bears enough experience of other polities, going back to his youth in Macedon and his years in Lesbos, that he can picture reform and argue for it, prudentially, as an aid to stability.

9. As Bernard Yack (1993) notes, human communities do not consistently achieve their end. Indeed their successes are fraught with difficulties and the arrangement is never perfect. Cf. Goodman (1991, 33–39).

10. Cf. I.5.1254b.5–7: "The soul rules the body with a despotical rule, whereas the intellect rules the appetites with a constitutional and royal rule." Cf. Plato's Aeschylean image of reason's "persuasion" of necessity, *Timaeus* (47E–48A).

11. For the natural limits to acquisition, and wealth as a means to an end: I.8.1256b34.

12. Cf. Spinoza, *Tractatus Politicus* (chapter 6, 3; chapter 7, 4, 8–13).

13. Cf. *Nicomachean Ethics* (V.5).

WORKS CITED

Ackerman, Bruce. 1989. "Why Dialogue?" *Journal of Philosophy* 86:16–27.

Allen, Anita, and Milton Regan, eds. 1998. *Debating Democracy's Discontent*. New York: Oxford University Press.

Annas, Julia. 1993. *The Morality of Happiness*. New York: Oxford University Press.

Aristotle. *Politics*. P. L. P. Simpson Translation.

Atkins, A. H. W. 1991. "The Connection between Aristotle's Ethics and *Politics*." In *A Companion to Aristotle's* Politics, ed. D. Keyt and F. D. Miller, Jr., 75–93. Oxford: Blackwell.

Austin, Norman. 1975. *Archery at the Dark of the Moon*. Berkeley: University of California Press.

Avineri, Shlomo, and Avner de-Shalit, eds. 1992. *Communitarianism and Individualism*. New York: Oxford University Press.

Barber, Benjamin. 1984. *Strong Democracy*. Berkeley: University of California Press.

———. 1998a. *A Place for Us*. New York: Hill and Wang.

———. 1998b. *A Passion for Democracy*. Princeton, N.J.: Princeton University Press.

Barker, Ernest, trans. 1946. *The Politics of Aristotle*. Oxford: Oxford University Press.

———. 1958. *The Politics of Aristotle*. New York: Oxford University Press.

Bellah, Robert, et al. 1985. *Habits of the Heart*. Los Angeles: University of California Press.

Benhabib, Seyla. 2002. *The Claims of Culture*. Princeton, N.J.: Princeton University Press.

Boaz, David. 1997. *Libertarianism: A Primer*. New York: Free Press.

Bohman, James. 1996. *Public Deliberation*. Cambridge, Mass.: MIT Press.

———. 1999. "Democracy as Inquiry, Inquiry as Democratic." *American Journal of Political Science* 43, no. 2:590–607.

———. 2004. "Realizing Deliberative Democracy as a Mode of Inquiry." *Journal of Speculative Philosophy* 18, no. 1:23–43.

———, and William Rehg, eds. 1997. *Deliberative Democracy*. Cambridge, Mass.: MIT Press.

Bos, Deiter. 2001. *Privatization: A Theoretical Treatment*. Oxford: Oxford University Press.

Brown, C. 1992. *International Relations Theory: New Normative Approaches*. New York: Columbia University Press.

Brown, Vivienne. 2001. " 'Rights' in Aristotle's *Politics* and *Nicomachean Ethics*?" *The Review of Metaphysics* 55, no. 2:269–95.

Chan, Joseph. 1992. "Does Aristotle's Political Theory Rest on a 'Blunder'?" *History of Political Thought* 13, no. 2:189–202.

Charles, David. 1988. "Perfectionism in Aristotle's Political Theory: Reply to Martha Nussbaum." In *Oxford Studies in Ancient Philosophy*, supplementary volume. Oxford: Oxford University Press.

Cohen, Joshua. 1986. "An Epistemic Theory of Democracy." *Ethics* 97 (October): 26–38.

———. 1996. "Procedure and Substance in Deliberative Democracy." In Bohman and Rehg, eds.

———. 1998. "Democracy and Liberty." In Elster, ed.

Copp, D., J. Hampton, and J. Roemer, eds. 1993. *The Idea of Democracy*. Cambridge, UK: Cambridge University Press.

Cooper, John M. 1996. "Justice and Rights in Aristotle's Politics." *The Review of Metaphysics* 49, no. 4, issue 196:859–72.

Dennett, D. C. 1976. "Conditions of Personhood." In *The Identity of Persons*, ed. A. Rorty, 175–96. Berkeley: University of California Press.

———. 1987. *The Intentional Stance*. Cambridge, Mass.: MIT Press.

Dionne, E. J. 1991. *Why Americans Hate Politics*. New York: Simon and Schuster.

Dryzek, John. 2000. *Deliberative Democracy and Beyond*. New York: Oxford University Press.

Elshtain, Jean. 1981. *Public Man, Private Woman: Women in Social and Political Thought*. Princeton, N.J.: Princeton University Press.

———. 1982. "Aristotle, the Public-Private Split, and the Case of the Suffragists." In *The Family in Political Thought*, ed. Jean Elshtain. Amherst: University of Massachusetts Press.

———. 1995. *Democracy on Trial*. New York: Basic.

Elster, Jon, ed. 1998. *Deliberative Democracy*. Cambridge, UK: Cambridge University Press.

Epstein, Richard A. 2005. "One Step beyond Nozick's Minimal State: The Role of Forced Exchanges in Political Theory." *Social Philosophy and Policy* 22:1 (Winter):286–313.

Estlund, David. 1993a. "Who's Afraid of Deliberative Democracy?" *Texas Law Review* 71:1437–77.

———. 1993b. "Making Truth Safe for Democracy." In Copp, Hampton, and Roemer, eds.

———. 1997. "Beyond Fairness and Deliberation." In Bohman and Rehg, eds.

Etzioni, Amitai. 1993. *The Spirit of Community*. New York: Simon and Schuster.

———. 1998. "Moral Dialogues." In Allen and Regan, eds.

Everson, Stephen. 1988. *The Politics*. Cambridge, UK: Cambridge University Press.

Feigenbaum, Harvey, Chris Hamnett, and Jeffrey R. Henig. 1998. *Shrinking the State: The Political Underpinnings of Privatization*. Cambridge UK: Cambridge University Press.

Fischer, J. M. 1994. *The Metaphysics of Free Will*. Oxford: Blackwell.

Fish, Stanley. 1999. "Mutual Respect as a Device of Exclusion." In Macedo, ed.

Franken, Al. 2003. *Lies and the Lying Liars Who Tell Them*. New York: Dutton.

Frankfurt, H. G. 1969. "Alternate Possibilities and Moral Responsibility." *Journal of Philosophy* 66:829–39.

———. 1971. "Freedom of the Will and the Concept of a Person." *Journal of Philosophy* 68:5–20.

French, P. A. 1984. *Collective and Corporate Responsibility*. New York: Columbia University Press.

Frost, M. 1996. *Ethics in International Relations: A Constitutive Theory*. Cambridge: Cambridge University Press.

Galston, William. 1999. "Diversity, Toleration, and Deliberative Democracy." In Macado, ed.

Garver, Eugene. 2005. "Factions and the Paradox of Aristotelian Practical Science." *Polis* 22, no. 2:181–205.

Gauthier, D. 1986. *Morals by Agreement*. Oxford: Oxford University Press.

———, and R. Sugden, eds. 1993. *Rationality, Justice and the Social Contract*. New York: Harvester.

George, Robert. 1999. "Law, Democracy, and Moral Disagreement." In Macado, ed.

Goodin, R. 1989. "The State as a Moral Agent." In *The Good Polity: Normative Analysis of the State*, ed. A. Hamlin and P. Petit. Oxford: Blackwell.

Goodman, L. E. 1991. *On Justice: An Essay in Jewish Philosophy*. New Haven: Yale University Press.

Goodpaster, K. 1984. "The Concept of Corporate Responsibility." In *New Introductory Essays in Business Ethics*, ed. T. Regan, 291–323. New York: Random House.

Gould, Carol. 1988. *Rethinking Democracy*. Cambridge, UK: Cambridge University Press.

Graham, K. 2002. *Practical Reasoning in a Social World: How We Act Together*. Cambridge, UK: Cambridge University Press.

Gutmann, Amy. 1985. "Communitarian Critiques of Liberalism." In Avineri and de-Shalit, eds.

———, and Dennis Thompson. 1996. *Democracy and Disagreement*. Cambridge: Harvard University Press.

Habermas, Jurgen. 1990. "Discourse Ethics." In *Moral Consciousness and Communicative Action*. Cambridge, Mass.: MIT Press.

———. 1996. *Between Facts and Norms*. Cambridge, Mass.: MIT Press.

Hall, David, and Roger Ames. 1999. *The Democracy of the Dead*. Chicago and Lasalle: Open Court.

Halper, Edward. 1995. "The Substance of Aristotle's Ethics." In *The Crossroads of Norm and Nature: Essays on Aristotle's Ethics and Metaphysics*, ed. May Sim, 3–28. Lanham, Md.: Rowman and Littlefield.

———. 1999. "The Unity of the Virtues in Aristotle." *Oxford Studies in Ancient Philosophy* 17:115–43.

Hamburger, Max. 1959. "Aristotle and Confucius: A Comparison." *Journal of the History of Ideas* 20:236–49.

Hamilton, Alexander, James Madison, and John Jay. 1961. "The Federalist Papers." In *The Federalist Papers*, with an introduction by Clinton Rossiter. New York: New American Library.

Hardin, Garrett. 1972. "The Tragedy of the Commons." In *Exploring New Ethics of Survival*. New York: Viking.

Holmes, Stephen. 1993. *The Anatomy of Antiliberalism*. Cambridge: Harvard University Press.

Hsu, Francis L. K. 1986. "Confucianism and Its Culturally Determined Manifestations." In *The Psycho-Cultural Dynamics of the Confucian Family*, ed. Walter H. Slote. Seoul: International Cultural Society of Korea.

Husock, Howard. 1997. "Standards versus Struggle: The Failure of Public Housing and the Welfare-State Impulse." *Social Philosophy & Policy* 14, no. 2:69–94.

Iyengar, Shanto. 1991. *Is Anyone Responsible?* Chicago: University of Chicago Press.

Janowitz, Morris. 1983. *The Reconstruction of Patriotism.* Chicago: University of Chicago Press.

Johnson, James. 1998. "Arguing for Deliberation: Some Skeptical Considerations." In Elster, ed.

Jordan, David K. 1986. "Folk Filial Piety in Taiwan: The Twenty-four Filial Exemplars." In *The Psycho-Cultural Dynamics of the Confucian Family*, ed. Walter H. Slote. Seoul: International Cultural Society of Korea.

Keyt, David. 1987. "Three Fundamental Theorems in Aristotle's Politics." *Phronesis* 32:54–79.

King, Ambrose Y. C. 1985. "The Individual and Group in Confucianism: A Relational Perspective." In *Individualism and Holism: Studies in Confucian and Taoist Values*, ed. D. Munro. Ann Arbor: University of Michigan Press.

Knight, Jack. 1999. "Constitutionalism and Deliberative Democracy." In Macedo, ed.

Kraut, Richard. 1996. "Are There Natural Rights in Aristotle?" *The Review of Metaphysics* 49, no. 4, issue 196:755–74.

———. 2002. *Aristotle: Political Philosophy.* Oxford: Oxford University Press.

Lee, Sang-Im. 1999. "The Unity of the Virtues in Aristotle and Confucius." *Journal of Chinese Philosophy* 26, no. 2:203–23.

Legge, James, trans. 1971. *Confucius: Confucian Analects, The Great Learning and The Doctrine of the Mean.* New York: Dover.

Lewis, H. D. 1948. "Collective Responsibility." *Philosophy* 23:3–18.

Light, Paul Charles. 1999. *The True Size of Government.* Washington, D.C.: Brookings Institution Press.

Littman, Robert. 1974. *The Greek Experiment: Imperialism and Social Conflict 800–400 BC.* London: Thames and Hudson.

Lord, Carnes. 1982. *Education and Culture in the Political Thought of Aristotle.* Ithaca: Cornell University Press.

Macedo, Stephen, ed. 1999. *Deliberative Politics.* New York: Oxford University Press.

Machan, Tibor R., ed. 1982. *The Libertarian Reader.* Totowa, N.J.: Rowman and Littlefield.

MacIntyre, Alasdair C. 1981. *After Virtue.* Notre Dame, Ind.: University of Notre Dame Press.

Mansbridge, Jane. 1983. *Beyond Adversary Democracy.* Chicago: University of Chicago Press.

McLuhan, Marshall. 1962. *The Gutenberg Galaxy: The Making of Typographic Man.* Toronto: Toronto University Press.

Mead, Lawrence M. 1997. "Citizenship and Social Policy: T. H. Marshall and Poverty." *Social Philosophy & Policy* 14, no. 2:197–230.

Mill, John Stuart. 1947. *On Liberty.* New York: Appleton Century Crofts.

———. 1991. *On Liberty.* New York: Oxford University Press.

Miller, Fred D. Jr. 1989. "Aristotle's Political Naturalism." *Apeiron* 22:195–218.

———. 1995. *Nature, Justice, and Rights in Aristotle's Politics.* New York: Oxford University Press.

Moran, R. 2001. *Authority and Estrangement: An Essay on Self-Knowledge.* Princeton, N.J.: Princeton University Press.

Morris, Christopher W. 1998. *An Essay on the Modern State*. Cambridge, UK: Cambridge University Press.

Mouffe, Chantal. 2000. *The Democratic Paradox*. New York: Verso.

Mulgan, R. G. 1977. *Aristotle's Political Theory*. Oxford: Clarendon.

———. 1987. *Aristotle's Political Theory: An Introduction for Students of Political Theory*. Oxford: Clarendon.

Mulhall, Stephen, and Adam Swift. 1996. *Liberals and Communitarians*. New York: Blackwell.

Nagel, Thomas. 1991. *Equality and Partiality*. New York: Oxford University Press.

Nardin, T. 1983. *Law, Morality, and the Relations of States*. Princeton, N.J.: Princeton University Press.

Narveson, Jan. 1982. *The Libertarian Idea*. Philadelphia: Temple University Press.

Nietzsche, Friedrich. 1974. *Beyond Good and Evil: Prelude to a Philosophy of the Future*. Trans. R. J. Hollingdale. Harmondsworth, Middlesex, England: Penguin.

Nino, Carlos. 1996. *The Constitution of Deliberative Democracy*. New Haven: Yale University Press.

Novak, Michael. 1982. *The Spirit of Democratic Capitalism*. New York: Simon and Schuster.

Nozick, Robert. 1974. *Anarchy, State, and Utopia*. New York: Basic.

Nussbaum, Martha. 1988. "Nature, Function, and Capability: Aristotle on Political Distribution." In *Oxford Studies in Ancient Philosophy*, supplementary volume. Oxford: Oxford University Press.

Olson, Mancur. 1965. *The Logic of Collective Action*. Cambridge: Harvard University Press.

O'Reilly, Bill. 2001. *The No Spin Zone*. New York: Broadway Books.

Page, Benjamin. 1996. *Who Deliberates?* Chicago: University of Chicago Press.

Phaar, Susan, and Robert Putnam, eds. 2000. *Disaffected Democracies*. Princeton, N.J.: Princeton University Press.

Putnam, Robert. 1995. "Bowling Alone." *Journal of Democracy* 6, no. 1 (January):65–78.

Rand, Ayn. 1964. *The Virtue of Selfishness*. New York: New American Library.

———. 1966. *Capitalism: The Unknown Ideal*. New York: New American Library.

Rawls, John. 1989. "The Domain of the Political and Overlapping Consensus." In Freeman, ed.

———. 1996. *Political Liberalism*. Paperback ed. New York: Columbia University Press.

———. 1999. *Law of Peoples*. Cambridge: Harvard University Press.

Reeve, C. D. C., trans. and ed. 1998. *Aristotle. Politics*. Indianapolis: Hackett.

Reus-Smit, C. 1999. *The Moral Purpose of the State: Culture, Social Identity, and Institutional Rationality in International Relations*. Princeton, N.J.: Princeton University Press.

Robinson, R., trans. 1995. *Aristotle's Politics, Books III and IV*. With an introduction and comments by Richard Robinson. Oxford: Clarendon.

Rothbard, Murray. 1982. *The Ethics of Liberty*. Atlantic Highlands, N.J.: Humanities.

Rovane, C. A. 1994. "The Personal Stance." *Philosophical Topics: The Philosophy of Daniel Dennett* 22:351–96.

———. 1998. *The Bounds of Agency: An Essay in Revisionary Metaphysics*. Princeton, N.J.: Princeton University Press.

Sandel, Michael, ed. 1982. *Liberalism and Its Critics*. New York: New York University Press.

———. 1984. "The Procedural Republic and the Unencumbered Self." In Avineri and de-Shalit, eds.

———. 1996. *Democracy's Discontent*. Cambridge: Harvard University Press.

———. 1998a. "A Response to Rawls's Political Liberalism." Appendix to the second edition of *Liberalism and the Limits of Justice*. Cambridge: Cambridge University Press.

———. 1998b. "Reply to Critics." In *Debating Democracy's Discontent*, eds. Anita Allen and Milton Regan. Cambridge: Harvard University Press.

Sim, May. 2001. "Aristotle in the Reconstruction of Confucian Ethics." *IPQ* 41, no. 4, issue 164:453–68.

———. 2002. "Ritual and Realism in Early Chinese Science." *Journal of Chinese Philosophy* 29, no. 4:501–23.

———. 2003. "The Moral Self in Confucius and Aristotle." *IPQ* 43, no. 4, issue 172:439–62.

———. 2004a. "A Confucian Approach to Human Rights." *History of Philosophy Quarterly* 2, pt. 1, no. 4:337–56.

———. 2004b. "Categories and Commensurability in Confucius and Aristotle: A Response to MacIntyre." In *Categories: Historical and Systematic Essays*, ed. M. Gorman and J. Sanford. Washington, D.C.: Catholic University of America Press.

———. 2004c. "Harmony and the Mean in the *Nicomachean Ethics* and the *Zhongyong*." *Dao: A Journal of Comparative Philosophy* 3, no. 2:253–80.

———. Forthcoming. "Confucian Rights in Practice."

Simpson, Peter. 1998. *A Philosophical Commentary on the* Politics *of Aristotle*. Chapel Hill: University of North Carolina Press.

Singer, P. 1995. *How Are We to Live? Ethics in an Age of Self-interest*. Amherst, N.Y.: Prometheus.

Slater, Philip. 1971. *The Glory of Hera: Greek Mythology and the Greek Family*. Boston: Beacon.

Spinoza, Baruch. 1982. *The Ethics and Selected Letters*. Trans. Samuel Shirley. Indianapolis: Hackett.

Strauss, Leo. 1953. *Natural Right and History*. Chicago: University of Chicago Press.

Sunstein, Cass. 2001a. *Republic.com*. Princeton, N.J.: Princeton University Press.

———. 2001b. *Designing Democracy*. New York: Oxford University Press.

———. 2003a. *Why Societies Need Dissent*. Cambridge: Harvard University Press.

———. 2003b. "The Law of Group Polarization." In *Debating Deliberative Democracy*, eds. James Fishkin and Peter Laslett. London: Blackwell.

Swanson, Judith. 1992. *The Public and the Private in Aristotle's Political Philosophy*. Ithaca: Cornell University Press.

Thornton, Bruce. 2000. *Greek Ways*. San Francisco: Encounter.

Tu Weiming. 1986. "An Inquiry on the Five Relationships in Confucian Humanism." In *The Psycho-Cultural Dynamics of the Confucian Family*, ed. Walter H. Slote. Seoul: International Cultural Society of Korea.

Tullock, Gordon. 2005. *The Rent-Seeking Society*. Indianapolis: Liberty Fund.

Vallentyne, P., ed. 1991. *Contractarianism and Rational Choice*. Cambridge, UK: Cambridge University Press.

Vallentyne, Peter, and Hillel Steiner, eds. 2000a. *Left-Libertarianism and Its Critics: The Contemporary Debate*. Houndmills, UK: Palgrave.

———. 2000b. *The Origins of Left-Libertarianism: An Anthology of Historical Writings*. Houndmills, UK: Palgrave.

Watson, James D. 1980. *The Double Helix: A Personal Account of the Discovery of DNA*. Ed. Gunther S. Stent. New York: Norton.

Weber, Max. 1947. *Theory of Social and Economic Organization*. New York: Free Press.

Wendt, A. 1994. "Collective Identity Formation and the International State." *American Political Science Review* 88, no. 2:384–95.

Yack, Bernard. 1993. *The Problems of a Political Animal: Community, Justice and Conflict in Aristotelian Political Thought*. Berkeley: University of California Press.

Young, Iris Marion. 2000. *Inclusion and Democracy*. New York: Oxford University Press.

CONTRIBUTORS

EUGENE GARVER is Regents Professor of Philosophy at Saint John's University in Minnesota. He is the author of *Confronting Aristotle's Ethics: Ancient and Modern Morality* (2006), *For the Sake of Argument: Practical Reasoning, Character and the Ethics of Belief* (2004), and *Aristotle's Rhetoric: An Art of Character* (1994). His contribution to this volume will become part of a book on Aristotle's *Politics*.

LLOYD P. GERSON is Professor of Philosophy at the University of Toronto. Gerson works on ancient philosophy, especially Plato, Platonism, and Aristotle. The author of several articles on topics in ancient philosophy, Gerson's most recent books are *Aristotle and Other Platonists* (2005) and *Ancient Epistemology* (2007).

LENN E. GOODMAN is Professor of Philosophy and Andrew W. Mellon Professor in the Humanities at Vanderbilt University. He is the author of several books, including *Islamic Humanism* (2003), *In Defense of Truth: A Pluralistic Approach* (2002), *Jewish and Islamic Philosophy: Crosspollinations in the Classic Age* (1999), and *Judaism, Human Rights and Human Values* (1998). His 2005 Gifford Lectures are forthcoming, under the title *Love Thy Neighbor as Thyself*.

EDWARD C. HALPER is the Josiah Meigs Distinguished Teaching Professor of Philosophy at the University of Georgia. Much of his published work is in ancient philosophy, but he has written on a wide range of subjects. His work is guided by an interest in metaphysics that expresses itself even in papers on political philosophy. Some forty-five of his articles have appeared in journals and books. His first book, *One and Many in Aristotle's* Metaphysics: *The Central Books* was reissued at the end of 2005. A companion volume, *One and Many in Aristotle's* Metaphysics: *Books A–Δ*, is now in press, and the final volume of the trilogy covering *Metaphysics* I–N will appear in the next couple of years.

FRED D. MILLER, JR., is Professor of Philosophy at Bowling Green State University. In addition to numerous articles on the history of philosophy and on political philosophy, he is the author of *Nature, Justice, and Rights in Aristotle's Politics* (1995), coeditor (with David Keyt) of *A Companion to Aristotle's*

Politics (1991), and coeditor (with Carrie-Ann Biondi) of *A History of the Philosophy of Law from the Ancient Greeks to the Scholastics* (2006). He is associate editor of the journal *Social Philosophy and Policy*.

MAY SIM is Associate Professor of Philosophy at the College of the Holy Cross. She is the contributing editor of *The Crossroads of Norm and Nature: Essays on Aristotle's Ethics and Metaphysics* (1995) and *From Puzzles to Principles? Essays on Aristotle's Dialectic* (1999). Her most recent book, *Remastering Morals with Aristotle and Confucius* (2007) is a comparison of Aristotle and Confucius on the ethical life. Her current research focuses on human rights in Confucianism.

PETER L. P. SIMPSON is Professor of Philosophy and Classics at the Graduate Center of the City University of New York. He is the author of a translation and commentary on Aristotle's *Politics* (1997 and 1998), of a book on ethics, and *Vices, Virtues and Consequences* (2001), and of a book on the late pope, *On Karol Wojtyla* (2001). His current research is centered on the origins and foundations of metaphysics and on the relation of music to morals.

ROBERT B. TALISSE is Associate Professor of Philosophy at Vanderbilt University. His research is focused on contemporary political philosophy, especially democratic theory. He is the author of several articles and two books: *Democracy After Liberalism* (2005) and *A Pragmatist Philosophy of Democracy* (2007).

INDEX LOCORUM

INDEX

Made in the USA
San Bernardino, CA
22 July 2013